D0864494

The Art of
POLICYMAKING

CQ Press, an imprint of SAGE, is the leading publisher of books, periodicals, and electronic products on American government and international affairs. CQ Press consistently ranks among the top commercial publishers in terms of quality, as evidenced by the numerous awards its products have won over the years. CQ Press owes its existence to Nelson Poynter, former publisher of the *St. Petersburg Times,* and his wife Henrietta, with whom he founded Congressional Quarterly in 1945. Poynter established CQ with the mission of promoting democracy through education and in 1975 founded the Modern Media Institute, renamed The Poynter Institute for Media Studies after his death. The Poynter Institute (*www.poynter.org*) is a nonprofit organization dedicated to training journalists and media leaders.

In 2008, CQ Press was acquired by SAGE, a leading international publisher of journals, books, and electronic media for academic, educational, and professional markets. Since 1965, SAGE has helped inform and educate a global community of scholars, practitioners, researchers, and students spanning a wide range of subject areas, including business, humanities, social sciences, and science, technology, and medicine. A privately owned corporation, SAGE has offices in Los Angeles, London, New Delhi, and Singapore, in addition to the Washington DC office of CQ Press.

SECOND EDITION

The Art of POLICYMAKING

TOOLS, TECHNIQUES, and PROCESSES in the MODERN EXECUTIVE BRANCH

GEORGE E. SHAMBAUGH, IV
Georgetown University

PAUL J. WEINSTEIN, Jr.
Johns Hopkins University

Los Angeles | London | New Delhi
Singapore | Washington DC

Los Angeles | London | New Delhi
Singapore | Washington DC

FOR INFORMATION:

CQ Press

An Imprint of SAGE Publications, Inc.

2455 Teller Road

Thousand Oaks, California 91320

E-mail: order@sagepub.com

SAGE Publications Ltd.

1 Oliver's Yard

55 City Road

London EC1Y 1SP

United Kingdom

SAGE Publications India Pvt. Ltd.

B 1/I 1 Mohan Cooperative Industrial Area

Mathura Road, New Delhi 110 044

India

SAGE Publications Asia-Pacific Pte. Ltd.

3 Church Street

#10-04 Samsung Hub

Singapore 049483

Copyright © 2016 by CQ Press, an Imprint of SAGE Publications, Inc. CQ Press is a registered trademark of Congressional Quarterly Inc.

All rights reserved. No part of this book may be reproduced or utilized in any form or by any means, electronic or mechanical, including photocopying, recording, or by any information storage and retrieval system, without permission in writing from the publisher.

Printed in the United States of America

Library of Congress Cataloging-in-Publication Data

Shambaugh, George E., 1963-

The art of policymaking: tools, techniques and processes in the modern executive branch / George E. Shambaugh IV, Georgetown University, Paul Weinstein Jr., Johns Hopkins University.—Second edition.

pages cm
Includes bibliographical references and index.

ISBN 978-1-4833-8551-8 (pbk.: alk. paper)

1. Political planning—United States. I. Weinstein, Paul J. II. Title.

JK468.P64S47 2016
352.3'40973—dc23   2015028656

This book is printed on acid-free paper.

Acquisitions Editor: Sarah Calabi
Editorial Assistant: Raquel Christie
Production Editor: Veronica Stapleton Hooper
Copy Editor: Diana Breti
Typesetter: C&M Digitals (P) Ltd.
Proofreader: Dennis W. Webb
Indexer: Marilyn Augst
Cover Designer: Gail Buschman
Marketing Manager: Amy Whitaker

16 17 18 19 20 10 9 8 7 6 5 4 3 2 1

BRIEF CONTENTS

DETAILED CONTENTS

LIST OF BOXES

BOXES

ACRONYMS

ACA	Affordable Care Act
AFDC	Aid to Families With Dependent Children
APA	Administrative Procedure Act
BTU	British Thermal Unit
CBO	Congressional Budget Office
CEA	Council of Economic Advisers
CENTCOM	Centralized Joint Command of the U.S. Military With Jurisdiction in the Middle East
CEQ	Council on Environmental Quality
CIA	Central Intelligence Agency
COLA	Cost of Living Adjustment
COS	Chief of Staff
CRA	Community Reinvestment Act
DNC	Democratic National Committee
DNI	Director of National Intelligence
DOD	Department of Defense
DPC	Domestic Policy Council
DPP	Democratic Progressive Party of Taiwan
DSCC	Democratic Senatorial Campaign Committee
EEZ	Exclusive Economic Zone
EOP	Executive Office of the President
EPA	Environmental Protection Agency
EU	European Union

FCC	Federal Communications Commission
FEC	Federal Elections Commission
FEMA	Federal Emergency Management Agency
GAO	General Accounting Office
GSA	General Services Administration
HHS	U.S. Department of Health and Human Services
HUD	U.S. Department of Housing and Urban Development
INS	Immigration and Naturalization Service
ISF	Iraq Security Forces
JCS	Joint Chiefs of Staff
LRM	Legislative Referral Memorandum
NAFTA	North American Free Trade Agreement
NASA	National Aeronautics and Space Administration
NATO	North Atlantic Treaty Organization
NEC	National Economic Council
NEPA	National Environmental Policy Act
NGA	National Governors' Association
NSC	National Security Council
NSS	National Security Staff
NSTC	National Science and Technology Council
OC	Office of Communications
OCA	Office of Congressional Affairs
OCAF	Office of Cabinet Affairs
OIRA	Office of Information and Regulatory Review
OIA	Office of Intergovernmental Affairs
OLA	Office of Legislative Affairs
OMB	Office of Management and Budget
ONDCP	Office of National Drug Control Policy

OPA	Office of Political Affairs
OPD	Office of Policy Development
OPE	Office of Public Engagement
OPEC	Organization of Petroleum Exporting Countries
OPL	Office of Public Liaison
OSTP	Office of Science and Technology Policy
PCAST	President's Committee of Advisors on Science and Technology
PO	Press Office
PRC	People's Republic of China
Q&As	Question and Answer Sheets
RNC	Republican National Committee
ROC	Republic of China on Taiwan
SAP	Statement of Administrative Policy
SBA	Small Business Administration
SO	Speechwriting Office
SOTU	State of the Union
SSA	Social Security Administration
SSI	Supplemental Security Income
UN	United Nations
UNSC	United Nations Security Council
USIP	United States Institute of Peace
WTO	World Trade Organization

PREFACE

The first edition of *The Art of Policymaking: Tools, Techniques, and Processes in the Modern Executive Branch* hit bookstore shelves early in 2002. It provided students and practitioners with a detailed explanation of the specific tools, techniques, and processes used to create, analyze, and implement policy in the United States. The second edition expands the scope and depth of the first edition in multiple ways.

- **New presidents**. We expanded "Part I: The Policymakers" to reflect upon and compare the organizational structures and policymaking processes in the executive branch as they evolved under Presidents William J. Clinton, George W. Bush, and Barack H. Obama. Just as the original edition offered important information and guidelines on how the White House policymaking process worked to a new president, the second edition is designed to assist President Obama's successor.
- **Rise of the budget process in policymaking**. We expanded "Part II: Tools of the Trade" by adding a new chapter on the budget process and economic policymaking. We also expanded "Part III: Case Studies" to include a case study that focuses on budget negotiations in the Obama administration.
- **Cross-administration comparisons**. The second edition provides case studies regarding social policy, economic policy, and foreign security policy during different administrations. In particular, we supplement our analysis of the Clinton economic plan with an assessment of the Bowles-Simpson deficit reduction commission (on which co-author Paul J. Weinstein, Jr. served as senior adviser) during the Obama administration. In addition, we supplement our chapter on the beginning of U.S. war in Iraq during Desert Shield and Desert Storm with one analyzing President George W. Bush's decision to change U.S. strategy and dramatically increase the number of U.S. personnel on the ground in Iraq through a

policy that became known as "the surge." With these additions, students can compare how economic and security policymaking varies across multiple administrations.

Why is this book still needed? While students of American government and public policy are generally well informed about the institutional characteristics of the American political system, and most understand basic political science theories about politics and governance, many lack a practical understanding of how to assimilate and apply this knowledge to the actual formation and implementation of policy. Furthermore, the extreme polarization of politics today has led many students, scholars, and practitioners to focus on executive-legislative relations. Although this is important, many are entering government and politics with strong ideological positions but little understanding about the role that the executive branch plays in actually creating and implementing policy.

The second edition of our book addresses these problems by explaining how senior officials within the executive branch of government manage the policymaking process. We also provide practitioners and students with a detailed description of the tools and techniques used throughout the executive branch to create and implement policy.

The art of policymaking is the art of leading people and managing problems by using a process that enables the president to make and implement the best possible decisions for the nation. When used effectively, the tools, techniques, and processes of policymaking enhance the president's ability—and the abilities of those he charges with the responsibility to act—to lead the policymaking process by promoting the president's agenda, by serving as an honest broker among competing stakeholders, and by acting as an incubator of ideas. The tools, techniques, and processes also help the president manage policymaking by providing staffing functions, by coordinating the agencies and departments within the Executive Office of the President, by designating accountability, and by monitoring policy implementation and execution. We argue, in particular, that the policymaking process operates best when the authority, responsibility, and accountability for a particular policy are clearly specified and all policymakers with a stake in the policy believe that the process provides a legitimate and effective means of voicing their concerns to the president or those responsible for policy development.

Understanding the specific tools and techniques used in policymaking is critical because the likelihood that policymakers will support the formulation, adoption, and implementation of a particular policy is often as much a function of the perceived legitimacy and effectiveness of the process of policymaking as its substantive merits. When the process is considered to be illegitimate or ineffective, policymakers will circumvent the process and use other means—such as leaking information to the media, ignoring established chains of command, and/or using alternative means to contact the president or other key decision makers directly—to promote their objectives. Such activity undermines the policymaking process because it tends to present the president or other key decision makers with a biased view of the issue at hand and it often sparks retaliatory action by others who do not share that view. The end result is often either an ill-considered policy or, more likely, political deadlock on both the issue at hand and other policy proposals considered to be important to political opponents.

In order to prevent this problem, it is vital for the student and the practitioner to understand the process itself along with the tools and techniques that can make it work effectively. When applied appropriately, they can facilitate policymaking by providing a recognized means of communication among interested parties, thereby enhancing both efficiency and the perception of procedural legitimacy. In contrast, when the tools and techniques are ignored, the process unravels. An effective process does not guarantee that the final policy decision will be the best of all possible decisions, but it increases the probability that the decisions made will reflect the input and evaluation of a variety of competing values and objectives. This, in turn, increases the likelihood that the policy will be supported and adopted. The goal of this book is, thus, to complement existing studies and theories of the policymaking process by providing students and practitioners with the tools, techniques, and processes necessary to make the policymaking process function effectively. By doing so, it also seeks to demonstrate the impact of procedural legitimacy on the policymaking process and the corresponding fruitfulness of incorporating the tools, techniques, and processes of policymaking into extant theories of the policymaking process.

We could not have written this book without the insights and contributions made by many individuals within the administrations of George H. W. Bush, William J. Clinton, George W. Bush, and Barack H. Obama. Paul J. Weinstein, Jr. would particularly like to thank former Vice President Albert Gore, Jr.—who gave him his first opportunity to work in government and politics—and former President William J. Clinton for giving him the opportunity to serve his country and to hone the skills that are presented in this book. In addition, the authors would like to thank all those who helped make this book possible. Although it is not possible to list all those who contributed to this project, a few people deserve special recognition: Kris Balderston, Erskine Bowles, John Bridgeland, Victor Cha, Marc Dunkelman, Peter Feaver, Tom Freedman, Al From, Ben Ginsberg, Stephen Hadley, Mark Jacobsen, Colin Kahl, Matthew Kroenig, James Kvaal, Lindsay Lewis, Gene Ludwig, Will Marshall, Thurgood Marshall, Jr., C. Thomas McMillen, Dana Milbank, Sarah O'Byrne, Jay Parker, Bruce Reed, and Alan Simpson. We thank Kelsey Larsen and Sirvart Tokatlian for their research and editorial assistance on the second edition. In addition, we would like to offer special thanks to Jacquelyn Shambaugh and Jessica Milano; George Shambaugh, III; Lynne Weinstein; William Straus; and Paul Weinstein, Sr. for their tireless support throughout this endeavor.

We also greatly appreciate the input and support of the editors at CQ Press.

ABOUT THE AUTHORS

Dr. George E. Shambaugh, IV is associate professor of international affairs and government in the Edmund A. Walsh School of Foreign Service and former chairman of the Department of Government at Georgetown University. He holds a Ph.D. and M. Phil. in political science and an M.A. in international affairs from Columbia University, and a B.A. in government and physics from Oberlin College. His research focuses on topics of international political economy, international politics, foreign policy, and the environment.

Dr. Shambaugh is the author of *States, Firms, and Power: Successful Sanctions in U.S. Foreign Policy* (SUNY, 1999), co-author of the first edition of *The Art of Policymaking: Tools, Techniques, and Processes in the Modern Executive Branch* (Longman, 2003), co-editor of *Anarchy and the Environment: The International Politics of Common Pool Resources* (SUNY, 1999), and co-editor of three issues of *Taking Sides: Clashing Views on Controversial Issues in American Foreign Policy* (McGraw-Hill, 2006, 2008, 2010). His articles have appeared in a range of journals including the *American Journal of Political Science, International Studies Quarterly, The Journal of Peace Research, Review of International Studies, Analyses of Social Issues and Public Policy, International Politics, Environmental Politics, International Interactions,* and *Security Dialogue.* He has received grants and awards from the National Science Foundation, the Smith Richardson Foundation, the Social Science Research Council, the MacArthur Foundation, the International Studies Association, the American Political Science Association, and the Oberlin Alumni Foundation, and he has been a MacArthur Foundation and Dwight D. Eisenhower/Clifford Roberts Fellow.

Paul J. Weinstein, Jr. is the director of the M.A. in Public Management program at Johns Hopkins University. He holds a M.A. in international affairs from Columbia University and a B.S. in foreign service from Georgetown University. A veteran of two presidential administrations, he was senior adviser to the National Commission on Fiscal Responsibility and Reform (Simpson-Bowles), which was created by President Obama to address the nation's mid- and long-term fiscal challenges. Weinstein formerly served as special assistant to the president and chief of staff of the White House Domestic Policy Council and then later as senior advisor for policy planning to the vice president during the Clinton-Gore administration. Prior to that, Weinstein served as a legislative aide to then-Representative C. Thomas McMillen (D-MD) and then-Senator Albert Gore, Jr. (D-TN).

Since 2001, Weinstein has served as a senior fellow at the Progressive Policy Institute, where he was chief operating officer for five years. He also consults for the Promontory Interfinancial Network. He has advised numerous elected officials, including former governors Jennifer Granholm and Christine Gregoire. Weinstein has taught at Johns Hopkins University since 2003 and has also lectured at Columbia University and Georgetown University. He is co-author of the first edition of *The Art of Policymaking: Tools, Techniques, and Processes in the Modern Executive Branch* (Longman, 2003). He has written chapters in a number of other books, and his writing also has appeared in *The Atlantic, The Boston Globe, The Baltimore Sun, New York Newsday, Forbes, Investor's Business Daily, San Francisco Chronicle, Washington Monthly, New York Daily News,* and *Politico,* among others.

We dedicate this book to Emily, Natalie, Parker,
and the next generation of political leaders in the executive branch.

SAGE was founded in 1965 by Sara Miller McCune to support the dissemination of usable knowledge by publishing innovative and high-quality research and teaching content. Today, we publish over 900 journals, including those of more than 400 learned societies, more than 800 new books per year, and a growing range of library products including archives, data, case studies, reports, and video. SAGE remains majority-owned by our founder, and after Sara's lifetime will become owned by a charitable trust that secures our continued independence.

Los Angeles | London | New Delhi | Singapore | Washington DC

WHY THE POLICYMAKING PROCESS MATTERS

OBJECTIVE

During the first six months of the William J. Clinton administration in 1993, disorganization, disarray, confusion, and general chaos were the rules rather than the exceptions. For twelve years, Democrats had been absent from the halls of power in the executive branch. A young president and an even younger staff were unfamiliar with the decision procedures and systems within the Executive Office of the President. Faced with a large agenda that included an economic stimulus package, universal health care coverage, welfare reform, anti-crime legislation, and national service, the White House became bogged down and incapable of setting priorities and developing and implementing coherent policies. It took almost a year before the president's staff became proficient in the tools and techniques of the decision-making systems within the administration.

George W. Bush entered office intending to focus on tax breaks and other domestic economic policy issues, but he was thrust into unknown territory when terrorists attacked the World Trade Center and the Pentagon on September 11, 2001. The attacks drove domestic security and foreign policy to the top of the Bush administration's policy agenda. They motivated major land wars in Afghanistan and Iraq as well as an open-ended Global War on Terror. To manage these issues, President Bush had to bring together multiple **stakeholders** in the Department of Defense, the Department of State, and the intelligence community who often disagreed about the best means for achieving his objectives. When conditions on the ground in Iraq deteriorated, the president and his senior advisors adapted the policymaking process to build support for a policy change—a "surge" of forces—that ran contrary to both congressional and public opinion.

President Barack Obama campaigned on an anti-war agenda, yet he soon faced foreign policy challenges in Afghanistan, Iraq, Syria, and Russia. In addition, while still promoting his signature health care reform, he had to set other economic priorities aside to manage the worst financial crisis to hit the United States since the Great Depression. Like presidents before him, President Obama faced disagreement among his **principals** and stiff opposition from Congress to many of his policy initiatives. In some areas, like trade policy, President Obama used the policymaking process to build a consensus among competing stakeholders.[1] In others, policymaking was concentrated in the hands of a small number of so-called policy czars in the executive branch, some of whom were situated in the existing policy council structures while others were not. Although the administration continues to hold interagency policy meetings, this centralization and tendency to focus on policy crisis management rather than long-range policy planning has raised concerns from some stakeholders over whether these meetings provide useful conduits to the president's inner circle.[2]

The experiences of the George H. W. Bush, William J. Clinton, George W. Bush, and Barack H. Obama administrations suggest that presidents often face challenges and opportunities that they did not anticipate. To be successful, they must manage these situations and lead people effectively. Doing so requires them to master the art of policymaking. Our primary objective is to provide students and practitioners with an introduction to the tools and techniques used to make policy in the executive branch of the U.S. government. At a pragmatic level, a basic understanding of the tools of the policymaking trade—including how to write and when to use decision memoranda, how to place an issue on the legislative agenda, how to get policies through the legislative clearance and coordination processes, when and how to use polling during the policymaking process, and how to communicate and market policies—is necessary to function effectively within the executive branch. These tools,

---

1. James P. Pfiffner, "Decision Making in the Obama White House," *Presidential Studies Quarterly* 41, 2 (June 2011), pp. 244–262.

2. Mark J. Rozell and Mitchel A. Sollenberger, "Obama's Executive Branch Czars: The Constitutional Controversy and a Legislative Solution," *Congress and the Presidency* 39 (2012), pp. 74–99.

techniques, and processes are the primary means by which the policymaking process is initiated, ideas and concerns of policy stakeholders are expressed and debated, and policy options are presented, chosen, and implemented. In addition to enabling the president to acquire the inputs needed to make the best decisions possible, mastering these skills will help drive policies through the process and improve the chances that they will be implemented as desired in a timely manner.

Given time and experience, practitioners and students of policymaking who are offered an opportunity to work in the White House will become familiar with these tools and techniques. As the cases below demonstrate, Presidents William J. Clinton and George W. Bush became more proficient users of the policymaking process over time. This book is intended to accelerate the learning of those who are entering the executive branch from other arenas as well as guide those who are interested in how to develop and implement policy in general.[3] It is also intended to further the understanding of students and practitioners of policymaking regarding how stakeholders in the executive branch interact throughout the policymaking process and the impact that their behavior has on the policymaking process itself. Policymaking involves a wide range of actors in a variety of venues. These include Congress, think tanks, interest groups, and many others. We acknowledge that all of these actors and institutions matter, but we will focus on policymaking within the executive branch.

Our book is heavily informed by the insights and experiences of policymakers in the George H. W. Bush, William J. Clinton, George W. Bush, and Barack H. Obama administrations. Like them, new presidents will enter office with specific policy goals and the ambition to reshape the policy process in particular ways.[4] While presidential management styles differ and the organizational structure of policymaking evolves over time, there has been a high degree of

---

3. This is particularly important in the White House because few, if any, of the core staff from the previous administration remain when a new president enters office. For a discussion of the difficulties of organizing the White House in a new administration, see Martha Joynt Kumar, "The White House as City Hall: A Tough Place to Organize," *Political Studies Quarterly* 31, 1 (March 2001), pp. 44–55; and John Burke, "Lessons From Past Presidential Transitions: Organization, Management and Decision Making," in *The White House World: Transitions, Organization and Office Operations*, ed. Martha Joynt Kumar and Terry Sullivan (College Station, TX: Texas A&M University Press, 2003), pp. 25–44.

4. For a broader discussion, see B. Guy Peters, *American Public Policy: Promise and Performance* (Thousand Oaks, CA: SAGE, 2012).

consistency in the tools, techniques, and processes of policymaking in the modern executive branch.[5] Especially when considering the past four administrations, the similarities in tools, techniques, and processes of policymaking far outweigh the differences. Thus, lessons learned from the last four administrations can help current and future policymakers make and implement the best possible policy decisions.

The book is divided into three parts: In Part I, we identify key players in the executive branch and the roles they perform in the policymaking process. In Part II, we introduce the tools that enable policymakers to communicate with one another. In Part III, we analyze a series of case studies based on real-world situations to demonstrate how the tools are used and how the individuals interact throughout the policymaking process.

Over the years, control over policy development has become increasingly centered in the White House and the policy councils. Consequently, we begin Part I by introducing three White House policy councils—Domestic Policy, National Economic, and National Security (which includes the now-defunct Homeland Security Council)—and describing their chief leadership and management responsibilities.

Chapter 3 focuses on the White House staff. This chapter describes the roles of the various offices in the White House and what their relationships are to one another. It also explains the flow and control of information within the White House. Chapter 4 focuses on the roles and responsibilities of agencies in the policymaking process. It discusses the role of agencies and the White House in the implementation of policy decisions via drafting regulations, filling in the details on legislation submitted by the president to Congress, carrying out presidential decisions presented in executive orders, and other means. Chapter 5 discusses the role of the policy management models utilized by the policy councils and cabinet agencies and their importance in the policymaking process.

Part II introduces the fundamental tools needed to create policy. Chapter 6 presents the decision memorandum. This chapter describes how to write decision and other types of memoranda for senior government officials using the formats developed by the Office of the White House Staff Secretary.

Chapter 7 discusses the importance of the budget and the State of the Union address as policymaking and implementation tools. Because both

---

5. Charles E. Walcott and Karen M. Hult, "White House Structure and Decision Making: Elaborating the Standard Model," *Presidential Studies Quarterly* 35, 2 (June 2005), pp. 303–318.

are annual processes, they provide a regular mechanism for policymakers to launch new or change existing policies. Chapter 8 discusses the array of authorizing and implementation tools available to policymakers. Policy tools can be broken down into carrots (incentives), sticks (disincentives), and sermons (bully pulpit). Each of these has its strengths and weaknesses. In addition, policy authorization tools—how policies become legally authorized—are a key but often neglected part of the policymaking process.

Chapter 9 discusses the relevance of statements of administration policy (SAPs), legislative referral memoranda (LRMs), and other policymaking facilitators. It explains how administration policy is cleared through the executive branch and the role of the Office of Management and Budget (OMB) in circulating proposals to be adopted as "administration policy." OMB is where the day-to-day activities of the entire government can be routinely monitored and rendered reasonably accountable. In addition, OMB has the power to clear legislation and major regulations, as well as issue administration positions on various policy matters.

Chapter 10 analyzes polling. Good polling data help policymakers refine, test, and market their policy ideas. Inaccurate or incomplete polling data can doom a good proposal. The chapter describes the role pollsters play in the policymaking process and presents a set of polling do's and don'ts.

Chapter 11 analyzes the art of communicating and marketing policy. In this chapter, we analyze the role of the press and communications office in the policymaking process. We also discuss how to draft press statements, question and answer sheets (Q&As), and "backgrounders" the press office can use to sell a policy agenda to the general public.

Part III examines case studies in three issue areas based on real-world situations. Each case is a step-by-step analysis of an actual executive branch decision as seen through the eyes of a practitioner involved in the policymaking process. The case studies demonstrate how to apply the models, tools, and techniques and how the models that were presented in Part I are used in the policymaking process. The cases include the following:

- **A pressing social policy issue:** welfare reform during the Clinton administration (Chapter 12);
- **Important economic issues across administrations:** the development of President Clinton's economic plan in 1993 (Chapter 13) and

the Simpson-Bowles Commission and the fiscal cliff in 2010–2012 (Chapter 14);

- **Vital national security crises across administrations:** the transition from Desert Shield to Desert Storm in Iraq under the George H. W. Bush administration in 1991 (Chapter 15) and the decision during the George W. Bush administration in 2006 to escalate the war in Iraq through the troop "surge" despite widespread opposition to the war (Chapter 16).

Part IV develops a ten-step policymaking checklist that summarizes the lessons presented in this book. It also presents a series of sample policy scenarios. This unique and special feature enables you to rehearse the tools and techniques provided in the book to hone your policy skills. Each scenario includes maps of the policymaking process that readers can use to check their understanding and application of the tools and techniques they have learned. The fictitious scenarios include the following:

- **An important domestic political issue:** a proposal to ban handheld phone texting in motor vehicles;
- **An international political/military scenario:** the crisis in Ukraine;
- **An important multilateral issue:** a multilateral environmental initiative.

SITUATING THE TOOLS, TECHNIQUES, AND PROCESSES IN THE EXISTING LITERATURE

By focusing on the basic tools of the trade of policymaking, this book provides a unique complement to the plethora of superb textbooks and scholarly studies of the executive branch.[6] Political scientists and policy analysts have also

---

6. Prominent texts in the field include George C. Edwards, III and Stephen J. Wayne, *Presidential Leadership: Politics and Policymaking,* 9th edition (New York, NY: Cengage Learning, 2014); Erwin C. Hargrove and Michael Nelson, *Presidents Politics and Policy* (New York, NY: Knopf, 1984); Samuel Kernell, *Going Public,* 4th edition (Washington, DC: The Congressional Quarterly, 2007); Martha Joynt Kumar and Terry Sullivan, eds., *The White House World: Transitions, Organization and Office Operations* (College Station, TX: Texas A&M University Press, 2003); Michael Nelson, *The Presidency and the Political System* (Washington, DC: The Congressional Quarterly, 1997); Richard E. Neustadt, *Presidential Power and the Modern Presidents* (New York, NY: Free Press, 1990); Alexander George and Juliette George, *Presidential Personality and Performance* (Boulder, CO: Westview Press, 1998).

developed a variety of useful frameworks to help practitioners and scholars alike understand the policymaking process.[7] One classic approach describes the policymaking process as a series of sequential stages—problem identification, policy formulation, adoption, implementation, and evaluation—and categorizes policy actions as they vary from stage to stage.[8] Another focuses on the impact of the organizational process, bureaucratic politics, and presidential management styles on the policymaking process.[9] There are also increasingly sophisticated theories that emphasize strategic rationality[10] and

7. For a review of prominent theories of policymaking, see Paul A. Sabatier and Christopher Weible, eds., *Theories of the Policy Process*, 2nd edition (Boulder, CO: Westview Press 2007), pp. 1–17; Kevin Smith and Christopher Larimer, *The Public Policy Theory Primer*, 2nd edition (Boulder, CO: Westview Press, 2013), pp. 1–23; and James P. Pfiffner, "Presidential Decision Making: Rationality, Advisory Systems, and Personality," *Presidential Studies Quarterly* 35, 2 (2005), pp. 217–228.

8. The **sequential approach**, also known as the "stages heuristic" or "the textbook approach," was developed by James Anderson, Charles Jones, Gary Brewer, and Peter deLeon. See James E. Anderson, *Public Policymaking: An Introduction* (Boston, MA: Houghton Mifflin, 1990); and Peter deLeon, "The Stages Approach to the Policy Process: What Has it Done? Where is it Going?" in *Theories of the Policy Process*, 2nd edition, eds. Paul Sabatier and Christopher Weible (Boulder, CO: Westview Press, 2014), pp. 19–32. For a critique of this approach, see Paul Sabatier, "Toward Better Theories of the Policy Process," *PS Political Science and Politics* 24, 2 (June 1991), pp. 147–156.

9. Classics in this tradition include I. M. Destler, *Presidents, Bureaucrats, and Foreign Policy* (Princeton, NJ: Princeton University Press, 1972), and Neustadt, *Presidential Power*. For a review of the organizational process model, the bureaucratic politics model, and the presidential management model, see William Newmann, "Causes of Change in National Security Processes: Carter, Reagan, and Bush Decision Making on Arms Control," *Presidential Studies Quarterly* 31, 1 (March 2001), pp. 69–103.

10. This includes theories about the source of policymaker preferences as well as rational choice and institutional rational choice theories about how individuals pursue actions that maximize their preferences and interests within a set of institutional constraints. On the former, see Graham Allison and Philip Zelikow, *Essence of Decision: Explaining the Cuban Missile Crisis* (New York, NY: Longman, 1999), and Roger Hilsman with Laura Gaughran and Patricia A. Weitsman, *The Politics of Policymaking in Defense and Foreign Affairs: Conceptual Models and Bureaucratic Politics*, 3rd edition (Englewood Cliffs, NJ: Prentice Hall, 1993). On the latter, see Kenneth Shepsle, *Analyzing Politics* (New York, NY: W. W. Norton, 1997) and Sabatier and Weible, *Theories of the Policy Process*, pp. 25–58. For a critique of rational choice approaches to policy analysis, see Deborah Stone, *Policy, Paradox, and Political Reason* (Glenview, IL: Scott, Foresman and Company, 1988).

the dynamics of individual and collective decision making.[11] In a variant of this genre, some scholars argue that bounded rationality and a variety of institutional, informational, and contextual constraints make policymaking "sticky" and prone to periods of punctuated equilibrium.[12] This punctuated equilibrium theory posits that policy change is expected to be incremental in the absence of significant social, political, or related events that break inertia, such as elections, economic crises, or wars.[13] Others go further to argue that the policymaking process reflects "organized anarchy" more than a rational process of strategic interaction.[14] From this perspective, policy problems and solutions are often ambiguous. Success is difficult to predict because it requires gaining sustained attention and **buy-in** from key stakeholders, and it is often done under significant information and time constraints. Policymaking outcomes reflect the blending of independent streams of problems, potential solutions, participants, and opportunities in what can be characterized as a "garbage can" model of organizational dynamics.[15] From this perspective, policymaking is most likely to be successful when three streams intersect: policy problems come to the attention of policymakers, a policy process is developed and policy proposals are generated, and the political environment (elections, leadership, public opinion, etc.) enable the participants to act.

Combined, the literature provides useful insights into how a wide range of historical, legal, institutional, organizational, psychological, and political factors

---

11. For example, the Advocacy Coalition Framework developed by Sabatier and Jenkins-Smith focuses on the interaction between advocacy coalitions in the policymaking process. See Paul Sabatier and Hank Jenkins-Smith, *Policy Change and Learning: An Advocacy Coalition Approach* (Boulder, CO: Westview Press, 1993); Sabatier and Weible, *Theories of the Policy Process*, pp. 225–266. In addition, Jeffrey Pressman and Aaron Wildavsky analyze the problems that arise as a result of having multiple participants and perspectives involved in policy implementation. See Jeffrey Pressman and Aaron Wildavsky, *Implementation*, 2nd edition (Berkeley: University of California Press, 1979).

12. Sabatier and Weible, *Theories of the Policy Process*, pp. 183–224.

13. Frank Baumgartner and Bryan D. Jones, *Agendas and Instability in American Politics* (Chicago, IL: University of Chicago Press, 1993).

14. For early work in this area, see Michael D. Cohen, James G. March, and Johan P. Olsen, "A Garbage Can Model of Organizational Choice," *Administrative Science Quarterly* 17, 1 (March 1972), pp. 1–25.

15. John Kingdon, *Agendas, Alternatives, and Public Policy* (Boston, MA: Little Brown, 1984). See also Sabatier and Weible, *Theories of the Policy Process*, pp. 59–104.

affect policymaking in the executive branch.[16] It is, however, relatively silent about the tools and techniques that policymakers in the executive branch use to achieve their ends and on the impact that these have on the process. By highlighting the tools and techniques of policymaking, we do not suggest that the factors emphasized in this diverse literature are unimportant. Indeed, many of these factors rely on or influence the tools, techniques, and processes used by policymakers in the modern executive branch. Rather, we argue that whether one evaluates policymaking through the lens of management styles; bureaucratic or organizational politics; strategically rational individuals acting in the context of institutional and informational constraints; or as the result of the convergence of streams of policy problems, ideas, participants, and opportunities; putting these insights into practice requires a practical understanding of the nuts and bolts of the actual policymaking tools, techniques, and processes at the policymaker's disposal. Mastering the art of policymaking enables stakeholders to lead and manage the policymaking process so that the president receives the best information possible and can generate and implement policies that address long-term strategic goals and adapt to changing circumstances. Our book thus contributes to work by recent scholars by informing these theoretical debates with insights and perceptions of policymakers regarding the role and structure of important institutions and actors within the executive branch.[17]

One of the most enduring and broadly recognized characteristics of policymaking since President Franklin D. Roosevelt reasserted the executive branch's role in the policymaking process is the gap between the high public demands and expectations placed on the president and the president's comparatively limited legal, political, and institutional capabilities to meet them.[18] Whether it

---

16. For a summary of this literature, see George C. Edwards, III and Stephen J. Wayne, "Appendix A: Studying the Presidency," in *Presidential Leadership: Politics and Policy Making*, 9th edition (New York, NY: St. Martin's/Worth, 2014), pp. 487–499.

17. Prominent among these is the Presidency Research Group. The PRG's objective is to provide a detailed job description of some of the most important positions in the White House. Beginning in December 2001 with the publication of guidelines for planning a transition to power for the new president, its findings have been published in *Presidential Studies Quarterly*. Many of these findings are synthesized in Kumar and Sullivan, *The White House World*.

18. See Neustadt, *Presidential Power*; Joseph A. Pika and Norman C. Thomas, "The Presidency Since Mid-Century," *Congress and the Presidency* 19, 1 (Spring 1992), pp. 29–46; Karen M. Hult, "Strengthening Presidential Decision-Making Capacity," *Presidential Studies Quarterly* 30, 1 (March 2000), pp. 27–46. Recent critics of this viewpoint, including Terry Moe and

is due to a honeymoon period of hope or a rally-around-the-flag effect in response to a national trauma or national success, public confidence in the president is often fleeting. For example, the percentage of the American public who have "a great deal" or "quite a lot" of confidence in the president has declined from a high of 72% in 1991 to 29% in 2015.[19] It peaked for President Clinton in 1998 (toward the end of his administration), it peaked for President George W. Bush in 2002 (after 9/11), and it peaked for President Obama in 2010 (in his first term in office). In every case, it declined thereafter (see Box 1-1).

Paradoxically, the president has little direct influence over many of the people whose support and expertise he needs to close the gap and effectively formulate and implement executive branch policy initiatives.[20] He also often has to make policy choices that disappoint many of his constituents, raising doubts among supporters while exciting critics. Understanding the tools, techniques, and processes can help policymakers reduce this problem and bridge the performance-expectations gap by leading people and managing policy problems effectively.

William Howell, argue that modern presidents have a great institutional capacity to act unilaterally and make law on their own. See Terry M. Moe and William G. Howell, "Unilateral Action and Presidential Power: A Theory," *Presidential Studies Quarterly* 29, 4 (1999), pp. 850–872. Others, including Charles O. Jones, argue that presidents may be able to take advantage of the competition among different units in the federal government to assert influence over the policy agenda. See Charles O. Jones, "Reinventing Leeway: The President and Agenda Certification," *Presidential Studies Quarterly* 30, 1 (March 2000), pp. 6–26. For some of the potential problems resulting from this gap, see Colin Campbell, *The U.S. Presidency in Crisis: A Comparative Perspective* (New York, NY: Oxford University Press, 1998); Hult, "Strengthening Presidential Decision-Making Capacity," pp. 27–46; Larry M. Lane, "The Public Administration and the Problem of the Presidency," in *Refounding Democratic Public Administration: Modern Paradoxes, Postmodern Challenges*, ed. Gary L. Wamsley and James F. Wolf (Thousand Oaks, CA: SAGE, 1996); and Paul C. Light, *Thickening Government: Federal Hierarchy and the Diffusion of Accountability* (Washington, DC: Brookings Institution, 1995).

19. Public confidence in Congress declined from 30% in 1991 to 7% in 2014. See GALLUP Politics, "Americans Losing Confidence in All Branches of U.S. Gov't: Confidence hits six-year low for presidency; record lows for Supreme Court, Congress," last modified June 30, 2014, accessed May 29, 2015, http://www.gallup.com/poll/171992/americans-losing-confidence-branches-gov.aspx.

20. Stephen J. Wayne, G. Calvin MacKenzie, David M. O'Brien, and Richard L. Cole, *The Politics of American Government*, 3rd edition (New York, NY: St. Martin's/Worth, 1999), p. 498. See also Hult, "Strengthening Presidential Decision-Making Capacity," pp. 27–46; Terry M. Moe, "The Politicized Presidency," in *The New Directions in American Politics*, ed. John Chudd and Paul Peterson (Washington, DC: Brookings Institution, 1985); and Bert A. Rockman, *The Leadership Question* (New York, NY: Praeger, 1984).

BOX 1-1	Americans' Level of Confidence in the Three Branches of Government

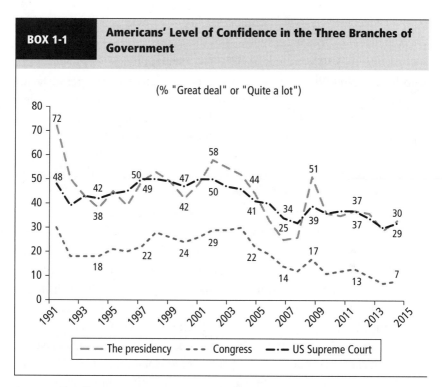

Source: Gallup, "Americans Losing Confidence in All Branches of U.S. Gov't," June 30, 2014. Copyright © 2014 Gallup, Inc. All rights reserved. The content is used with permission; however, Gallup retains all rights of republication. Updated data are available online at http://www.gallup.com/poll/1597/confidence-institutions.aspx.

PROMOTING PRESIDENTIAL LEADERSHIP AND MANAGEMENT THROUGH THE POLICYMAKING PROCESS

The president is the leader of the country and its chief policymaker. As President Truman argued in his farewell address in 1953, "The President—whoever he is—has to decide. He can't pass the buck to anybody. No one else can do the deciding for him. That's his job."[21] The art of policymaking is the art of leading people and managing problems using a process that enables the president to make and implement the best possible decisions for the nation.

---

21. For a photograph of "The Buck Stops Here" sign on President Truman's desk in the Oval Office, see the Truman Library online at http://www.trumanlibrary.org/buckstop.htm.

Used effectively, the tools, techniques, and processes of policymaking enable and enhance the president's ability—and the abilities of those he charges with the responsibility to act—to lead the policymaking process by performing at least three critical roles:

1. **Promoting the president's agenda**

   The White House staff and policy councils are custodians of the president's initiatives and are responsible for driving them through the policymaking process. This requires a working knowledge of the roles of the policy councils, key policymakers within the White House staff, and the agencies and departments of the executive branch.

2. **Acting as an honest broker among competing stakeholders**

   The White House staff and policy councils are also conduits to the president for the multiple stakeholders throughout the executive branch. An honest broker process is one that enables stakeholders to participate and be heard by the president.[22] At a minimum, this increases the level of consultation and reduces biases inherent in decision making in small groups of people. It also builds consensus and generates higher levels of political support among stakeholders even when the policies chosen do not reflect each stakeholder's views. This is especially important when the context changes and/or stakeholders' disagreements about the problems, policy solutions, or politics at hand persist.

3. **Incubating new ideas**

   The White House staff and policy councils are responsible for making sure that the president has the best information possible before making a policy decision. Different stakeholders will offer different perspectives, insights, and information. Giving the president access to the resulting ideas will generate better-articulated and better-vetted policies. Decisions taken without inclusive deliberations are prone to individual or group biases and are less well-considered.[23]

---

22. John P. Burke, "The Neutral/Honest Broker Role in Foreign-Policy Decision Making: A Reassessment." *Presidential Studies Quarterly,* 35, 2 (2005), pp. 229–258; and John P. Burke, *Honest Broker? The National Security Advisor and Presidential Decision Making* (College Station, TX: Texas A&M University Press, 2009).

23. James P. Pfiffner, "The Contemporary Presidency: Decision Making in the Bush White House," *Presidential Studies Quarterly,* 39, 2 (2009), pp. 363–384.

An effective process can also help the president manage policymaking and policy implementation. It does so by providing three functions:

1. **Staffing the president**

   The White House staff and policy councils prepare memos, vet his or her speeches, conduct policy briefings, and organize his or her daily schedule. To be effective, they need a working knowledge of legislative clearance and coordination procedures and the ability to communicate and market policy. As former National Security Advisor Stephen Hadley noted, "Serving as the National Security Advisor is a great and important job, but it is ultimately a staff position."[24]

2. **Coordinating the agencies and departments within the Executive Office of the President**

   This may involve arranging meetings and briefings among the highest levels of commissioned officers who work directly for the president. They include the assistants to the president (principals), the deputy assistants to the president (deputies), and the special assistants to the president (specials). It may also include coordinating stakeholders in other departments and agencies such as the Department of Defense, Department of State, and Central Intelligence Agency.

3. **Designating accountability and monitoring implementation and evaluating execution**

   This oversight function involves making sure that the president's initiatives are implemented as directed in a timely manner. Once the president has made a decision and set a strategy, the appropriate policy council needs to break it down, determine which agencies are responsible for the tasks, when they are due, who has the lead, and who is accountable. Without oversight and a sense of urgency, daily demands will likely swamp policy changes and the policy may never come to fruition.

The combination of these leadership and managerial roles creates a hexagon of responsibilities, reflected in Box 1-2. Although all White House staff and policy councils serve these roles, the relative weight given to each role varies as a function of the president's management style and the management styles of

---

24. Stephen Hadley (former national security advisor), interview with the author, January 12, 2015.

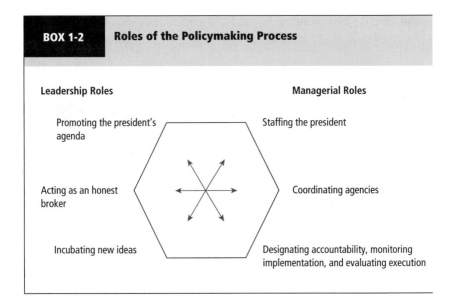

BOX 1-2   **Roles of the Policymaking Process**

Leadership Roles   **Managerial Roles**

Promoting the president's   Staffing the president
agenda

Acting as an honest   Coordinating agencies
broker

Incubating new ideas   Designating accountability, monitoring
                                             implementation, and evaluating execution

the president's chief of staff, the assistant to the president who directs the policy council in question, and the directors of other agencies and departments in the executive branch. The relative weight also varies with the specificity, urgency, and general nature of the situation at hand. Some principals in some circumstances emphasize the honest broker and policy incubator roles, while in different circumstances they or others in their position may choose to delegate responsibility to a particular department or agency and place greater emphasis on implementing the president's policies. The relative importance of different roles played by the National Security Council, for example, varies significantly over time.[25] Some national security advisors, like Bundy, Scowcroft, and Hadley, emphasized the managerial roles of overseeing policy accountability, implementation, and execution.[26] Some, like Lake and Hadley, acted more like honest brokers when incubating policy ideas; some, like Brzezinski, took a more assertive position when confronting others with competing perspectives. Still others, like Rice, sought to organize the policymaking process rather than impose views or encourage others do so.[27] Thus, different

25. Burke, "The Neutral/Honest Broker," pp. 229–258; Burke, *Honest Broker?*

26. Ivo H. Daalder and Irving M. Destler, *In the Shadow of the Oval Office: Profiles of the National Security Advisers and the Presidents They Served—From JFK to George W. Bush* (New York, NY: Simon and Schuster, 2009), p. 9.

27. Daalder and Destler, *In the Shadow of the Oval Office*, pp. 257, 281.

policy councils may find themselves in different locations within the hexagon at different times throughout a particular administration.

THE IMPORTANCE OF PROCEDURAL LEGITIMACY IN BUILDING POLICY SUPPORT

The process of molding an idea into a policy within the executive branch involves the collective action of a wide range of individuals, policy councils, agencies, and departments who have a stake in its outcome. The majority of these executive branch stakeholders share some common policy goals most of the time. Indeed, the degree of compatibility of the goals among executive branch members is likely to be much greater than the degree of compatibility between those in the executive branch and those in the legislative or judicial branches.[28] As noted above, policy problems and policy solutions can be ambiguous. Existing policies may also need to be adapted to changing circumstances. Consequently, while the majority of the individuals, policy councils, agencies, and departments within the executive branch share some common goals most of the time, they may (and often do) disagree about the relative importance of bringing one issue versus another to the president's attention.

Even if there is agreement that something must be done on a particular issue, stakeholders in the executive branch often disagree about precisely what the specific objectives of an administration's policy response should be or how best to achieve those objectives. For example, in 1993, President Clinton's policymaking team did not agree on the relative merits of pursuing welfare versus health care reform and, even when welfare reform eventually was given priority, the Domestic Policy Council and the Department of Health and Human Services did not agree on the structure that welfare reform policy should take. In 2006, President Bush's foreign policy team disagreed on how best to fight the war in Iraq. National Security Advisor Stephen Hadley argued for a "surge" of troops, Secretary of State Rice expressed concerns that a surge was not viable, and General Casey argued that the existing "stand up [Iraqi forces], stand down [U.S. forces]" policy should be continued. In 2010, senior members of the Obama administration disagreed on how best to manage the economy and deficit reduction. Senior economic advisor

---

28. The division of powers and preferences into these the executive, legislative, and judicial branches were, of course, part of the system of checks and balances established by the original framers of the Constitution to keep any one group from gaining pervasive influence over another. For a discussion of policymakers and the policy environment, see James Anderson, *Public Policymaking: An Introduction* (Boston, MA: Houghton Mifflin, 1990), pp. 41–76.

Lawrence Summers and Treasury Secretary Timothy Geithner favored continued economic stimulus while others, including former budget director Peter Orszag and political advisers David Axelrod and David Plouffe, favored deficit reduction.[29] Thus, regardless of administration, the policymaking environment is often characterized by multiple groups with common and competing viewpoints vying to influence the form and content of policy ideas. To complicate matters further, power and responsibility are distributed unevenly and tend to shift among these groups over time and across issues.[30]

At the same time, there are powerful incentives for these groups to **strain toward agreement** and reach a collective solution to the problems at hand.[31] Policymakers have shared ideas, especially about the importance and role of the executive branch in policymaking. Most also recognize that their integrity as policymakers and the integrity of the system as a whole lie in the ability to function and respond to the problem at hand.

The president has a strong incentive to create buy-in among his team. Above all, presidents want to be right. If a trusted advisor does not agree with a chosen policy, something likely needs to be reconsidered. Presidents also want to avoid splits among their senior advisors. Even if the disagreements do not become public, they can raise concerns about access to the president and biases in the information he receives. This matters because these stakeholders are also likely to play a critical role in advocating the president's policy, shepherding that policy through the process, and monitoring its implementation. All of these functions will be better done if those involved are convinced that the policy is appropriate.

In such a complex environment, it is often difficult to achieve a general consensus about a particular policy goal or the best means to achieve that goal. All else equal, however, stakeholders are more likely to support the formulation, adoption, and implementation of a particular policy when accountability is clear and multiple stakeholders are able to voice their policy ideas and concerns. When accountability is unclear or the tools fail to provide an effective means for

---

29. Jackie Calmes, "Obama's Deficit Dilemma," *New York Times,* February 27, 2012, http://www.nytimes.com/2012/02/27/us/politics/obamas-unacknowledged-debt-to-bowles-simpson-plan.html.

30. For a discussion of different aspects of fragmentation within the executive branch, see Roger Porter, *Presidential Decision Making* (Cambridge, UK: Cambridge University Press, 1980), pp. 11–25.

31. Roger Hilsman et al., *The Politics of Policymaking in Defense and Foreign Affairs,* pp. 80–81; Warner Schilling, "The Politics of National Defense: Fiscal 1960," in *Strategy, Politics and Defense Budgets,* ed. Warner R. Schilling, Paul Y. Hammond, and Glenn H. Snyder (New York, NY: Columbia University Press, 1962), p. 23; and Stone, *Policy, Paradox, and Political Reason,* p. 7.

those with opposing viewpoints to participate in policy development, disgruntled stakeholders tend to circumvent the process and use other means—such as leaking information to the media, circumventing or ignoring bureaucratic hierarchies, and attempting to contact the president (or the decision makers responsible for policy development) directly—to promote their objectives.[32] Such activity undermines the policymaking process because it tends to present the president (or the decision makers responsible for policy development) with a biased view of the issue at hand, and it often sparks similar retaliatory action by others who do not share that view.[33] This wastes time, sends signals of uncertainty to Congress, and may result in the public reducing their willingness to support executive actions.[34] The end result may be an ill-considered policy or, more likely, political deadlock and a decline in the president's reputation in Washington and his prestige with the general public. While it is certainly true that the existence of an accountable and representative policymaking process does not guarantee that the final policy decision will be the best of all possible decisions, it increases the probability that the decisions made will reflect the input and evaluation of a variety of competing values and objectives; this, in turn, increases the likelihood that the policy will be supported and adopted.[35]

An effective policymaking process can increase **procedural legitimacy** by coordinating relevant agencies and departments, assigning accountability, and monitoring implementation. It can also increase buy-in by serving as an honest broker among competing stakeholders and acting as an incubator of ideas for the president. Sociological, legal, and policy studies suggest the perceived legitimacy of the tools, techniques, and procedures of complex decision-making processes have a significant impact on the willingness of people to take part in the decision-making process. It also affects their willingness to implement or comply with a

---

32. In the words of Albert O. Hirschman, the ability to voice one's concerns tends to be associated with increased loyalty, while the inability to do so is associated with a tendency to exit. Albert O. Hirschman, *Exit, Voice, and Loyalty: Responses to Decline in Firms, Organizations, and States* (Cambridge, MA: Harvard University Press, 1970).

33. In political science jargon, the failure of the chief decision maker to weigh all options in an unbiased manner reduces his or her ability to act in a fully rational manner.

34. Richard Neustadt, one of the most influential scholars of the presidency, argues that the president's power to lead is greatly affected by his reputation for competency in Washington and his prestige with the general public. In support of this contention, George Edwards found that popular presidents received more congressional support regardless of party affiliation. George C. Edwards III, *At the Margins* (New Haven, CT: Yale University Press, 1989), p. 124; Neustadt, *Presidential Power*.

35. Porter, *Presidential Decision Making*, p. 1.

given policy. For example, in a 1984–1985 survey of 2,379 people who were involved with the U.S. legal system, Tom Tyler found that perceptions of procedural legitimacy had a significant impact on how people evaluated the decisions made and the decision-making processes used by politicians, the courts, and the police.[36] He found that the more "fair" and "appropriate" the procedures were perceived to be, the more people were willing to accept and comply with a particular interpretation of the law, even when the outcome was undesirable. The perception of procedural legitimacy mattered more when the issues were contentious and less when they were not, more when compliance with a given set of procedures or rules was voluntary than when it was enforced, and far more when the participants valued a particular outcome highly versus when they did not (regardless of whether or not the decision was favorable). Consistent with this finding, studies of international law suggest that even in the absence of a central authority or viable enforcement mechanism in international politics, nation-states are likely to accept and conform to international rules and norms when they perceive them to have a high degree of legitimacy.[37] Conversely, when international rules and norms are not considered to be legitimate, compliance decreases substantially.

Political scientists have argued, further, that the political significance of legitimacy is one of the most fundamental components of political interaction. For example, Alan Lamborn argues that how people will react to a particular set of policy outcomes in a political context will vary depending on the importance they attach to creating or sustaining legitimate relationships, their beliefs about legitimate procedures and outcomes, and their perceptions of how legitimate their existing relationships are.[38] Consistent with individuals' perceptions of the law discussed above, Lamborn argues that the political importance of the legitimacy of a specific policy outcome and the legitimacy of the policy process from which it evolved is inversely related: the lower the legitimacy of an outcome, the greater the political significance of perceived procedural legitimacy.[39] If people place a high value on sustaining legitimate relationships (as competing policymakers in the executive branch do when they "strain toward agreement" on collective decisions)

---

36. Tom Tyler, *Why People Obey the Law* (New Haven, CT: Yale University Press, 1990), p. 105.

37. International legal scholars emphasize the importance of legitimacy as a property of a rule or rule-making institution, which itself exerts a pull toward compliance. See Thomas Franck, *The Power of Legitimacy Among Nations* (Oxford, UK: Oxford University Press, 1990), p. 25.

38. Alan Lamborn, "Theory and the Politics of World Politics," *International Studies Quarterly* 41 (1997), pp. 187–214.

39. The converse is also true.

and their relationships are perceived to be legitimate, then they are more likely to accept outcomes that adversely affect their short-term policy preferences.[40]

Given the importance of legitimacy to the policymaking process, it is important to understand how policymakers define fair or legitimate procedures. Some take an instrumental view and argue that "fairness" may be defined in terms of the policy outcome and the degree to which the outcome reflects the specific interests of particular policymakers. The ends, thus, justify and motivate the means. Others take an institutional perspective and argue that legitimacy may be explained in terms of the specific institutional process of action, defined in terms of rules about how laws are made, how decision makers are chosen, and how public participation is achieved.[41] In support of the second of these two viewpoints, Tyler's statistical study suggests that people actually value the ability to obtain a particular outcome less than the opportunity to present their arguments, be listened to, and have their views considered by those responsible for policy development.[42] The study also found that perceptions of legitimacy and fairness were linked to judgments about the neutrality of the chief decision maker and the unbiased nature of the decision-making process. Individuals who felt that they played a role in the decision-making process and that the process was unbiased or neutral were more accepting of the outcome, regardless of what the outcome was. People who felt that the process was biased or that their views were not being considered by those responsible for policy development were more apt to exit the formal decision-making process and evade its decisions.

These findings have important implications for policymaking in the executive branch. Policymakers in the executive branch often negotiate over highly contentious and politically volatile issues, they generally act voluntarily rather than being compelled to do so, and they often have a high stake in particular outcomes. Consequently, based on the survey results, one would expect procedural legitimacy to matter greatly to policymakers in the executive branch. The policymaking process is, thus, likely to be evaluated in terms of how it operates

---

40. Lamborn, "Theory and the Politics of World Politics," p. 193.

41. This view builds on Max Weber's conception of legitimacy in terms of a specific process. See Franck, *The Power of Legitimacy*, p. 17. Legitimacy is conventionally defined as a belief on the part of citizens that the current government represents a proper form of government and a willingness on the part of those citizens to accept the decrees of the government as legal and authoritative. See Peters, *American Public Policy*, p. 95; Michael Kraft and Scott R. Furlong, *Public Policy: Politics, Analysis, and Alternatives*, 4th edition (Thousand Oaks, CA: SAGE, 2013), pp. 97–98.

42. Tyler, *Why People Obey the Law*, p. 163.

as well as by what it produces. Effective operation involves management—using the appropriate tools of the trade, managing the agencies and departments, assigning accountability, and overseeing implementation—as well as leadership—serving as an honest broker among competing stakeholders and serving as an effective incubator of ideas for the president. Extending this beyond the executive branch, Michael Kraft and Scott R. Furlong argue that this process of legitimation is important for virtually all policy initiatives:

> A careful assessment of any policy analyses or other technical studies might be part of this process of discussion and debate. So too might public participation through public meetings, hearings, and citizen advisory bodies, or endorsement by respected community or national leaders. Sometimes lawmakers call on cultural elites, athletes, and other celebrities to convince the public of the worthiness of the issue under consideration. . . . Policies that are adopted without such legitimation face serious hurdles. They may well fail to command public support, affected interest groups may oppose them or even challenge them in court, and their implementation could be adversely affected.[43]

We, thus, join prominent scholars and practitioners and define legitimacy in terms of how things are done (i.e., whether proper procedures are used) as well as what is actually being done.[44] As noted by Thomas Franck, for example, fairness of any legal system will be judged

> first by the degree to which the rules satisfy the participant's expectations of justifiable distribution of costs and benefits [substance], and secondly, by the extent to which the rules are made and applied in accordance with what the participants perceive as the right process [procedure].[45]

Perceptions of the right process will be greatest when policymakers believe that "decisions about the distributive and other entitlements will be made by those duly authorized and in accordance with procedures which protect against corrupt, arbitrary, or idiosyncratic decision-making or decision-executing."[46]

---

43. Kraft and Furlong, *Public Policy*, pp. 97–98.

44. Anderson, *Public Policymaking*, p. 110.

45. Thomas M. Franck, *Fairness in International Law and Institutions* (Oxford, UK: Clarendon Press, 1995), p. 7.

46. Franck, *Fairness in International Law*, p. 7.

Procedural legitimacy is important in a variety of places including the administrative process, the legislative process, the regulatory process, the courts, and direct democracy.[47] Many of the rules and procedures of the policy-making process are codified in the Constitution, determined by Congress, or specified in executive orders or other legal processes. When policymaking is conducted outside of established rules and procedures, its legitimacy is likely to be questioned. At the same time, however, acting within the bounds of one's legal authority is not sufficient to guarantee that the process will be perceived as legitimate. Indeed, as James Anderson argues, "Some actions of government, even when within the legal or constitutional authority of officials, may not be regarded as legitimate because they depart too far from prevailing notions of what is acceptable."[48] Many Americans, for example, considered the use of tor-ture and inhumane treatment at Abu Ghraib prison in Baghdad during the second Iraq War to be illegitimate, even though Deputy Assistant U.S. Attorney General John Yoo wrote memos justifying the military interrogation of alien unlawful combatants.[49]

One of the hallmarks of an effective political process is that it enables the president to make potentially controversial decisions with the best available input so mistakes can be avoided. While the perception that the policymaking process is legitimate can help buffer decision makers who deliver undesirable outcomes, the perception that the process is corrupt can undermine support for the decision and decision makers, even if the policy itself is ultimately popular.[50]

CONCLUSION

The ability of all executive branch policymakers to navigate and manage the policymaking process is complicated by the fact that ideas for a particular policy may come from virtually any source—members of the president's staff, executive agencies and departments, Congress, the media, academic scholars, special interest groups, and more.[51] All of these groups provide input and compete to influence the ideas, information, and proposals presented for the

---

47. Peters, *American Public Policy*, p. 96.

48. Anderson, *Public Policymaking*, p. 110.

49. ACLU, "Memo Regarding the Torture and Military Interrogation of Alien Unlawful Combatants Held Outside the United States," last modified March 14, 2003, accessed May 29, 2015, https://www.aclu.org/files/pdfs/safefree/yoo_army_torture_memo.pdf.

50. Tyler, *Why People Obey the Law*, p. 106.

51. Smith and Larimer, *The Public Policy Theory Primer*, pp. 73–97.

policy issue at hand. Paradoxically, the president has little direct influence over many of the people whose support and expertise he needs to formulate and implement executive branch policy initiatives effectively.

The art of policymaking is the art of leading people and managing problems using a process that enables the president to make and implement the best possible decisions for the nation. When used appropriately, the tools, techniques, and processes of policymaking can help the president and his principals lead the people on his team and manage the policy problems effectively. Using the tools, techniques, and processes appropriately also increases procedural legitimacy. This, in turn, increases that likelihood that all stakeholders will accept and support a given policy throughout its development and implementation.

Key Terms

Buy-in

Principals

Procedural legitimacy

Sequential approach

Stakeholders

Strain toward agreement

Review Questions

1. Discuss three ways in which the tools and techniques of policymaking affect the policymaking process.
2. Name six ways that the policymaking process can assist the president.
3. Why does procedural legitimacy matter?

THE WHITE HOUSE POLICY COUNCILS

THE POLICY COUNCILS AND THE STRUCTURE OF THE EXECUTIVE BRANCH

Since the end of World War II, control over policy development has become increasingly centered in the White House. Presidents George H. W. Bush, Bill Clinton, George W. Bush, and Barack Obama continued this trend by centralizing management of the policymaking process in the White House and the Executive Office of the President.[1]

This trend has been driven, in part, by three factors:

- The United States' outsized role in the global community;
- The rapidly increasing responsibilities and size of the federal government;
- The evolution of the president as "policymaker-in-chief."

Although all executive branch **departments** and **agencies** have input into the policymaking process, the White House policy councils are by far the most influential. The most relevant among these are the National Security Council (NSC), the National Economic Council (NEC), and the Domestic Policy Council (DPC). The policy councils play six primary roles:

---

1. For a discussion of the evolution of the staffing, organization, and roles of players within the executive branch, see George C. Edwards III and Stephen J. Wayne, *Presidential Leadership: Politics and Policy Making* (New York, NY: St. Martin's/Worth, 1999), pp. 184–215.

Leadership roles:

- Promoting the president's agenda
- Acting as honest brokers
- Incubator for new ideas

Management roles:

- Staffing the president
- Coordinating the agencies
- Holding stakeholders, agencies, and others accountable for policy implementation and evaluating execution

Unlike other agencies and departments, the policy councils have no programmatic or specific constituencies beyond the president. The intended unbiased nature of the policy councils helps to increase their ability to serve as arbiters and brokers among competing stakeholders, and it suggests that they can provide an unbiased conduit to the president or his principals. These factors, in turn, tend to increase perceived legitimacy of the process and increase support for policy outcomes. In addition, they serve the substantive function of providing conduits and incubators for ideas, policy proposals, and recommendations from executive agencies and departments to the president. This serves the principal goal of providing the president with the best available information before he makes a decision. The perception of procedural legitimacy and the benefits it brings is, however, very fickle. It can easily be lost if the White House councils do not act as honest brokers among competing stakeholders or otherwise fail to fulfill their leadership and management functions.

The staffs of the policy councils are primarily made up of political appointments that are not subject to the delays and tribulations of Senate confirmation. As such, policy council staffs are highly accountable to the president, and they have the ability to impact the decision-making process on the first day of the administration. However, although the councils are more flexible, they can also lack the expertise of agencies, and turnover is relatively high, creating a lack of continuity on policy matters. In his recent memoir, former Secretary of Defense Robert Gates argues, for example, that principals in Obama's White House staff often made judgments themselves rather than deferring to the Department of Defense or other agencies with the relevant areas of expertise:

> Most of my conflicts with the Obama administration during the first two years weren't over policy initiatives from the White House, but rather the NSS's [National Security Staff] micromanagement and operational meddling, which I routinely resisted. For an NSS staff member to call a four-star combatant commander or field commander would have been unthinkable when I worked at the White House—and probably cause for dismissal. It became routine under Obama. I directed commanders to refer such calls to my office.[2]

On the other hand, the lack of expertise on the policy councils also provides an opportunity for agencies to influence the councils by providing policy experts in a number of fields to work with the councils. Indeed, one of the arts of policymaking is designing a policymaking process that brings experts in while keeping the president and his agenda at the center of the process. While Gates's criticism was directed at the Obama NSS staff, it is not an uncommon complaint and could easily have been made of the White House staff and policy councils in many of the administrations that came before him.

In parallel to the central roles they play in the policymaking process, the White House councils are situated at the inner core of the policymaking apparatus. The organizational structure of the Executive Office of the President (EOP) can be compared to an egg (see Box 2-1). The president sits at the center and is surrounded by the White House Office, which includes the Policy Councils and several other offices (which we will discuss in the next chapter). Together these make up the "egg yolk." The yolk is surrounded by "egg white," which contains the EOP. The EOP consists of agencies of different size and importance. Agencies in the EOP are congressionally chartered, their top political appointees are confirmed by the Senate, they are required to testify before Congress on policy matters, and they have regulatory and/or reporting responsibilities (see Box 2-1). In contrast to agencies within the EOP, policy councils within the White House Office are presidentially appointed, they are not confirmed by the Senate, they run no programs, set no regulations, and there is a longstanding tradition based in the doctrine of "separation of powers" that staff members do not have to testify on policy issues (though they can be subpoenaed by Congress

---

2. Robert Gates, *Duty: Memoirs of a Secretary at War* (New York, NY: Knopf, 2014), cited in "The Quiet Fury of Robert Gates: Bush and Obama's Secretary of Defense Had to Wage War in Iraq, Afghanistan—and Today's Washington," *Wall Street Journal*, January 7, 2014, http://www.wsj.com/articles/SB10001424052702304617404579306851526222552.

BOX 2-1	The Structure of the Executive Branch

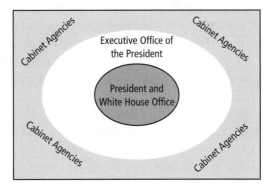

The White House Office

Domestic Policy Council

- Office of National AIDS Policy
- Office of Faith-Based and Neighborhood Partnerships
- Office of Social Innovation and Civic Participation
- White House Rural Council

National Security Council
National Economic Council
Office of Cabinet Affairs
Office of the Chief of Staff
Office of Communications

- Office of the Press Secretary
- Media Affairs
- Research
- Speechwriting

Office of Digital Strategy
Office of the First Lady

- Office of the Social Secretary

Office of Legislative Affairs
Office of Management and Administration

- White House Personnel
- White House Operations
- Telephone Office
- Visitors Office

Oval Office Operations
Office of Presidential Personnel
Office of Public Engagement and Intergovernmental Affairs

- Office of Public Engagement
- Council on Women and Girls
- Office of Intergovernmental Affairs

- Office of Urban Affairs
- Office of Scheduling and Advance

Office of the Staff Secretary

- Presidential Correspondence
- Executive Clerk
- Records Management

Office of the White House Counsel

Executive Office of the President

Office of Management and Budget
Council on Environmental Quality
Office of National Drug Policy Control
Council of Economic Advisers
Office of Science and Technology Policy
United States Trade Representative
Office of Administration
Office of the Vice President

Cabinet Agencies

State Department
Treasury Department
Defense Department
Justice Department
Interior Department
Agriculture Department
Commerce Department
Labor Department
Department of Health and Human Services
Department of Housing and
  Urban Development
Department of Transportation
Department of Education
Department of Energy
Department of Veteran Affairs
Department of Homeland Security

when there is evidence of illegal or unethical behavior). In addition, unlike the agencies, the policy councils thus are not beholden to Congress and do not have specific programmatic interests. These distinctions are important because it makes them better able to defend the president's position and to act as honest brokers between other actors in the policymaking process.

BOX 2-2   **Executive Office of the President vs. White House Policy Councils**

Councils within the Executive Office of the President (such as the Council of Economic Advisers and Council on Environmental Quality) are distinct in three ways from the White House policy councils:

- Top political appointees must be confirmed;
- They can have reporting, regulatory, and in some instances programmatic responsibilities;
- Their top appointees can be asked to testify before Congress on matters of policy.

The shell of the egg includes all the cabinet departments and agencies that are not under the authority of the president, with the exception of fully independent agencies such as the Federal Reserve. In the past, the secretary of the cabinet was responsible for coordinating cabinet policymaking. But as the cabinet has grown in size—it is now too large for regular meetings and has become unwieldy and is often disjointed—the role of the secretary of the cabinet has shifted to one of scheduling. The role of coordinating the policy development and decision-making process within the cabinet has shifted to the policy councils within the White House Office. Indeed, the growth of policy councils was, in part, a response to the growth in issues and number of cabinet agencies with interest in a large range of policy matters.

HOW THE POLICY COUNCILS OPERATE AND WHY THEY ARE IMPORTANT

Lyndon Johnson was the first president to begin concentrating policymaking control in the White House.[3] This shift was reflected in the rise of Joseph Califano, who became known as a freewheeling, all-purpose domestic policy

---

3. I. M. Destler, *Presidents, Bureaucrats, and Foreign Policy* (Princeton, NJ: Princeton University Press, 1972); Richard Neustadt, *Presidential Power: The Politics of Leadership* (New York, NY: Wiley, 1960).

czar in the Johnson White House.[4] Following the Johnson administration, how-ever, the shift toward more centralized policymaking was slow and uneven. It was not until the early 1970s that the Office of Policy Development (OPD) became an institutional entity in the White House.[5] And, despite being institu-tionalized, the OPD lacked a clear mandate from the president, its role was unclear, and its influence was minimal. The OPD gained importance during the Carter administration under the leadership of Stu Eizenstat, but it once again declined in importance during the Reagan and Bush administrations when it was overshadowed by the Office of Management and Budget.

The role and significance of the White House domestic policymaking staff increased dramatically after President Clinton took office in 1993. President Clinton entered his office with a desire to create a more coordinated policy development and planning apparatus. He also sought to centralize control over policymaking by placing primary responsibility for policy development and planning in the hands of political appointees rather than career civil servants. Motivated by the end of the Cold War and the onset of economic globalization, the president separated the OPD into two distinct offices: the NEC and the DPC. As Clinton envisioned, these two councils were modeled on the NSC and served three primary missions. First, the NEC and DPC serve as arbiters on policy decisions that could not be resolved at lower levels. Because they do not manage any programs, they have none of the "programmatic baggage" that could hinder the ability of other cabinet agencies to mediate disputes. In particular, because the policy councils are made up of cabinet agencies and some of the smaller non-cabinet departments, like the Small Business Administration, they can resolve disputes through the direct involvement of the department heads and the chair of the relevant agency. This increases the capacity for all parties to participate in the policymaking process, thereby increasing the perceived legitimacy of the process itself and the likelihood that parties will buy into the process and the results it produces. Second, the policy councils serve as "think tanks" and develop new ideas that fit the president's agenda. The policy councils are responsible for integrating executive agencies such as the Office of Management and Budget (OMB), Department of the Treasury, Department of Health and Human Services (HHS), the Department of Labor, and the Environmental Protection Agency (EPA) into the policy development structure.

---

4. Charles L. Heatherly and Burton Yale Pines, eds., *Mandate for Leadership III: Policy Strategies for the 1990s* (Washington, DC: The Heritage Foundation, 1989).

5. Heatherly and Yale Pines, *Mandate for Leadership III.*

They were also to work in conjunction with the Office of Congressional Affairs (OCA) to develop a legislative strategy on initiatives that require congressional approval. Finally, the councils are responsible for overseeing the OMB to ensure that the president's agenda is being implemented by the agencies. These roles create a specific point of contact and responsibility for policymaking. As such, they increase the efficiency and manageability of the policymaking process.

The day-to-day running of government programs largely resides with the various cabinet, noncabinet, and independent agencies, and outside analysis of the management and performance of these programs is mainly the responsibility of the OMB and, outside the executive branch, Congress. But as a general rule, the councils are not supposed to be involved in operational activities (although on numerous occasions they have ignored this dictum). Beyond other considerations, this is a practical matter of bandwidth. Micromanaging is highly inefficient and one issue could—if people let it—easily absorb all of a council member's attention. Consequently, deciding what issues merit the attention of the policy councils is critical. Three people can make these decisions: the president, his chief of staff, or the head of the relevant policy council. Often a cabinet agency will seek policy council involvement because it brings the cachet of presidential interest. Other times cabinet agencies will avoid involving the councils in order to protect turf or to keep the process from slowing down.

One of the chief responsibilities of the policy councils is to develop new policy proposals for the president that are consistent with his or her political agenda. This underscores the need for a council head who is ideologically and politically in tune with the president. Avoiding turf battles and overly contentious ideological conflict was part of President Clinton's motivation for increasing the role that the policy councils played in the policymaking process. Building consensus is important, given the prominent role of the policy councils in establishing the policymaking agenda, preparing of the State of the Union address, and submitting the president's proposed fiscal budget every year. The State of the Union address every January and the submission of the president's budget every February are critical events because they provide the president with highly visible and widely publicized platforms for presenting his or her policy agendas to the American people and the Congress. The president can, of course, propose new policies at White House conferences or through the presentation of government studies, and so on. However, the State of the Union address and the president's budget are the two primary, annual vehicles, and they are widely recognized as the definitive declaration of presidential initiatives and priorities for the coming year.

The policy councils are intimately involved in the preparation of the State of the Union address and work in conjunction with the OMB to develop the president's proposed budget. The policy councils begin their preparation by setting up a variety of **interagency working groups** in late August, usually after Congress leaves for its summer recess. These interagency groups consist of all agencies with an interest in a potential policy initiative and are directed by a deputy assistant or special assistant to the president on one of the policy councils. The working groups are often jointly run by two policy councils. For example, the NEC and the NSC may jointly chair an interagency working group on trade, while the NEC and DPC may chair jointly a working group on poverty or welfare. Typically, the policy councils ask each participating agency to develop and prioritize new policy proposals that require either legislative, executive (presidential action via **executive orders** or memoranda), legal (via the courts), or regulatory action. The policy councils will also develop a set of new proposals, working independently. The policy councils will then meet over the course of August and September to develop a consensus regarding which proposals will be included in the State of the Union address.

At the same time, the OMB will be running its budget process, through which it will evaluate all the other non–presidential-level initiatives or maintenance of existing programs. At the end of this process, the policy councils and the OMB will merge their efforts into a fiscal budget proposal. While the policy councils and the OMB work together throughout this phase, the policy councils can be responsible for presenting any disagreements over how much to spend on any particular item in the budget to the president. With regard to proposals for the State of the Union, the Councils will try to resolve most of the issues at either the **deputy level** or the **principal level** (agency heads). To ensure a fair process, however, any agency can ask for an issue to be presented to the president for resolution. In these circumstances, a memo is prepared by the head of the relevant council and his or her staff and sent to the president for his decision. The decision regarding what policies will be included in the State of the Union or the president's budget are finalized in mid-January. Appeals to the president are typically submitted in December or early January.

After the State of the Union and the submission of the president's budget, the policy councils work with the relevant White House Offices to secure action on each policy item. Some Councils have regular bimonthly principals' and deputies' meetings, while others prefer to meet on an as-needed basis. On some occasions, rather than have all the principals meet to discuss all issues, meetings will be broken down by issue, such as education or welfare. In either case, the **deputy** or special assistant to the president in charge of the working group is responsible for maintaining contact and exchanging information with all relevant parties. Throughout the year, the chief of staff will ask for updates on each major policy initiative. If legislative action is required, the councils will team with Legislative Affairs and develop a congressional strategy. They will then brief members and their staffs throughout the winter. The councils will also work with the Office of Public Engagement to build support among state, local, and tribal governments and interest groups. If the action requires a presidential directive, White House Counsel becomes involved. Follow-up media events designed to build support for proposals are put together with the assistance of White House Communications, Press, and Speechwriting Offices. In all cases, however, the councils serve as the linchpin.

THE WHITE HOUSE POLICY COUNCILS

BOX 2-3   **How the White House Ranks Staffers**

In the White House, senior staffers are ranked as commissioned officers to the president.

The highest rank is that of assistant to the president. The White House chief of staff, press secretary, head of White House Counsel, the chairs of the DPC and NEC, and the national security advisor are all assistants to the president and have roughly the same rank as cabinet secretaries.

The next rank is that of deputy assistant to the president, followed by special assistant to the president.

Most staffers in the White House are not commissioned. This includes most policy analysts, schedulers, and press assistants.

The term *principal* refers to the head of a council, agency, or department.

National Security Council

The NSC is the president's principal forum for considering national security and foreign policy matters with his senior national security advisors and cabinet officials.[6] The NSC also serves as the president's principal arm for coordinating policies among these various government agencies. It is the oldest and largest-staffed of all the policy councils. The NSC was established during the Truman administration by the National Security Act of 1947 (PL 235—61 Stat. 496; U.S.C. 402), amended by the National Security Act Amendments of 1949

---

6. The NSC web site is http://www.whitehouse.gov/nsc/.

(63 Stat. 579; 50 U.S.C. 401 et seq.). Later in 1949, as part of the Reorganization Plan, the council was placed in the EOP. The following information is from the NSC's official description of its roles and responsibilities.[7]

The NSC is chaired by the president. In addition to the president, its statutory and nonstatutory members include the vice president and the secretaries of state, defense, and treasury. The chairman of the Joint Chiefs of Staff is the statutory military advisor to the council, and the director of National Intelligence (DNI) is the intelligence advisor. The chief of staff to the president, counsel to the president, and the assistant to the president for economic policy are invited to attend any NSC meeting. The attorney general and the director of the OMB are invited to attend meetings pertaining to their responsibilities. The heads of other executive departments and agencies, as well as other senior officials, are invited to attend meetings of the NSC when appropriate. The NSC staff (or the NSS, from May 2009 to February 2014) serves as the president's primary national security and foreign policy advisers in the White House (see Box 2-4). The NSC staff receives its direction from the president through the national security advisor (also known as the assistant to the president for national security affairs). The NSC staff performs a variety of activities in advising and assisting the president and the national security advisor. It is responsible for preparing briefing materials (including the preparation of meeting agendas, decision papers, and discussion papers) for the president and the national security advisor to assist them in making decisions regarding national security policy and operations. The NSC staff also serves as an initial point of contact for departments and agencies who wish to bring a national security issue to the president's attention. Staff members participate in interagency working groups organized to assess policy issues in a coordinated fashion; they prepare analysis and recommendations for the deputy

---

| **BOX 2-4** | **National Security Council** |

The National Security Council is the president's principal forum for considering national security and foreign policy matters with his senior national security advisors and cabinet officials. Since its inception under President Truman, the function of the council has been to advise and assist the president on national security and foreign policies. The council also serves as the president's principal arm for coordinating these policies among various government agencies.

Source: White House web site, https://www.whitehouse.gov.

---

7. See the NSC web site, http://www.whitehouse.gov/nsc/.

assistants to the president for national security affairs, the assistant to the president for national security affairs, and the president.

The executive secretary of the NSC is its chief manager and administrative officer;[8] he assists in directing the activities of the NSC staff on the broad range of defense, intelligence, and foreign policy matters, including the preparation necessary for meetings with foreign leaders in connection with the president's foreign travel. He also assigns, reviews, and ensures proper coordination of all information and action memoranda submitted by the NSC staff to the national security advisor and the president. The executive secretary is the principal point of contact between the NSC and other government agencies and with the EOP. Most divisions are headed by a special assistant to the president/senior director. Under President Clinton and President George H. W. Bush, staffing levels approximated 100 individuals. Under President George W. Bush, staffing levels originally dropped to around 70 people. After 9/11, staff levels rose again, reaching 200.[9]

Under President Obama, a number of important changes occurred. Shortly after taking office, he promulgated Presidential Policy Directive 1, which established the procedures for assisting the president in carrying out his responsibilities in the area of national security. He also merged the Homeland Security Council staff and the National Security Council staff, creating a combined team called the National Security Staff (NSS).[10] To recognize the successful merger of these two units, the NSS was renamed the National Security Council staff in February of 2014.[11] Consequently, although the Homeland Security Council (which was created by President Bush) still exists on paper, it is now staffed by the NSC. This added bureaucratic complexity to the NSC and contributed to its growth to approximately 400 employees.[12] The Obama

---

8. The NSC web site, http://www.whitehouse.gov/nsc/.

9. Karen D. Young, "How the Obama White House Runs Foreign Policy," *The Washington Post*, August 5, 2015, https://www.washingtonpost.com/world/national-security/how-the-obama-white-house-runs-foreign-policy/2015/08/04/2befb960-2fd7-11e5-8353-1215475949f4_story.html.

10. Alan G. Whittaker, Shannon A. Brown, Frederick C. Smith, and Ambassador Elizabeth McKune, *The National Security Policy Process: The National Security Council and Interagency System* (Charlottesville, VA: University of Virginia, 2011).

11. Caitlin Hayden, "The NSC Staff, the Name is Back! So Long, NSS," *The White House Blog* (February 10, 2014), https://www.whitehouse.gov/blog/2014/02/10/nsc-staff-name-back-so-long-nss.

12. Young, "How the Obama White House Runs Foreign Policy."

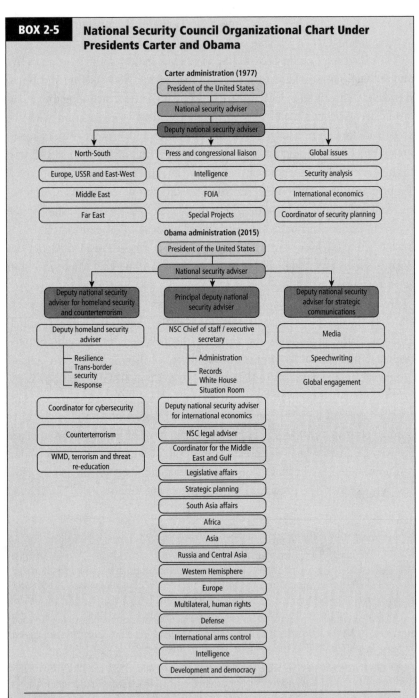

| BOX 2-5 | **National Security Council Organizational Chart Under Presidents Carter and Obama** |

Carter administration (1977)

President of the United States

National security adviser

Deputy national security adviser

North-South	Press and congressional liaison	Global issues
Europe, USSR and East-West	Intelligence	Security analysis
Middle East	FOIA	International economics
Far East	Special Projects	Coordinator of security planning

Obama administration (2015)

President of the United States

National security adviser

Deputy national security adviser for homeland security and counterterrorism

Principal deputy national security adviser

Deputy national security adviser for strategic communications

Deputy homeland security adviser

NSC Chief of staff / executive secretary

Media

— Resilience
Trans-border security
— Response

— Administration
— Records
White House Situation Room

Speechwriting

Global engagement

Coordinator for cybersecurity

Deputy national security adviser for international economics

Counterterrorism

NSC legal adviser

WMD, terrorism and threat re-education

Coordinator for the Middle East and Gulf

Legislative affairs

Strategic planning

South Asia affairs

Africa

Asia

Russia and Central Asia

Western Hemisphere

Europe

Multilateral, human rights

Defense

International arms control

Intelligence

Development and democracy

Source: "The Growth of the National Security Council," *The Washington Post* (August 4, 2015), https://www.washingtonpost.com.

administration also has three deputy assistants to the president who now serve under the national security advisor/assistant to the president for national security. These include a principal deputy, a deputy for strategic communications, and a deputy for homeland security and counterterrorism. A comparison of the Obama NSC and Carter NSC developed by *The Washington Post* is shown in Box 2-5.[13]

Some have criticized the Obama NSC of overly centralizing national security policy in the White House and conducting diplomacy on its own rather than through the State Department. For example, two senior NSC officials—deputy national security adviser Benjamin J. Rhodes and then–Latin American director Ricardo Zuniga—reportedly handled secret talks regarding normalization of relations with Cuba, rather than the State Department and Secretary Kerry.[14] Such forays into policy implementation and operations may weaken the credibility of the NSC with the agencies it is supposed to help coordinate and damage the legitimacy of the policy process.

National Economic Council

The NEC was created by presidential executive order on January 25, 1993.[15] The principal functions of the council are as follows:

- To coordinate the economic policymaking process with respect to domestic and international economic issues;
- To coordinate economic policy advice to the president;
- To ensure that economic policy decisions and programs are consistent with the president's stated goals, and to ensure that those goals are being effectively pursued;
- To monitor implementation of the president's economic policy agenda.

The NEC is chaired by the president and consists of eighteen members. Under Clinton, the staff size was roughly thirty individuals, considerably smaller than the NSC (which has historically been staffed by about 100 people). Because it is smaller and newer, the NEC is considerably less bureaucratic and somewhat more freewheeling than the NSC (see Box 2-6). This gives it some advantages, including a more innovative approach to policymaking, but the smaller staff means it has fewer resources available than the NSC.

---

13. Whittaker et al., *The National Security Policy Process.*

14. Young, "How the Obama White House Runs Foreign Policy."

15. The NEC web site, http://www.whitehouse.gov/nec/.

BOX 2-6 **Cookies**

The key to knowing who the players are at any meeting with the president is to watch who eats the cookies. When a proposal is being presented to the president, the White House mess staff—who cook for the president—bring out two trays of cookies. One goes in front of the president, and the other is for the staff. Most staffers won't touch the cookies, for fear that they will be caught with their mouth full right at the moment the president asks them a question. However, those staffers who are truly comfortable in the presence of the president have no qualms about stuffing a few chocolate chip macadamia nut cookies into their mouths. By the way, when the meeting with the president is over and he has left the room, the cookie tray is picked clean by famished staff.

By creating the NEC, President Clinton instituted the most significant, broad purpose, policy-staff initiative since President Nixon mandated the transformation of the NSC under Henry Kissinger in 1969.[16] The creators of the NEC used the NSC as a model and intended it to coordinate economic policymaking in the same manner that the NSC coordinated foreign policymaking. Under the initial leadership of Robert Rubin, the NEC quickly became a powerful force inside the White House. Its role was enhanced by the general power vacuum of the first year of the Clinton White House—at which time the offices of the chief of staff and White House communications were weak, and the Office of Legislative Affairs was largely ignored due to a lack of strategic thinking and overreliance on the Democrats in the Congress. In the context of the day-to-day chaos in the Clinton White House, Rubin followed a well-orchestrated, businesslike approach to policymaking and systematically expanded the NEC's role beyond that of designing policy proposals on behalf of the president to include the creation and implementation of the legislative and communications strategies that accompanied these proposals.

Rubin created teams of NEC staffers who focused on core issues including education and training, transportation, banking and finance, economic development and housing, energy and environment, defense conversion, and international trade. Each team consisted of three or four individuals who were directed by a special assistant to the president. Rubin also appointed two deputies, one who focused on day-to-day management and the other who focused

---

16. I. M. Destler, "National Economic Council: A Work In Progress," *Policy Analyses in International Economics #46* (Washington, DC: Institute for International Economics, 1996), p. IIE.

on long-range strategic planning. Under Rubin, the NEC's power grew, and it became the only channel through which decisions were forwarded to the president, even those with no economic impact. For example, the meetings to discuss the policy initiatives involving campaign finance reform were chaired by Rubin and the NEC, even though the majority of the discussion was led by then–DPC Deputy Bruce Reed and the policy initiatives had been developed by members of the DPC.

Early on, the extension of the NEC's role often clashed with the OMB and the Council of Economic Advisers (CEA), particularly over the issue of which body was to serve as the "coordinator" of economic policy for the president. The OMB had controlled economic policy development under the Bush administration, and the CEA had a tradition of providing economic analysis to presidents, yet the NEC usurped the roles of both agencies under the Clinton administration. It succeeded in doing so, first, because many of the agencies outside the executive branch resented the influence that the career staff at OMB had over the president's agenda. These agencies preferred working directly with the political appointees of the NEC because they had some direct or independent connection to the president. Second, Rubin made it clear that the NEC would be an "honest broker" and would ensure that all views were presented to the president (see Box 2-7). This was something OMB had a reputation for not doing, especially since the agency's mandate to fit programs within a budget (preferably a balanced one) sometimes conflicted with the president's policy agenda. Finally, the CEA became increasingly marginalized because its congressional mandate conflicted with the Clinton administration's desire to center decision making within the White House.

BOX 2-7	**Establishment of the National Economic Council**

January 25, 1993

EXECUTIVE ORDER

ESTABLISHMENT OF THE NATIONAL ECONOMIC COUNCIL

By the authority vested in me as president of the United States by the Constitution and the laws of the United States of America, including sections 105, 107, and 301 of title 3, United States Code, it is hereby ordered as follows:

Section 1. Establishment. There is established the National Economic Council ("the Council").

(Continued)

(Continued)

Sec. 2. Membership. The Council shall comprise the:

  (a) President, who shall serve as Chairman of the Council;
  (b) Vice President;
  (c) Secretary of State;
  (d) Secretary of the Treasury;
  (e) Secretary of Agriculture;
  (f) Secretary of Commerce;
  (g) Secretary of Labor;
  (h) Secretary of Housing and Urban Development;
  (i) Secretary of Transportation;
  (j) Secretary of Energy;
  (k) Administrator of the Environmental Protection Agency;
  (l) Chair of the Council of Economic Advisers;
  (m) Director of the Office of Management and Budget;
  (n) United States Trade Representative;
  (o) Assistant to the President for Economic Policy;
  (p) Assistant to the President for Domestic Policy;
  (q) National Security Advisor;
  (r) Assistant to the President for Science and Technology Policy; and
  (s) Such other officials of executive departments and agencies as the President may, from time to time, designate.

Sec. 3. Meetings of the Council. The President, or upon his direction, the Assistant to the President for Economic Policy ("the Assistant"), may convene meetings of the Council. The President shall preside over the meetings of the Council, provided that in his absence the Vice President, and in his absence the Assistant, will preside.

Sec. 4. Functions. (a) The principal functions of the Council are: (1) to coordinate the economic policy-making process with respect to domestic and international economic issues; (2) to coordinate economic policy advice to the President; (3) to ensure that economic policy decisions and programs are consistent with the President's stated goals, and to ensure that those goals are being effectively pursued; and (4) to monitor implementation of the President's economic policy agenda. The Assistant may take such actions, including drafting a Charter, as may be necessary or appropriate to implement such functions.

(b) All executive departments and agencies, whether or not represented on the Council, shall coordinate economic policy through the Council.

(c) In performing the foregoing functions, the Assistant will, when appropriate, work in conjunction with the Assistant to the President for Domestic Policy and the Assistant to the President for National Security.

(d) The Secretary of the Treasury will continue to be the senior economic official in the executive branch and the President's chief economic spokesperson. The Director of the Office of Management and Budget, as the President's principal budget spokesperson, will continue to be the senior budget official in the executive branch. The Council of Economic Advisers will continue its traditional analytic, forecasting and advisory functions.

Sec. 5. Administration. (a) The Council may function through established or ad hoc committees, task forces or interagency groups.

(b) The Council shall have a staff to be headed by the Assistant to the President for Economic Policy. The Council shall have such staff and other assistance as may be necessary to carry out the provisions of this order.

(c) All executive departments and agencies shall cooperate with the Council and provide such assistance, information, and advice to the Council as the Council may request, to the extent permitted by law.

WILLIAM J. CLINTON

THE WHITE HOUSE, January 25, 1993.

Source: National Archives, Federal Register, January 27, 1993, http://www.archives.gov/federal-register/executive-orders/pdf/12835.pdf

Domestic Policy Council

After establishing the NEC, President Clinton placed the remainder of the staff from the now-defunct Office of Policy Development into the DPC.[17] Officially, the DPC was established by executive order on August 16, 1993, although it existed de facto shortly after President Clinton's inauguration in January of 1993. Like the NSC and NEC, the DPC is chaired by the president but run by an assistant to the president—in this case, the assistant to the president for domestic policy.

The DPC plays a role at every stage of the policymaking process to ensure policies reflect and carry out the goals of the president. The principal functions of the DPC are to coordinate the domestic policymaking process, to relay domestic policy advice to the president, to ensure that the president's stated

---

17. The DPC web site, http://www.whitehouse.gov/dpc/.

goals are being effectively pursued, and to monitor implementation of the president's domestic policy agenda. The DPC consists of twenty-four agencies, more than either the NSC or the NEC. On the other hand, when it was first created, it only had approximately ten staffers. Reflecting its increasing importance within the White House, it grew to around thirty staffers under President Clinton, approximately the same size as the NEC. The DPC was responsible for managing President Clinton's anti-crime package and the welfare reform proposal late in his first term. Passage of both those bills, combined with the departure of Robert Rubin to the Treasury Department in 1995, put the DPC on par with the NEC in terms of its importance within the White House.

Under President Clinton, the DPC was divided into the following teams, each headed by a special assistant to the president: education and training; welfare reform; policy planning; crime and drug policy; children and families; health care and management. Policy planning specifically focuses on new ideas and policy issues that do not fall within the structure of the other teams. The management team supports the assistant to the president for domestic policy and is similar in purpose to the executive secretary of the NSC. Like the NSC and NEC, the DPC has two deputies who oversee the management of the policy process.

After taking over the DPC in 1997, Bruce Reed believed the office should concentrate on issues most important to the president and allow the agencies and OMB to concentrate on the implementation of policy matters outside the president's primary agenda. Recognizing that thirty staffers could never effectively oversee the development and implementation of every policy, and that any attempt to do so would only lead to slower, more bureaucratic decision making, Reed decided to empower the team and have a very small "management staff" supporting him directly. He chose the team structure intentionally to encourage individual creativity and to increase the effectiveness of team management. The goal was to eliminate the hierarchical structure of the old DPC and replace it with one that fostered a considerable amount of horizontal interaction between the teams involved with different problems or issues.

During the Clinton administration, the role of the NEC in the White House policymaking process continued first under Laura Tyson and later Gene Sperling. Under the leadership of Tyson (between 1995 and 1996) and Sperling (from 1997 to early 2001), the director's staff was increased to two assistants, a press secretary, a chief of staff, and a deputy chief of staff. While the concentration of limited staff resources may have slightly weakened the NEC's role in policy development, the prominence of its directors combined with the tradition of holding deputies' meetings enabled the NEC to build and maintain its role as an honest broker in the policy arena. In the meantime, the DPC under Bruce Reed rose to be a major force behind the creation of "new ideas" in the White House. The DPC developed policy initiatives regarding the hottest issues of President Clinton's second term, including the K–12 education reform and class size reduction initiative; health care reform, containing both Medicare and the Patient's Bill of Rights; and the tobacco legislation and litigation efforts.

During the second term, the DPC also gained control over several issues that had been given to the NEC. Education and health care, which had been handed to the NEC after the failed health care reform effort of the First Lady Hillary Clinton, were placed under the control of the DPC in 1997. In addition, the DPC became a major proponent of using presidential authority (e.g., executive orders and memoranda, the publishing of studies, and the creation of task forces or holding of White House conferences) to promote issues such as Medicare, youth violence, child care, and the use of litigation in lieu of legislative remedies in the suit against the tobacco companies.

The Bush Administration and the NEC and DPC

During the 2000 campaign, it was unclear whether George W. Bush would continue to keep the NEC and DPC or whether he would revert to the structure of the pre-Clinton White House and combine both councils into a single entity. Interestingly, President Bush chose to maintain the structure put in place by President Clinton rather than adopt the single policy entity used by his father. Both the NEC and the DPC were maintained under the umbrella of the Office of Policy Development. In addition, despite his rhetoric to raise the level of importance of his cabinet, the NEC continued to play a very large role in policymaking, as did the DPC while under the direction of John Bridgeland.

One important difference between the Bush and Clinton administrations was that both councils reported directly through the deputy chief of staff for policy rather than directly to the chief of staff.[18] This is not to say that the Councils and their directors did not have access to the chief of staff or the president, but rather that the reporting system was more centralized than under President Bush, at least in the first term.

During the first years under President George W. Bush, the NEC played a significant policymaking and coordination role. Yet, the role of the NEC under Lawrence Lindsey (Bush's first NEC director) was significantly different that it

18. John Bridgeland, former assistant to President George W. Bush, interview with the author, January 2015.

had been under Robert Rubin (Clinton's first NEC director). Rubin saw a main function of the NEC as a consensus builder among agencies and other principals. The NEC was often the "go-to" to resolve policy differences. Lindsey saw the NEC as an enforcer of the president's wishes. This approach often led to conflicts between the Treasury Department and other agencies. Lindsey was eventually removed as part of an overhaul of the economic team and was replaced first by Stephen Friedman and later by Allen Hubbard.

The DPC under Bush was led by John Bridgeland even though the assistant to the president for domestic policy was Margaret Spellings, and it was the assistant to the president for domestic policy Bruce Reed who had led the DPC during the Obama administration.[19] The DPC was very active in the first few years under Bush, leading the policy effort for the administration's major K–12 initiative, No Child Left Behind, as well as the president's volunteer/service program expansion, which was ramped up after 9/11. After Spelling and Bridgeland left the DPC, the office became less active. And because of 9/11, both the NEC and the DPC began to take back seats because of the administration's increased focus on security issues.

The Obama Administration and the NEC and DPC

The Obama administration maintained the NEC and DPC structure. Indeed, it arguably strengthened them by funding both through the White House budget and eliminating the dormant Office of Policy Development. Obama folded the USA Freedom Corps (a policy council created by President Bush) into the DPC. He also moved the Office of Social Innovation and Civic Participation into the DPC (it had been independent under Bush). At the same time, however, he created potential competitors to the DPC and NEC by appointing policy czars to handle priorities outside of the policy council structure. For example, Nancy-Ann Min Deparle was designed as the health policy czar and reported directly to the chief of staff, Rahm Emanuel. Similarly, Carol Browner (the former head of the Environmental Protection Agency under Clinton) was appointed as the czar for climate and energy policy. These czars created some confusion and weakened the policy structure that was designed to facilitate

---

19. The directorship of the DPC under the Bush administration is confusing because the DPC is not led by the assistant to the president for domestic policy, as it had been under the Clinton Administration. For a discussion of the controversy, see Timothy Noah, "Who Is Director of the Domestic Policy Council? A Chatterbox investigation," *Slate.com*, January 15, 2003, http://www.slate.com/articles/news_and_politics/chatterbox/2003/01/who_is_director_of_the_domestic_policy_council.html.

decision making and create a legitimate process. While the czars focused accountability, they often did so at the expense of the honest broker role served by the councils.

Obama first picked Larry Summers, the former treasury secretary, to lead the NEC. Summers also acted as a policy czar. As such, he operated the NEC as a very "activist" entity, rather than the consensus-building model of his former mentor Robert Rubin. Summers left in 2010 and was eventually replaced by Gene Sperling, who focused more on bridging the differences between the various leaders of the economic team. His replacement, Jeff Zients, has followed a similar strategy, although Zients has kept a much lower public profile than either Summers or Sperling.

Besides the rise in policy czars within and outside the policy councils, another change under President Obama was title inflation. Whereas the NEC and DPC had previously made do with one assistant to the president and two deputy assistants to the president, under Obama both councils have seen an increase in individuals with those titles. At one point, the NEC had two assistants to the president, and both councils have had more than two deputies. Interestingly, the DPC currently has one primary deputy assistant to the president (James Kvall), but a number of policy areas are now headed up by deputy assistants to the president along with special assistants to the president (who typically handled those functions under Presidents Bush and Clinton).

KEY AGENCIES WITHIN THE EXECUTIVE OFFICE OF THE PRESIDENT

There are several agencies within the EOP that serve the president yet were established and are overseen by Congress. Unlike their executive-appointed counterparts, these agencies typically run programs related to reporting requirements established by Congress, such as the *Budget of the United States* and the *Economic Report of the President.* They also implement regulations. Prior to the Clinton administration, these agencies coordinated policy for the president. During the Clinton administration, the role of policy coordination was usurped by the policy councils in order to reduce the conflict of interest resulting from serving both Congress and the president. The exception to this rule has been the OMB and the Office of the Trade Representative, both of which are cabinet agencies that are housed in the EOP. In addition, environmental policy has in some instances been left outside the purview of the policy councils.

Some specialized entities exist outside of the policy councils. They tend to be run by career or expert staff who have no political allegiance to the president and often have little policy or political experience. Four prominent examples are the

Council on Environmental Quality (CEQ), Council of Economic Advisers (CEA), the Office of National Drug Control Policy (ONDCP), and the Office of Science and Technology Policy (OSTP).

Council on Environmental Quality

Congress first established the CEQ within the EOP as part of the National Environmental Policy Act (NEPA) of 1969. Additional responsibilities were provided by the Environmental Quality Improvement Act of 1970. The Council is headed by a chair, who is appointed by the president with the advice and consent of the Senate.

Specific functions of CEQ include the following:[20]

- Advise and assist the president in the development of environmental policies and proposed legislation, as requested by the president;
- Oversee federal agency implementation of the environmental impact assessment process and act as a referee for interagency disputes regarding the adequacy of such assessments;
- Report regularly to the president on the state of the environment;
- Interpret the NEPA and the CEQ regulations in response to requests from federal, state, and local agencies and citizens; and
- Approve NEPA procedures and issue guidance to address systemic problems.

Council of Economic Advisers

Although the term *council* conjures up the image of a large committee, the CEA actually consists only of a chairman and two members. The chairman is legally responsible for establishing the positions taken by the council. The other two members direct research activities of the council in particular fields, represent the council at meetings with other agencies, and generally work with the chairman to formulate economic advice.[21]

In addition to the chairman and two other members, the CEA has a professional staff that is both small and unusual. A group of about ten economists, generally professors on one- or two-year leaves from their universities, acts as the senior staff economists. They, in turn, are assisted by additional junior staff economists, typically advanced graduate students, who also spend only a

---

20. See the Council on Environmental Quality web site, http://www.whitehouse.gov/ceq/.

21. See the Council of Economic Advisers web site, http://www.whitehouse.gov/cea/.

year or two at the CEA. Several permanent economic statisticians assist the economists in the interpretation and identification of economic data.

The academic nature of the staff and of most CEA members distinguishes the CEA from other government agencies. It generally assures a higher level of technical economic sophistication and familiarity with current developments in economic thinking. Members and staff also use their strong links in the academic community to obtain advice on technical issues throughout their time in Washington. They often come to the CEA without the institutional knowledge of some of the issues with which they will deal and without any experience in the bureaucratic process of decision making. Experience suggests, however, that most of the senior staff economists learned quite quickly how to be effective participants and make an important contribution to the policy debates because of their ability to apply economic analysis to the issues being discussed and to develop new economic proposals that had not occurred to non-economist participants from the agencies.[22]

Office of National Drug Control Policy

The principal purpose of the ONDCP is to establish policies, priorities, and objectives for the nation's drug control program, the goals of which are to reduce illicit drug use, manufacturing, and trafficking; drug-related crime and violence; and drug-related health consequences. To achieve these goals, the director of the ONDCP is charged with producing the National Drug Control Strategy, which directs the nation's anti-drug efforts and establishes a program, a budget, and guidelines for cooperation among federal, state, and local entities.[23]

By law, the director of the ONDCP also evaluates, coordinates, and oversees both the international and domestic anti-drug efforts of executive branch agencies and ensures that such efforts sustain and complement state and local anti-drug activities. The director advises the president regarding changes in the organization, management, budgeting, and personnel of federal agencies that could affect the nation's anti-drug efforts and regarding federal agency compliance with their obligations under the Strategy.[24]

---

22. See the Council of Economic Advisers web site, http://www.whitehouse.gov/cea/.

23. See the Office of National Drug Control Policy web site, http://www.whitehousedrug policy.gov.

24. Ibid.

Office of Science and Technology Policy

The OSTP mission is set out in the National Science and Technology Policy, Organization, and Priorities Act of 1976 (Public Law 94–282). It calls for the OSTP to provide scientific and technological analysis and judgment for the president with respect to major policies, plans, and programs of the federal government.

The Act authorizes OSTP as follows:

- Advise the president and others within the EOP on the impacts of science and technology on domestic and international affairs;
- Work with the private sector to ensure federal investments in science and technology contribute to economic prosperity, environmental quality, and national security;
- Build strong partnerships among federal, state, and local governments; other countries; and the scientific community;
- Evaluate the scale, quality, and effectiveness of the federal effort in science and technology.

OSTP's Senate-confirmed director also serves as assistant to the president for science and technology. In this role, he co-chairs the President's Committee of Advisors on Science and Technology (PCAST) and supports the President's National Science and Technology Council (NSTC). A Senate-confirmed associate director leads each of OSTP's four divisions covering the areas of environment, national security and international affairs, science, and technology.[25]

CONCLUSION

In an effort to centralize the policymaking process and strengthen the role of presidential appointees, the Clinton administration dramatically increased the role and power of the policy councils within the White House Office. For the most part, this trend continued under Presidents Bush and Obama, although to a lesser extent. The DPC and NEC now play a central role in developing the president's policymaking agenda. They provide conduits for the flow of ideas, policy proposals, and recommendations from executive agencies and departments. They also act as honest brokers and mediators between competing policymakers. When this system is used appropriately, the policy council–centered

---

25. See the Office of Science and Technology Policy web site, https://www.whitehouse.gov/administration/eop/ostp.

organizational system enhances both the effectiveness and perceived legitimacy of the policymaking process. The role of other members of the White House staff in the policymaking process and their interaction with the policy councils is the topic of the next chapter.

Key Terms

Agencies

Departments

Deputy

Deputy level

Executive orders

Interagency working group

Principal level

Review Questions

1. Who chairs the NEC? How many members does the NEC have?
2. Describe the seven teams that comprised President Clinton's DPC.
3. How did President George W. Bush change the policy councils that existed or were created by the Clinton administration?
4. How do the White House policy councils and their counterparts in the EOP differ?

THE WHITE HOUSE STAFF

Pressure, low pay, long hours, and the constant threat of a subpoena. Welcome to the White House.[1]

WORKING ON THE WHITE HOUSE STAFF

Stockbrokers on Wall Street claim they have the most challenging and high-pressure jobs in the world. Members of the White House staff are, however, likely to disagree. The following is a typical morning for a policymaker in the White House.

Your supervisor emerges from a dawn meeting with the president and tells you that the **West Wing** wants a proposal for a new college tuition scholarship in time for the president's commencement address at his alma mater in two weeks. Your proposal will be limited to $2 billion in scarce taxpayer dollars, even though conservative estimates of the amount of money needed to actually solve the problem are ten to twenty times that amount. You identify five agencies that have a stake in the proposal (Department of Education, Department of the Treasury, Office of Management and Budget, Veterans Affairs, Department of Defense). You have to get their support for the proposal as well as buy-in from as many members of the groups as possible, to avoid having some cabinet secretary rip you to shreds behind your back to the White House chief of staff. You establish an inter-agency working group and begin identifying points of consensus and disagreement among those involved.

Almost immediately, the White House communications director begins asking for an early version of the proposal to leak to the press. You do not want to

---

1. Comment from a White House staffer in the Clinton administration.

give it out because you have not even called your first meeting of the working group, but the press office does not care. You are lucky they felt the need to check with you at all. Besides, if you do not leak the proposal to reporters, then they will likely criticize the idea in the press and dampen public support. In addition, the Office of Legislative Affairs is calling because they want you to brief thirty members of Congress who might be cosponsors. Of course, this means that you will have to make at least thirty changes to the proposal to get their support. You meet with the White House Counsel's office and describe one idea that involves eliminating nonprofit status for colleges that are raising tuition faster than inflation. They question your sanity as well as the constitutionality of the proposal and simultaneously hand you a subpoena for all your files concerning the housing policy project you worked on last month. So you call your lawyer at $500 per hour just to chat and reassure yourself that you have done everything by the book. By the way, it is only lunchtime. If you would like to work in this kind of environment, keep reading this chapter.

The White House staff has become an institutionalized component of policymaking in the modern executive branch, and it is critical to the president's success.[2] As executive branch policymakers, including Richard Cheney and David Gergen, have argued, the president's staff empowers him "to guide and direct government, to interact with the cabinet, to deal effectively with Congress, [and] to manage his relationship with the press." They become his "intelligence-gathering operation, it's his media management team, it's his congressional team, it's his formulation of his policy."[3] To be effective, the staff must recognize who the players are, what roles they play, and the tools, techniques, and processes they use to interact. This is vital because although no individual agency or department has the capacity to make policy solely on its own, except in some unique cases, many have the capacity to inhibit its development or stall its implementation.[4]

---

2. See Shirley Ann Warshaw, *The Domestic Presidency: Policymaking in the White House* (Boston, MA: Allyn & Bacon, 1997).

3. John H. Kessel, "The Presidency and the Political Environment," *Presidential Studies Quarterly* 31, 1 (March 2001), p. 25.

4. In addition, it is important to note that although the tools, techniques, and processes we describe in this book have been used by multiple presidents, each commander-in-chief has had his own working style. White House staff must adapt to the individual working habits of its president as well as the needs of external institutions and players with which the president has had to interact.

OTHER KEY PLAYERS IN THE WHITE HOUSE

On Pennsylvania Avenue, west of the White House executive residence, is a small, nondescript, three-story building known as the West Wing. Since it was first constructed under President Roosevelt, the West Wing of the White House has served as the office building of the White House staff. This building contains the Oval Office, the vice president's office, and the National Security Council's situation room, where the president's staff monitors the world. The ever-growing White House staff forced Franklin Roosevelt to add a third floor during World War II, and in the sixties large portions of the staff were moved across the street to the Eisenhower Executive Office Building.

Today, the White House office consists of around twenty different offices. In Chapter 2, we discussed the role of the White House policy councils—the National Economic Council (NEC), National Security Council (NSC), and the Domestic Policy Council (DPC). In this chapter, we will focus on the responsibilities and functions of the ten other major White House offices with responsibilities that relate to the policy development process.

Chief of Staff

As the size of the White House staff has grown, so has the power of the chief of staff (COS). Traditionally there have been three roles that the president's COS has played in the White House.[5]

1. *Confidant.* The COS is the president's closest adviser. The COS serves as a "behind-the-scenes" adviser whom the president trusts with special assignments and uses as a sounding board for ideas and policy proposals.
2. *Manager.* The COS selects and manages key members of the White House staff. He or she also coordinates and in some cases controls personal access, information flows, and the decision-making processes on behalf of the president. This power can be substantial. For example, the COS can act as a surrogate for the president and can often decide which decisions are worthy of presidential consideration and which are not.

---

5. For a review of the roles played by chiefs of staff and additional insights based on interviews with several former chiefs of staff, see Charles E. Walcott, Shirley Anne Warshaw, and Stephen J. Wayne, "The Chief of Staff," *Presidential Studies Quarterly* 31, 3 (September 2001), pp. 464–489.

3. *Principal.* The COS also functions much like an agency or department head. This differs from the function of personal confidant for the president in that the COS plays this role both publicly and within the confines of the White House. For example, the COS may negotiate with Congress and hold press conferences on behalf of the administration. Internally, the president sometimes designates the COS as a member of his cabinet, which allows him/her to participate in formal policy decision-making meetings. In this capacity, the COS presents and protects the president's interests, while also operating as an honest broker among members of the executive branch and other stakeholders.

In recent years, the COS has played an increasingly important role in the policymaking process. The COS provides his or her input through participation in the policy council deliberations or when a decision memorandum is circulated to the president through the White House staff secretary's office. For example, Leon Panetta, the COS for President Clinton, was the lead negotiator on the budget with Congress in the early to mid-1990s. Andrew Card, COS for President George W. Bush, participated in NSC meetings on the war in Afghanistan. President Obama's last two COSs, Jack Lew and Dennis McDonough, both came from policy backgrounds (Lew was head of OMB twice before becoming Treasury Secretary and McDonough was the deputy at the NSC) rather than the political or management side of government.

As the role of the COS has expanded so has the size of his or her personal staff, which has varied from single to double digits in recent administrations. Indeed, the size has grown large enough that some COS have had their own chief of staff. Most now have their own policy advisers on staff, including a foreign policy expert and individuals who are responsible for special projects that are of particular interest to the COS, such as climate change or technology policy. McDonough, Obama's COS as of June 2015, continued the practice started under President Clinton of designating one of his deputy COS to focus on policy and the policy councils.

Office of Legislative Affairs

The Office of Legislative Affairs (OLA) was established to manage all dealings between the president and Congress, specifically to coordinate the relationship with the White House policy offices and Congress. This function involves three responsibilities. First, it serves as an intermediary that manages the policy interaction between the White House and Congress (and their staffs). Every member of Congress wants to be involved in what the president is doing, and just listening and responding to all their input is a full-time job. The OLA staffs are usually the first in the White House to take calls from members of Congress. It is up to the OLA whether to pass the contents of a call or e-mail on to the appropriate White House staffer or simply to "hold onto" the information until it becomes timely.

Second, the OLA is responsible for maintaining good relations. This includes everything from ensuring the "right" members are given access to the president's box at the Kennedy Center, to briefing the president on what to say when he meets with a Senator or Representative on a particular piece of legislation.

Third, the OLA is intended to be the chief legislative strategist. This is a difficult role to fulfill. The OLA often becomes so closely tied to the party leadership in Congress that its staff is unable to understand or provide unbiased interpretations of conflicts between members of Congress in the president's party and the White House. A good OLA director will know how to build changing coalitions of members of Congress to pass or defeat legislation of importance to the president. In contrast, a weak or inexperienced OLA director will simply recommend that the president follow his party leadership in Congress. Although this may temporarily deflect him/her from criticisms from the Hill, party leadership does not always have the same interests or goals as the president. During the first two years of the Clinton administration, the OLA pursued a strategy intended to tie the president to the legislative agenda of the Democratic congressional leadership. As a result, many of President Clinton's chief legislative priorities, including welfare reform, the crime bill, health care reform, and campaign finance reform, languished. Only after the president showed a willingness to break with Democrats in Congress did he begin to experience greater legislative success. In the George W. Bush White House, OLA was placed under the direct control of Karl Rove, who oversaw the other three main political offices in the White House: the Office of Intergovernmental Affairs, the Office of Public Liaison, and the Office of Political Affairs. This new structure was designed to improve coordination of political strategy in the White House and to ensure one political message was delivered to the Congress; state, local, and tribal officials; and interest groups.

President Obama, as the first sitting Senator to become president since John F. Kennedy, was also very deferential to the Democratic leadership in the House and Senate, particularly during the first two years of his administration when Democrats held large majorities. The administration followed a strategy on health care reform that allowed then-Senator Baucus, Chairman of Senate

Finance, to take the lead on the health care bill. In fact, the administration did not send up an actual bill to Congress; it issued principles instead. This may have contributed to a protracted debate over the bill. However, in the end the Obama administration won passage of the Affordable Care Act (ACA), the largest health care reform bill since the creation of Medicare and Medicaid in 1965.

The relationship between the OLA and the policy councils is one of the most important in the White House. The policy councils maintain their role in the legislative process by running the interagency working groups on which the OLA sits. Though the OLA does not have a seat on any of the policy councils, it has an open offer to attend any meeting the Councils hold. If a decision memorandum (which we will discuss in Chapter 6) is drafted on legislation, the views of the OLA are almost always included. Even on nonlegislative policy matters, such as an executive order issued by the president on federal hiring, the views of the OLA will be sought out because Congress is responsible for overseeing the executive branch, which encourages every member of Congress to express an opinion on the policies of the president.

There is often a great deal of tension between these offices. It is not unusual for the OLA to be relatively more concerned about keeping members of Congress happy than are the policy councils' staffs, which, in turn, tend to be relatively more concerned about preserving the administration's position with regard to the policy proposal at hand. Despite this tendency, these organizations can work well together. Indeed, even competing organizations often make efforts to strain toward agreement in order to get a policy initiated.[6] For example, both the OLA and the policy councils operated in strategic and not parochial terms in the beginning of the second term of the Clinton administration. As a result, the administration experienced a good deal of legislative success during that time.

Office of Public Engagement and Intergovernmental Affairs

Under President Obama, the Office of Public Liaison became the Office of Public Engagement and was combined with the Office of Intergovernmental Affairs under presidential adviser Valerie Jarrett. Although combined, the two offices have very distinct roles, which we will discuss separately.

---

6. Roger Hilsman with Laura Gaughran and Patricia A. Weitsman, *The Politics of Policymaking in Defense and Foreign Affairs: Conceptual Models and Bureaucratic Politics,* 3rd edition. (Englewood Cliffs, NJ: Prentice Hall, 1993), pp. 80–81; Warner Schilling, "The Politics of National Defense: Fiscal 1960," in *Strategy, Politics and Defense Budgets,* ed. Warner R. Schilling, Paul Y. Hammond, and Glenn H. Snyder (New York, NY: Columbia University Press, 1962), p. 23.

Intergovernmental Affairs

In parallel to the OLA's role of managing the relationship between the White House and Congress, the Office of Intergovernmental Affairs (OIA) is charged with maintaining relationships between the White House and the nation's governors; state, county, and local legislators; county and local officials including mayors; and Native American tribal governments. Like the OLA, the OIA serves as a conduit and intermediary. The OIA is responsible for servicing and providing access to officials on various levels and communicating their concerns to the appropriate White House office. The OIA also works to convince state, local, and tribal governments to support the president's agenda. It works both with individual elected officials and with umbrella organizations such as the National Governors' Association and the Conference of Mayors. In the Bush White House, the OIA was downgraded in relation to other White House offices. The head of the OIA was a deputy assistant to the president, rather than an assistant to the president, in rank and reported directly to Senior Advisor Karl Rove. In the Obama administration, the head of the OIA has remained a deputy assistant to the president, but the office has been given greater focus because of the administration's commitment to issues affecting state and local governments.

The policymaking role of the OIA, and its interactions with the policy councils themselves, is centered on issues of particular concern to state, local, and tribal governments. For example, on issues of tobacco policy and welfare reform, the OIA played an important role in managing the interaction between individual governors, the National Governor's Association, and the policy councils. The OIA is often not the only point of contact between the policy councils and non-federal governments. Sometimes the policy councils deal directly with representatives from state, local, and tribal governments. But the OIA and the policy councils often work closely together, particularly when there is a meeting of one of the umbrella organizations on policy matters. For example, the National Governor's Association has two meetings each year in which policy resolutions are raised. Usually the policy councils and the OIA work together to respond to those resolutions.

Public Engagement

The Office of Public Engagement (OPE) serves as the go-between for the ever-growing number of interest groups that play important roles in our democracy.[7]

---

7. Charles Heatherly and Burt Pines, *Mandate for Leadership* (Washington, DC: American Heritage Institute, 1989).

It was first created to help build support among the public for major presidential initiatives. In fulfillment of this role, the OPE pursues three primary missions: consensus building, policy advocacy, and policy facilitation. Constituency building is the primary mission of the OPE. The success of a presidential proposal is often determined by whether or not constituency groups can be brought into the fold. Policy advocacy is the second most important mission of the OPE. Specifically, the OPE is responsible for generating public understanding and support for presidential initiatives. Policy facilitation is its third mission. In reality, this means providing "access" and "services" to constituency groups with the policy councils and other White House offices.

The OPE also facilitates the policymaking process by gathering information from a variety of private sector organizations that is not readily available from published sources. The OPE provides a conduit for private sector organizations to express their concerns to the White House, but it does not act as an advocate for specific interest groups or concerns. While decision memorandums do reflect, in some cases, the concerns of interest groups, the policy councils, rather than the OPE, usually make the judgment as to how relevant those concerns are. Nonetheless, by providing a means for communicating the concerns of private sector organizations, the OPE helps to promote the public perception of legitimacy of the policymaking process that, in turn, increases the likelihood of support for policy outcomes. It also helps identify people for policy positions in government based on their expertise and ideological compatibility.

Office of Political Affairs

Originally designed to fulfill a parallel role to that of the OLA, the Office of Political Affairs (OPA) is responsible for keeping the president apprised of political issues that arise throughout the country. It serves as liaison to the various party entities such as the Republican National Committee (RNC), Democratic Senatorial Campaign Committee (DSCC), and the Democratic National Committee (DNC). The office is broken down into regions, with a staffer covering each part of the country.

The OPA's task is to provide a political assessment of policy matters. As the role of outside political consultants has grown, however, the OPA's role has declined. Today, most consultants go around OPA and deal directly with the president or the office of the COS. The OPA's role is further undercut by a general belief of everyone in the White House that he or she is politically adept and has little need for its input. As a consequence, the OPA currently has little or no direct involvement in the policymaking process. Most of the political input that actually goes into the policy decision-making process comes from other places within the White House, such as the COS or the OLA. In part recognizing its decreasing relevance, OPA was downgraded relative to other White House offices by the Bush administration. President Obama actually closed the office for several years but decided in 2014 to reopen it under the leadership of David Simas.[8] It will be interesting to see if the latest incarnation of OPA means the office will become relevant again.

INTERACTION WITH THE MEDIA

While the additional White House offices—including the Office of Communications, the Press Office, and the Office of Cabinet Affairs—do not play a direct role in the policy formation process, they help to promote both the perception of legitimacy and efficiency of the system by providing points of contact and channels of communication between the White House and the public.

Office of Communications, the
Speech Writing Office, and the Press Office

People often ask what the difference is between the Office of Communications (OC) and the Press Office (PO). In principle, the roles are distinct, though in practice they often overlap. The OC is charged with developing the long-term and daily communications strategy for the president.[9] Its role is to coordinate people, programs, and institutions in a way that best publicizes the goals and achievements of the president and the White House.[10] The PO is charged with implementing this strategy and gathering and disseminating White House information to the press on behalf of the president.[11] It serves as the "firewall" between the press and the White House, and it is responsible for "servicing"

---

8. Michael Shear, "White House Comeback for Political Affairs Office," *New York Times,* January 24, 2014, http://www.nytimes.com/2014/01/25/us/politics/white-house-comeback-for-political-affairs-office.html.

9. Martha Joynt Kumar, "The Office of Communications," *Presidential Studies Quarterly* 31, 4 (December 2001), pp. 609–634; John Maltese, *Spin Control: The White House Office of Communications and the Management of Presidential News,* 2nd ed. (Chapel Hill, NC: University of North Carolina Press, 1994).

10. Joynt Kumar, "The Office of Communications," pp. 610–611.

11. For a useful discussion of the roles and functions of the Office of the Press Secretary, see Martha Joynt Kumar, "The Office of the Press Secretary," *Presidential Studies Quarterly* 31, 2 (June 2001), pp. 296–322.

press staff by granting formal interview requests and helping them make travel arrangements on presidential trips. It also helps present the views of the president, the White House staff, and the press to one another, and it devotes a substantial amount of time to staging events.

The administrative relationship between the PO and the OC has varied in recent administrations, with the press secretary sometimes taking over the role of communications director. For example, for much of the Carter administration, Jody Powell was directing communications operations.[12] Similarly, during the George H. W. Bush administration, Press Secretary Marlin Fitzwater took over the role. Sometimes, however, the hierarchy has been reversed. During the Clinton administration, for example, Press Secretary Dee Dee Myers reported to Communications Director George Stephanopoulos. Regardless, when the functions of these two organizations overlap, the resulting conflict can create misperception and result in a confused message to the public. In general, since the White House press secretary from the PO is the chief contact with the media, he or she often holds a great deal more leverage with the press than the head of the OC. On the other hand, the Speechwriting Office (SO) is typically under the authority of the OC. Because the president's speeches and remarks are the chief means of communication, the OC has a significant impact on the material the press is covering. This restores some of the balance in the relationship. The OC is also responsible for designing and creating presidential events that convey White House positions and messages. The competition in roles between access to the media by the PO and SO and presentation of presidential ideas by the OC invariably creates a significant amount of tension between the two offices.

Historically the press secretary has been responsible for communications planning within the White House—as was James Hagerty, who served as President Eisenhower's press secretary. Today the press secretary focuses primarily on gathering and delivering information to reporters and plays a secondary role in communications planning.[13] The role of planning events involves the Scheduling Office, the Office of the COS, the OC, and the relevant policy councils.

The PO and OC interact with the policy councils frequently. The PO is responsible for ensuring that the president is fully briefed before he or she goes before the press, and it is the policy council's responsibility to draft the Q&A

---

12. Joynt Kumar, "The Office of the Press Secretary."

13. Joynt Kumar, "The Office of the Press Secretary," p. 306.

sheet that is given to the president. Of course, the PO also has an opinion regarding the president's responses to statements. The policy councils are also heavily involved with the OC in the drafting of speeches, especially when new policy proposals are being announced.

The close relationship between the PO, OC, and policy councils is vitally important for the preparation and marketing of policy proposals. However, it is rare for either the press secretary or communications director to express views on policy matters in the decision-making process. For the most part, they weigh in only when they feel very strongly that the press will destroy a policy proposal. Similarly, speechwriting plays no role in the policy development process. Once the policy is agreed upon, the policy councils work closely with speechwriters to guarantee that the ideas are framed and marketed effectively.

Office of Cabinet Affairs

The Office of Cabinet Affairs (OCAF) was originally created for the purpose of serving as a deliberative body consisting of all the cabinet department heads. Because of its size and the disparate (and often conflicting) interests of all of the department heads, the Office of Cabinet Affairs has not operated effectively as a deliberate body. As a result, its role in policymaking has diminished significantly. During the Clinton administration and continuing with the Bush administration, the responsibility for policy coordination was largely taken over by the three White House policy councils, each of which include smaller subsections of the cabinet. Interaction between the OCAF and the policy councils is very minimal. The OCAF does not have a seat on any of the policy councils, and the councils themselves deal directly with the relevant federal agencies regarding policy matters. This has effectively negated the policymaking role of the OCAF.

Today, the OCAF functions principally as a clearinghouse of information for the various cabinet agencies and as a coordinator of federal response efforts to natural disasters such as earthquakes, hurricanes, and floods. The roles of coordinating communications among cabinet agencies and "Disaster Affairs" has restored some of the relevance of the OCAF. During disasters, the OCAF enhances the government's legitimacy by providing a point of contact for disaster relief; it increases the efficiency of disaster relief by centralizing disaster management; and it provides a means of communicating and amplifying the president's public communications.

WHITE HOUSE GATEKEEPERS

Even though their official role in policymaking is not their primary focus, the offices of the White House Counsel, Scheduling and Oval Office Operations, and Staff Secretary play important, if indirect, roles as gatekeepers in the policymaking process.

Office of Scheduling and Oval Office Operations

The Office of Scheduling and Oval Office Operations manage the president's calendar and his day-to-day interactions with staff, the press, and the public. When an organization or individual makes a request to meet the president, the request goes through the Office of Scheduling. Members of this office then coordinate its activities with all the other White House Offices and determine what person or event will be placed on the president's schedule. Although his or her function is primarily administrative, the White House scheduler has tremendous political influence because he or she controls public access to the president.

The Scheduling Office and Oval Office Operations are closely aligned with the Office of the COS, which directly oversees both. These offices provide the president's COS with the ability to control the president's policy agenda as well as day-to-day activities. Although the schedulers are concerned with ensuring that the president's day goes like clockwork and that the president has enough downtime, office time, and event time to fulfill his or her duties, they also can exert influence by proposing to eliminate policy events due to "time constraints." The level at which control of the schedule can influence policy depends on the management style and political strength of the White House COS. In highly centralized White House offices, autocratic COS used the Scheduling Office to control the policy agenda of agencies and White House policy advisers.

Typically, each week the president meets with his Director of Scheduling and the COS to review the scheduling requests coming from various White House offices and agencies within the executive branch. Any agency wanting to schedule a policy event for the president must submit a "scheduling decision memorandum." This memo summarizes the proposal, offers a recommendation (on an event site and type), and includes a check-off where the president can indicate his or her decision. The memo would also include background on the proposed event, a summary of the policy proposal, and a list of potential participants in the program.

In addition to the meetings with the president, the Scheduling Office (along with the CO) holds regular meetings of all relevant White House offices to coordinate policy and messages for each week. Sometimes these meetings are broken up into short-term scheduling meetings (a couple of weeks ahead) and long-term scheduling meetings (one to three months ahead). Some administrations tend to focus long-term scheduling from month to month, with the schedule changing more regularly. This was typical of the Clinton and sometimes the Obama administration.[14] In contrast, the George W. Bush administration initially tried to enforce more scheduling discipline by planning meetings on a three-month basis—although post 9/11 this proved to be more difficult.

Staff Secretary

The Staff Secretary controls the paper flow going to the president from his staff and from agency heads. Although the Staff Secretary plays a limited role in the early stages of the policy process, no paper or other materials get to the president without first going through the Staff Secretary. This role is functionally administrative, but it has important implications for policymaking.[15] For example, establishing a routing list or routing procedures that specify who is included or excluded from particular memos or meetings is highly political and can affect the outcome of the policy process. On sensitive issues like polling data, the circulation may be limited, but on less sensitive issues, the policy proposals or recommendations from one policy council or agency are generally circulated to others, who are the most likely critics.[16]

James Cicconi, Staff Secretary for president Bush in 1989 and 1990, summarized his role of an honest broker for stakeholders in the policymaking process. Once he received a draft memo from an agency or policy council, the Office of the Staff Secretary would circulate it for review, advice, and comments. Before sending it to the president, the Staff Secretary would circulate the comments to the authors of the memo to make sure they responded to or accommodated the comment. In an interview with Martha Joynt Kumar in 1999, Cicconi argued,

> If I wasn't satisfied with the answer, then I could overrule because I had the final responsibility for the paper that went to the president being full and complete and reflecting all the views of his advisers as honestly as possible.[17]

---

14. Karin Kullman (former White House scheduler), interview with the author.

15. Karen M. Hult and Kathryn Dunn Tenpas, "The Office of the Staff Secretary," *Presidential Studies Quarterly* 31, 2 (June 2001), p. 267.

16. Hult and Dunn Tenpas, "The Office of the Staff Secretary," pp. 266–269.

17. Cited in Hult and Dunn Tenpas, "The Office of the Staff Secretary," p. 269.

In order to explain the complexity and diversity of views, Staff Secretaries often add summary memos to the material that goes to the president, crystallizing the primary disagreements and issues to be decided.[18]

Furthermore, once a memo to the president is completed, the Staff Secretary is the one who circulates it—or with the sign-off of the COS chooses not to circulate it—to the president and other key officials. This control of access is quite important to all policymakers inside the White House and at the agencies. The Staff Secretary is handpicked by the president's COS, and former Staff Secretaries tend to move into positions of significance. Dick Darman, who later ran the Office of Management and Budget (OMB), was once Staff Secretary, as was president Clinton's COS and Obama top adviser John Podesta.

Like the Office of Scheduling, the Staff Secretary office is closely aligned with the White House COS. Whereas the National Security Adviser has his/her own power base, the Staff Secretary is dependent on the influence of the COS.

White House Counsel

The White House Counsel offers legal advice on official matters for the president and the White House staff. The office has grown over the years, especially as the number of Congressional investigations of the White House has increased, though its basic functions have remained the same since they were shaped by Counsel Fred Fielding during the Nixon administration.[19] These functions include advising the president and the White House staff on the exercise of presidential powers, defending the president's constitutional prerogatives, and overseeing presidential nominations and appointment to the executive and judiciary branches. In addition, the Counsel's Office decides what is appropriate and what is not, both legally and ethically, for the president and his staff. It also oversees training for all White House staff on ethics rules and records management and monitors their adherence when ethical issues arise. The Counsel's Office acts as a point of contact between the Executive Office of the President and the Justice Department and works with the Justice Department in determining the constitutional or other legal implications of policy proposals. Finally, the office works with White House personnel in "vetting" the qualifications of possible political appointees throughout the executive branch of government.

---

18. Hult and Dunn Tenpas, "The Office of the Staff Secretary," p. 268.

19. Mary Anne Borelli, Karen Hult, and Nancy Kassop, "The White House Counsel's Office," *Presidential Studies Quarterly* 31, 4 (December 2001), pp. 563–573.

The Counsel's Office sits at the intersection of law, politics, and policy. It is charged with advising the president and the White House staff on what is legally sound, yet politically astute.[20] When it is not totally mired in addressing scandals or confirmation matters, the White House Counsel is significantly involved in the policymaking process. The Counsel's Office does not draft legislation submitted by the White House to Congress. That is done by an agency, the OMB, or someone in the policy councils. The Counsel's Office does often draft executive orders or presidential memoranda that carry the same force of law as legislation. For example, the president can issue an executive order decreasing the size of the federal workforce without the approval of Congress, as President Clinton did early in his administration. Similarly, President George H. W. Bush made extensive use of executive orders when he responded to Iraq's invasion of Kuwait in 1991. President Obama, during his second term, turned to executive orders as legislation became bogged down in a hyper-partisan divide in Congress. In addition, the Counsel's Office often fulfills a variety of functions related to the legislative process. These include reviewing legislative proposals and bills presented for presidential signature or veto.[21] Furthermore, the Counsel's views are considered throughout the policy process, especially on policy matters before the courts—such as lawsuits against gun manufacturers that could impact gun control legislation.

In its gatekeeper role, the Counsel's Office will use its authority as the president's legal adviser to influence policy proposals. If the Counsel declares that a policy proposal developed by one of the policy councils is unconstitutional, the policy will have to be revamped or discarded. Policy councils rarely challenge the legal interpretations of the White House Counsel, unless they can get a different legal interpretation from the Justice Department. However, the Justice Department tends to adopt narrower interpretations of what is constitutional than the White House Counsel. In an effort to reduce some of the legal leverage of the Counsel's Office, the policy councils in the past have hired lawyers to provide legal ammunition. However, the Counsel's Office and its authority continue to grow as presidents rely on the office for more and more legal services.

CONCLUSION

In this chapter, we discussed the role of other White House offices in the policymaking process. These offices have distinct and important roles in the process. In particular, they serve as conduits through which the concerns of

---

20. Borelli et al., "The White House Counsel's Office," p. 562.

21. Borelli et al., "The White House Counsel's Office," p. 568.

various constituencies at the national, state, and local levels are transmitted to the president. The more these constituents believe that their views and concerns have been considered by the chief policymaker, the more likely they are to accept the process and the policy outcome. Consequently, although the role of the White House office in the policymaking process is less direct than that of the policy councils, it is no less important. In the next chapter, we analyze how policymakers build a consensus among the cabinet. We will describe how to set up a decision-making process, the role of interagency policy working groups, and how to determine who needs to be consulted in the process and who does not.

Key Terms

West Wing

Review Questions

1. What are the three primary roles of the OLA?
2. How can the Office of Public Engagement and the OIA facilitate the policy-making process?
3. What role does White House Counsel play in policymaking?

AGENCIES AND POLICY IMPLEMENTATION

EXECUTIVE AGENCIES AND DEPARTMENTS AND EXECUTIVE BRANCH POLICYMAKING

Even though the policymaking process since the presidency of Franklin Roosevelt has been increasingly centralized in the White House, federal agencies continue to play an important and dynamic role in the policymaking process. Because of the sheer number of government programs and decisions that need to be made, a large portion of the policymaking process remains outside the White House in executive branch agencies. The term *agency* refers to organizations with "Agency," "Department," or "Bureau" in their titles, like the Environmental Protection Agency or Central Intelligence Agency, the Department of State or Department of Defense, and the Federal Bureau of Investigation. All of these agencies control the programs that implement the policies decided by the president; they have the programmatic knowledge and expertise that are essential components of an effective decision-making process.[1] In addition, agencies control the budget, regulatory, and rule-making processes that make policy implementation a reality.

In this chapter, we will identify the roles and responsibilities of agencies in the policymaking process and analyze how they help to form and implement policy decisions. We will also discuss the role of agencies and the White House in the implementation of policy decisions. Once policy decisions are made by the president or his subordinates, agencies become the chief implementers of

---

1. For an overview of the problems and issues that the president faces when attempting to implement policy, see George Edwards and Stephen Wayne, *Presidential Leadership: Politics and Policy Making* (New York, NY: St. Martin's/Worth, 1999), pp. 283–322.

those policies. Agencies draft regulations, fill in the details on legislation sub-mitted by the president to Congress, and are often designated to carry out presidential decisions presented in executive orders. The four primary means of implementing policy decisions are (1) legislation; (2) executive actions, includ-ing issuing executive orders; (3) regulatory rule making; and (4) use of the presi-dential bully pulpit. In this chapter, we will analyze these implementation mechanisms and specify the conditions under which each is likely to be used.

THE ROLE OF AGENCIES

There are fifteen cabinet agencies and scores of agencies, commissions, and other government entities in the executive branch of government. These include cabinet-level agencies; non-cabinet-level agencies; and independent agencies, departments, and bureaus. The most prominent of these are cabinet-level agencies.

Cabinet-Level Agencies

Cabinet-level agencies are those whose programs and responsibilities have been determined by the Congress to be vital to the national interest and should serve as preeminent advisors to the president. The president can include the heads of particular agencies in his cabinet, but only Congress can grant the whole agency cabinet status. For example, President Clinton made the admin-istrator of the Environmental Protection Agency (EPA) a member of his cabi-net, but Congress failed to enact legislation that would provide the agency with cabinet rank. Box 4-1 provides a list of all the cabinet-level agencies.

BOX 4-1	Cabinet-Level Agencies
Department of Agriculture	Department of the Interior
Department of Commerce	Department of Justice
Department of Defense	Department of Labor
Department of Education	Department of State
Department of Energy	Department of Transportation
Department of Health and Human Services	Department of the Treasury
	Department of Veteran's Affairs
Department of Housing and Urban Development	Department of Homeland Security

Most agencies are organized into **program offices** and **non-program offices**. Program offices run the specific programs that Congress has established by statute, such as Head Start, Pell Grants, and food stamps. Non-program offices include an agency's budget office, the office of the general counsel, the office of the chief of staff, and an agency's policy and research office. Policy development in most federal agencies is coordinated by the office of the chief of staff and the policy development office. The budget process is directed by the budget office, while rule implementation (regulations) is controlled by an agency's general counsel office.

Like the White House office, cabinet agencies follow a specific set of internal processes and guidelines when developing policy. If a cabinet secretary wants an agency to prepare an options memorandum in a specific policy area, he or she will assign someone in the chief of staff's office or policy development office the task of setting up an intra-agency working group. The working group will usually include someone from the general counsel's office, the agency's budget office, and its relevant program office(s). In a fashion that mirrors the White House policy process, the intra-agency group will continue to meet until a memorandum is readied. Before the memo is submitted, however, a formal **concurrence/nonconcurrence sheet** is circulated to the agency senior staff. Each member of the senior staff *must* express his or her opinion before the memorandum is submitted to the Secretary.[2]

Non-Cabinet-Level Executive Agencies

The difference between cabinet agencies and agencies whose director is a member of a particular president's cabinet can seem confusing and arcane. The EPA, for example, has a larger budget than several other cabinet agencies. The Congress conducts regular oversight of the EPA, just as it does with cabinet departments. Furthermore, President Obama appointed the administrator of the EPA to his cabinet. Yet, Congress has never granted the EPA **cabinet-level status**. As a result, although the head of the EPA attends cabinet meetings, the EPA remains a non-cabinet-level agency. Consequently, for practical purposes, the difference between some cabinet departments and large non-cabinet agencies like the EPA is often nonexistent.

On the other hand, there is a distinct difference in the political clout of cabinet-level and non-cabinet-level agencies. For example, for reasons of continuity in government and clear lines of succession in the event of a catastrophe,

---

2. Jacquie Lawing (former Chief of Staff to the Secretary of Housing and Urban Development), interview with the author, May 7, 2001.

one cabinet officer always fails to attend the State of the Union address. The missing officer is always a congressionally designated cabinet agency.[3] Thus, even though President Clinton treated the head of the EPA as a cabinet officer, and even though his own Office of Cabinet Affairs (OCAF) believed that the president has the authority to make an agency a cabinet department without congressional approval, the OCAF did not allow the head of the EPA to be the missing cabinet official. This recognition of political clout carries over into policy meetings, where there is often a subtle difference in the way cabinet agencies are treated by White House staff versus non-cabinet agencies.

Many non-cabinet-level agencies tend to have a narrow program area or issue focus. The Federal Emergency Management Agency (FEMA), the General Services Administration (GSA), and the Peace Corps are examples of programs with a specific focus. FEMA is the agency responsible for coordinating the federal government's response to emergencies, including natural disasters. GSA manages all the administrative services for the federal government. It negotiates the leases for office space and purchases all the office furniture and supplies for all federal government agencies. The Peace Corps was founded under President Kennedy. It is very well known, yet it has a very small budget of only about $370 million. The Peace Corps logically could have been situated in the State Department, just as USAID is today. But there was concern that many developing countries would have balked at hosting Peace Corps volunteers if they thought they were really State Department diplomats or spies rather than engineers, teachers, and agricultural advisors. To minimize such misperceptions, the Peace Corps was developed as a new agency.

Box 4-2 lists most of the major non-cabinet-level agencies that report directly to the president. Some of the heads of these agencies serve on the president's cabinet, and others do not.

BOX 4-2	Major Non-Cabinet-Level Executive Agencies
Central Intelligence Agency Corporation for Community and National Service	Environmental Protection Agency Federal Bureau of Investigation
	(Continued)

---

3. Thurgood Marshall, Jr. (former Secretary to the Cabinet), interview with the author, April 3, 2001.

(Continued)

Federal Emergency Management Administration	Office of Personnel Management
	Peace Corps
General Services Administration	Small Business Administration
National Aeronautics and Space Administration (NASA)	Tennessee Valley Authority

Note: Some of the agencies on this list will assert they are independent because the statutes creating them describe them that way. But because they are not self-funded, they serve at the pleasure of the president (meaning they can be fired by the president), there are no terms of office, and political leadership is not limited by party, they are not truly independent in practice.

Some single-issue or program agencies have grown beyond their original mandates and could be cabinet agencies if Congress acquiesced. The EPA, for example, has become larger than several other cabinet departments and plays a much greater role in the policy process than originally envisioned. It is now involved in almost every interagency process regarding environmental policy— even when the discussion involves programs not run by the agency. This is unusual. Although cabinet agencies, such as Treasury, can participate in almost any discussion regardless of any direct responsibility for the programs being discussed, most single-issue or program agencies participate in policy processes only when the programs being discussed are ones run by their particular agencies.

Independent Agencies, Departments, and Bureaus

Independent agencies, departments, and bureaus exist within the executive branch, but their day-to-day operations are not overseen by the president and the White House staff. These agencies were created to ensure that they carried out their responsibilities without regular interference by the executive and legislative branches. They tend to be either regulatory enforcement agencies or government corporations that are chartered to provide a specific service to business or consumers (e.g., United States Postal Service). Independent regulatory agencies are also typically defined by term appointment rather than appointments at the pleasure of the presidency.[4] Below are the key characteristics of independent agencies:[5]

---

4. Thurgood Marshall, Jr, interview with the author, April 3, 2001.

5. Not all independent agencies exhibit each characteristic listed below.

- Fully or partially self-financed through user fees from industries they regulate;
- Agency leadership is nominated by president and confirmed by Senate, but serves for a term rather than at the pleasure of the president;
- Terms of office not concurrent with president;
- Membership limits based on party affiliation.

The best-known and arguably most powerful independent agency is the Federal Reserve Board, which serves as the nation's central bank. Others include the Federal Communications Commission (FCC), which regulates the telecommunications industry, and the Federal Elections Commission (FEC), which oversees our country's election laws. The president's primary authority over these agencies is his ability to nominate the heads and board members of these departments and, in some cases, his authority to designate their chairpersons. Although the president can formally request these agencies to take certain actions, he or she cannot order or direct them to do so. Furthermore, unlike non-independent agencies, independent agencies can simply ignore the president's request. For example, in 1997, President Clinton asked the FCC to require broadcasters to provide free television ads to candidates for federal office as part of his overall campaign finance reform agenda. FCC Chairman Bill Kennard expressed some initial interest in the proposal, but the Commission soon found that Hill appropriators were not so warm to the idea. Consequently, the FCC chose not to act on the president's official request. Box 4-3 lists the independent government agencies.

BOX 4-3	Independent Agencies

Commission on Civil Rights	Federal Deposit Insurance Corporation
Commodity Futures Trading Commission	Federal Election Commission
Consumer Product Safety Commission	Federal Maritime Commission
Defense Nuclear Facilities Safety Board	Federal Mediation and Conciliation Service
Federal Communications Commission	Federal Reserve System Board of Governors
	Federal Retirement Thrift Investment Board

(Continued)

(Continued)

Federal Trade Commission	Office of Government Ethics
Merit Systems Protection Board	Pension Benefit Guaranty
National Archives and Records	Corporation
Administration	Railroad Retirement Board
National Credit Union	Securities and
Administration	Exchange Commission
National Labor Relations Board	Selective Service System Trade and
National Railroad Passenger	Development Agency
Corporation	United States International Trade
National Transportation Safety Board	Commission
Nuclear Regulatory Commission	United States Postal Service

IMPLEMENTING POLICY DECISIONS

Once a policy decision has been made, the implementation process begins. A **decision-making memorandum** generally contains both policy recommendations and policy implementation recommendations. For example, in 1993, President Clinton was given a decision-making memorandum that recommended he reform the Community Reinvestment Act (CRA). Under the CRA, commercial banks and savings and loans are required to reinvest in the communities in which they charter and take deposits. The purpose of the law is to ensure that all communities have access to basic banking services. Yet throughout the 1980s, the CRA was criticized for being overly bureaucratic and focused more on paperwork than performance. President Clinton's advisers suggested that the CRA be streamlined and that the regulations be based on performance—tied to actual lending and investment benchmarks—instead of based on highly subjective criteria such as the number of meetings with community groups. In their decision-making memorandum to the president, his advisers suggested he send a presidential directive to the four banking regulators asking them to revise CRA regulations. Thus, the president's advisers provided him with not only a proposed policy change but a tool to implement those recommended changes. In the case of CRA reform, the tool of choice was a presidential directive. On other occasions it could be legislation, regulatory change, or simply the use of the presidential bully pulpit. Sometimes the choice of the tool is driven by the policies chosen and sometimes by the political climate. For example, presidents often rely on executive orders when they lack political support in Congress. In the remaining sections of this chapter, we will discuss the policy implementation process and the role of the White House offices and the agencies in this system.

Executive Orders and Other Executive Actions

The president is the chief executive of the executive branch of the federal government. As chief executive, he has ultimate supervision over the various administrative agencies. In addition, he has wide, if vague, authority to further the public interest (as an example, in the secession crisis of 1861, President Lincoln suspended, by proclamation, the writ of habeas corpus). Under the Constitution, the president is also the military commander-in-chief and head of state responsible for the directing of foreign relations. He also has considerable decision-making authority in matters regarding foreign trade. The primary means by which the president exercises his authority in these areas is through the issuance of **proclamations** and executive orders.

Proclamations and executive orders have much the same legal effect, but they are usually used for different purposes: proclamations for ceremonial or broad policy statements, executive orders for routine determinations under statutory authority. Proclamations are usually used for ceremonial statements of general interest (e.g., declaring National Flag Day), but occasionally they are used for substantive statements of general policy (e.g., Lincoln's Emancipation Proclamation) or for announcements of certain presidential decisions, especially in the fields of foreign relations and trade.

The first executive order was issued in 1789, but none were numbered or issued uniformly until 1907, when the State Department began a numbering system and designated an 1862 order as Executive Order #1. Orders issued between 1789 and 1862 are referred to as "unnumbered executive orders."[6] Executive orders are essentially presidential directives with the force of law and do not require the approval of Congress to take effect. The Constitution is silent on the subject of executive orders, but the courts have upheld them in principle, based on the implied powers inherent in the grant of "executive power" to the president in Article II, section 1 and in the constitutional language in Article II, section 3, that says presidents are "to take care that the laws be faithfully executed." In addition to this general constitutional authority, some executive orders are issued under direct statutory authority delegated specifically to the president by Congress in limited policy areas.[7]

---

6. University of Florida Levin College of Law web site, http://www.law.ufl.edu.

7. Ilona Nickels, Executive Orders, http://www.ilonanickels.com/CC_executiveorders.html

Congress often leaves considerable leeway to the executive branch to carry out its legislation. Details are often left out of statutory language, either because of a desire to give the federal agencies involved some flexibility in implementing a bill, or simply because Congress feels unable or unwilling to spell out every detail for a bill's execution. If members of Congress feel that an executive order contradicts the original legislative intent of the law or has no underlying statutory authority, they can file a lawsuit to change or rescind the order. Congress can also pass a bill repealing or modifying a specific executive order. That bill would, however, be subject to a presidential veto and a need to override.

Like the legislative drafting process, the process for preparing executive orders and other executive directives is generally controlled by the policy councils as long as the orders are policy related. On the other hand, when it comes to implementing policy, executive orders share all the same advantages as regulations. The process for issuing an executive order is not as long as it is for issuing a regulation, and there is no public comment period (see Box 4-4). At the same time, executive orders have the disadvantage of being restricted by statutory and constitutional limitations.

Submitting Legislation

When a president signs into law legislation he or she submitted to Congress, it is often considered a milestone event from a policy, political, and

---

BOX 4-4	**Executive Actions**

1. The president agrees to issue executive order or directive.
2. The relevant policy council identifies a lead entity to draft the executive order or directive. Potential lead entities include a policy council or an agency, the White House Counsel, or the OMB.
3. A draft executive order or directive is completed and sent back to the relevant policy council for editing and review.
4. A final draft is submitted to the White House staff secretary.
5. The White House staff secretary circulates to all White House and Executive Office of the President offices and, if appropriate, to the relevant agencies for concurrence or nonconcurrence recommendation.
6. The final executive order or directive is sent to the president with an information memorandum.
7. The president signs the executive order or directive.

communications perspective. Bill signings are big events, and legislative achievements are given high consideration by political commentators and historians. Using legislation to authorize policy has several advantages over executive orders and executive directives. First, legislation is generally broader in scope than executive orders or regulations. Executive orders and regulations are limited by statutes, but legislation can be as far reaching as its authors desire. It is limited only by the degree of political consensus in Congress and the White House and by constraints imposed by the Constitution. Second, legislation that is enacted into law carries an aura of legitimacy derived from the legislative process. Specifically, any legislation that becomes law has the support of majorities in the House and Senate and at least the acquiescence of the president. Executive actions and regulations, which are implemented solely by the executive branch, do not carry the same political weight because they lack the legitimacy that comes from wider participation in the policymaking process.

Despite the benefits of using legislation to implement policy, there are several drawbacks that make it inappropriate under certain circumstances. First, no legislation passes without compromise. Although a president can control executive actions, legislation must go through the congressional process. In some cases, what comes out at the end of the process may look very different from what the president proposed. Second, the legislative process is usually long and arduous. Sometimes bills take years to pass, and other times Congress just ignores them. In contrast, policy can be implemented very quickly using executive orders. For example, within twelve hours of being informed that Iraq had invaded Kuwait, President Bush had signed executive orders freezing Iraqi and Kuwaiti assets in the United States (see Chapter 15). Third, the president must spend political capital to get legislation enacted. Many presidents have wasted a great deal of political influence on legislation that never gets out of Congress. Despite these drawbacks, presidents continue to submit legislation to Congress because it offers them the best chance to achieve real, substantial changes in policies, programs, and systems.

Box 4-5 outlines the process by which legislation is drafted and then submitted to the Congress. Like the policymaking process discussed in earlier chapters, the Policy Councils lead an interagency process to develop the bill. A lead agency is designated to draft the language of the bill and a series of meetings is held to review, edit, and redraft the legislation until a consensus is reached.

Once the interagency group has completed its work, the bill is moved through the OMB LRM process for review by any interested party of government. If a disagreement cannot be resolved, a decision-memorandum is drafted and the president is presented with the recommendations of the group. However, several different groups of advisers meet in the hopes of resolving any differences before the president is required to engage. If a consensus is reached, the president receives an information memorandum that the bill is ready and a timetable for when it will be sent up.

BOX 4-5   Preparing Legislation

1. The president directs the appropriate White House policy council to implement his decision to draft legislation.
2. The White House Policy Office establishes a working group to write a draft of the legislation.
3. The chair of the White House working group chooses a lead agency to provide a first draft of the legislation.
4. The lead agency divides up drafting responsibilities between the general counsel's office, the relevant program office, and the relevant policy office.
5. An interagency working group meets to review first draft of the legislation. The policy council coordinates the revisions and recommendations received from other agencies in the working group. The policy council resolves any disagreements.
6. The lead agency incorporates the revisions.
7. The redrafted bill is submitted to the OMB legislative referral management process.
8. The OMB circulates the draft bill to the relevant agencies.
9. The OMB incorporates the revisions and recommendations it receives from the agencies. Unresolved issues go to policy councils. If major disagreement exists, the issue is bumped up to a principals-level meeting (agency heads). If disagreement still exists, the policy council drafts a decision-making memorandum for the president.
10. The final legislation is prepared by the lead agency. The lead agency identifies the members of Congress who will submit the legislation on behalf of the president.
11. The legislation is submitted. The congressional review process begins.

Regulations and the Rule-Making Process

Issuing regulations is one of the key means by which policies are implemented. Agencies can issue and revise regulations using existing statutory authority. They generally do so either when Congress has enacted legislation, when the president has asked for a new rule, or when the agency itself determines that a regulation should be reviewed and/or revised.

The advantages to the executive branch of using the regulatory process as a means of implementing policy are that the process is under the control of the rule-making agency and the impact can be immediate once the rule is completed. The limitations are that the impact of regulations is limited by the statutes on which they are based; the regulatory process can be long and arduous and is subject to public comment, which can often create political problems for the executive branch; and new regulations often create new requirements and paperwork burdens, which are generally politically unpopular (see Box 4-6).

BOX 4-6   The Rule-Making Process

1. An agency begins the rule-making process.
2. The appropriate agency program office and general counsel's office write a draft of the regulation.
3. The first draft of the regulation circulates within the agency.
4. Revisions and recommendations are sent back to the appropriate agency program office and general counsel's office.
5. The draft regulation is circulated through the agency again, along with a concur/not concur sheet. All senior agency staff personnel must reply before the process continues.
6. A final "drop dead" meeting takes place in which all final comments are made and reviewed.
7. The Secretary's or agency head's office clears the final rule.
8. The Office of Information and Regulatory Review (OIRA) coordinates the review of the regulation by the OMB and White House, though *only* economically significant regulations require OMB review.
9. OIRA establishes a regulatory working group to review the regulation that includes the White House policy councils and the Office of the Vice President.

(Continued)

(Continued)

10. OIRA assembles the revisions and sends them back to the agency that originated the regulation. If there is no disagreement, OIRA will provide the agency with a regulation number, which allows the regulation to be published in the Federal Register.[8] If there are disagreements over the revised regulation, the vice president's working group convenes and resolves the differences. In unique circumstances, a decision-making memorandum can be presented to the president.

11. The regulation is sent to the relevant congressional committees (authorizing committees) for a short waiting period.

12. The regulation is published in the Federal Register for public comment. On occasion, public hearings are held on proposed rules. Comment periods are at least sixty days.

13. The regulations are revised to incorporate public comments.

14. Steps 5 through 11 are repeated.

15. The final regulation is printed in the Federal Register. If parts of a regulation are set aside for further consideration, an interim final rule is published instead. Rules take effect no earlier than thirty days after publication.

Federal agencies are authorized to issue regulations by their enabling statutes, by statutes establishing new programs, and by statutes amending and extending the duties and responsibilities of those agencies. Most regulations are issued informally, under the notice-and-comment procedure established by the Administrative Procedure Act (APA). Less frequently, certain agencies are required to add elements of adjudicatory proceedings, such as cross-examination and rebuttal witnesses, to the notice-and-comment requirements. These agencies include the Federal Trade Commission, the Consumer Product Safety Commission, and the Occupational Safety and Health Administration. Very rarely, some agencies must conduct their rule-making exercises in a formal adjudicatory proceeding.[9]

More than 100 federal agencies and units within agencies issue regulations. Depending on their relationship to the president, the agencies may be divided into two categories: those subject to the president's direction and control (executive departments and independent agencies) and those relatively independent of such direction and control (independent regulatory agencies). The Consumer

---

8. Jacquie Lawing, interview with the author, May 7, 2001.

9. Rogelio Garcia, "Federal Regulatory Reform: An Overview," *The Semiannual Regulatory Agenda,* IB95035. (Washington, DC: Congressional Research Service Government and Finance Division, 2000).

Product Safety Commission, the Federal Energy Regulatory Commission, the Federal Reserve System, the Federal Trade Commission, and Securities and Exchange Commission are all examples of independent regulatory agencies.[10]

Approximately 90 percent of all regulations issued by agencies are subject to Executive Order 12866, which gives the president considerable oversight capability. Most of these agencies are involved with issuing the more costly social regulations. They include the EPA, the Occupational Safety and Health Administration and the Mine Safety and Health Administration (both in the Department of Labor), the Food and Drug Administration (Department of Health and Human Services), the Department of Energy, Department of the Interior, Department of Agriculture, and Department of Transportation (especially the National Highway Safety Administration).

Once the rule-making process starts, however, the White House cannot comment to the drafting agency on the proposed regulation until it has been sent to OIRA for review.[11] However, although OIRA controls the editing process for regulations, the White House offices and the policy councils in particular have tremendous influence over the process and the final outcome once the regulation is circulated by OIRA.[12] The knowledge that the policy councils are senior policy advisers to the president and can submit any dispute to him gives the councils a great deal of leverage in any negotiation over disagreements.[13] If there are disagreements between the drafting agency and a White House policy council, OIRA generally brings the parties together to negotiate a compromise rather than impose its will on them.

Presidents Nixon, Ford, and Carter directed agencies to consider costs and various regulatory alternatives to reduce those costs when developing regulations. But it was E.O. 12291 that dramatically changed the procedure under

---

10. Garcia, "Federal Regulatory Reform."

11. However, OIRA only reviews rules that are significant. A significant regulation is defined as one that may have an annual effect on the economy of $100 million or more, or adversely affect in a material way the economy, a sector of the economy, productivity, competition, jobs, the environment or public health or safety, or state, local, or tribal governments or communities (regulations in this category are considered economically significant, requiring detailed cost-benefit analyses and OMB review); interfere with an action taken or planned by another agency; or may materially alter the budgetary impact of entitlements, grants, user fees, or loan programs or the rights and obligations of recipients; or raise novel legal or policy issues arising out of legal mandates, the president's priorities, or the principles for regulatory planning and review specified in the order.

12. Cynthia Rice (former special assistant to the president for domestic policy), interview with the author, May 1, 2001.

13. Cynthia Rice, interview with the author, May 1, 2001.

which agencies develop and issue regulations. E.O. 12291 directed agencies to employ cost-benefit analysis when developing regulations and established centralized review of rule making. It also directed agencies, to the extent permitted by law, to issue only those regulations for which benefits outweigh costs and to prepare cost-benefit analyses when developing major regulations. To assure compliance, agencies were required to submit their proposed and final regulations to the OMB for review and clearance. When President Clinton assumed office in 1993, he continued the reform process by issuing Executive Order 12866 and revoking E.O. 12291. The new order maintained, with minor revisions, the cost-benefit analysis requirements as well as the requirement that regulations be reviewed and cleared by the OMB. Independent regulatory boards and commissions again were exempted from the order. In 2011, the Obama administration issued Executive Order 13563 that amended 12866 moderately. The **Congressional Review Act**, Subtitle E (110 Stat. 868), requires agencies to submit new regulations to the Congress and the General Accounting Office (GAO) before they can take effect. The GAO is to prepare a report on each major rule, which it sends to Congress, to assure that the agency has complied with procedural requirements regarding cost-benefit analysis, regulatory flexibility analysis, and specified sections of the Unfunded Mandates Reform Act. Congress has sixty session days in which to block the regulation by passing a joint resolution of disapproval, which must be signed by the president. The regulation goes into effect if the president vetoes the joint resolution and the veto is not overridden.[14]

Box 4-7 provides a copy of relevant sections of Executive Orders 13563 and 12866, which set forth the procedures for regulatory review in the executive branch of government.

BOX 4-7	The Regulatory Review Process

Executive Order 13563 of January 18, 2011—Improving Regulation and Regulatory Review

By the authority vested in me as president by the Constitution and the laws of the United States of America, and in order to improve regulation and regulatory review, it is hereby ordered as follows:

Section 1. General Principles of Regulation. (a) Our regulatory system must protect public health, welfare, safety, and our environment while promoting

14. Garcia, "Federal Regulatory Reform."

economic growth, innovation, competitiveness, and job creation. It must be based on the best available science. It must allow for public participation and an open exchange of ideas. It must promote predictability and reduce uncertainty. It must identify and use the best, most innovative, and least burdensome tools for achieving regulatory ends. It must take into account benefits and costs, both quantitative and qualitative. It must ensure that regulations are accessible, consistent, written in plain language, and easy to understand. It must measure, and seek to improve, the actual results of regulatory requirements. (b) This order is supplemental to and reaffirms the principles, structures, and definitions governing contemporary regulatory review that were established in Executive Order 12866 of September 30, 1993. As stated in that executive order and to the extent permitted by law, each agency must, among other things: (1) propose or adopt a regulation only upon a reasoned determination that its benefits justify its costs (recognizing that some benefits and costs are difficult to quantify); (2) tailor its regulations to impose the least burden on society, consistent with obtaining regulatory objectives, taking into account, among other things, and to the extent practicable, the costs of cumulative regulations; (3) select, in choosing among alternative regulatory approaches, those approaches that maximize net benefits (including potential economic, environmental, public health and safety, and other advantages; distributive impacts; and equity); (4) to the extent feasible, specify performance objectives, rather than specifying the behavior or manner of compliance that regulated entities must adopt; and (5) identify and assess available alternatives to direct regulation, including providing economic incentives to encourage the desired behavior, such as user fees or marketable permits, or providing information upon which choices can be made by the public. (c) In applying these principles, each agency is directed to use the best available techniques to quantify anticipated present and future benefits and costs as accurately as possible. Where appropriate and permitted by law, each agency may consider (and discuss qualitatively) values that are difficult or impossible to quantify, including equity, human dignity, fairness, and distributive impacts.

Sec. 2. Public Participation. (a) Regulations shall be adopted through a process that involves public participation. To that end, regulations shall be based, to the extent feasible and consistent with law, on the open exchange of information and perspectives among State, local, and tribal officials, experts in relevant disciplines, affected stakeholders in the private sector, and the public as a whole. (b) To promote that open exchange, each agency, consistent with Executive Order 12866 and other applicable legal requirements, shall endeavor to provide the public with an opportunity to participate in the regulatory process. To the extent feasible and permitted by law, each agency shall afford the public a meaningful opportunity to comment through the Internet on any proposed regulation, with

(Continued)

(Continued)

a comment period that should generally be at least 60 days. To the extent feasible and permitted by law, each agency shall also provide, for both proposed and final rules, timely online access to the rulemaking docket on regulations.gov, including relevant scientific and technical findings, in an open format that can be easily searched and downloaded. For proposed rules, such access shall include, to the extent feasible and permitted by law, an opportunity for public comment on all pertinent parts of the rulemaking docket, including relevant scientific and technical findings. (c) Before issuing a notice of proposed rulemaking, each agency, where feasible and appropriate, shall seek the views of those who are likely to be affected, including those who are likely to benefit from and those who are potentially subject to such rulemaking.

THE WHITE HOUSE

January 18, 2011.

Sources: Executive Order 13563 of January 18, 2011, "Improving Regulation and Regulatory Review," Government Printing Office, January 21, 2011, http://www.gpo.gov/fdsys/pkg/DCPD-201100031/pdf/DCPD-201100031.pdf.

CONCLUSION

Even though the policymaking process has been increasingly centralized in the White House, federal agencies continue to play an important and dynamic role in the policymaking process. In this chapter, we have underscored their programmatic expertise, their control of budgets, and their regulatory and rulemaking processes. Given these functions, agencies are essential players in the making and implementation of policy in the executive branch.

Key Terms

Cabinet-level status

Concurrence/nonconcurrence sheet

Congressional Review Act

Decision-making memorandum

Independent agencies, departments, and bureaus

Non-program offices

Proclamations

Program offices

Review Questions

1. How many executive branch agencies are cabinet-level agencies? What difference does that designation make?
2. What is a "single-issue" or "program" agency?
3. What is an independent regulatory agency?
4. When was the first executive order issued? How can executive orders be challenged?
5. What are the advantages and disadvantages of issuing executive orders?
6. Describe the eleven steps taken by the federal government in preparing legislating to be submitted to Congress.
7. What are some of the advantages to utilizing the rule-making process as a means of implementing policy?

POLICY MANAGEMENT

POLICY MANAGEMENT AND PROCEDURAL LEGITIMACY

The way in which the president (or for that matter a governor, mayor, or county executive) organizes and manages an executive branch may have significant implications for the level of procedural legitimacy granted to the policymaking process and, hence, the level of support that a policy proposal is likely to receive. One of the primary lessons learned from the policymaking experiences of the George H. W. Bush, William J. Clinton, George W. Bush, and Barack H. Obama administrations is that stakeholders in the federal executive branch are more likely to consider the process to be legitimate when it is well managed and well led. In particular, leadership is enhanced when the policymaking process helps promote the president's agenda and enables him and his principals to serve as honest brokers and incubators of ideas. Management is enhanced when the process fulfills the president's staffing needs, coordinates the relevant agencies, and establishes and monitors accountability, implementation, and execution. Notable examples of the effective use of the policymaking process include the National Economic Council (NEC) under Robert Rubin when it developed the 1993 economic plan (Chapter 13), the National Security Council (NSC) under National Security Advisor Anthony Lake in 1995 when it promoted an "End Game Strategy" for Bosnia, and the NSC under National Security Adviser Stephen Hadley in 2006 when it transformed U.S. policy in Iraq (Chapter 16). In these cases and others like them, the policy councils and their principals used the policymaking process to increase the level of support by stakeholders in the executive branch even when an initial policy consensus did not exist.

In contrast, when the policymaking process fails to fulfill its principal roles, internal conflicts persist. When, for example, the responsibility and account- ability for policy development are not clear, as was true with Clinton's welfare reform policy issue before 1994, internal conflicts are more likely (Chapter 12). Similarly, when policymakers are excluded or feel unable to express their views and concerns to the principals or the president as the policy develops, they often try to circumvent the process. This was true during Operations Desert Storm and Desert Shield as well as the 2003 invasion of Iraq (Chapter 15). In addition, even if an interagency process is used and various stakeholders take part in policy discussions, disagreements among stakeholders may persist if they do not believe the process provides a balance of representation, centralized management, and decisions that are clear and final. Though stakeholders who criticize the process or policy often resign or move on to other positions, some go to the press and other outlets to voice their concerns. The so-called Revolt of the Generals who criticized the president and senior policymakers for their actions in Iraq in September of 2007 is an example of this.[1] Others hold their comments until after they have left public service. In his recent memoir, for example, former Secretary of Defense Robert Gates supports President Obama but is critical of the policymaking process. In particular, he expresses frustra- tion over interagency meetings when he felt that policy decisions had been determined by the White House staff before the meetings took place, or when the final policy choices did not reflect the discussions that had taken place.[2]

MODELS OF POLICY MANAGEMENT

Much of the recent work on presidential decision making has emphasized the importance of institutional arrangements and organizational characteristics to policy choices.[3] Prominent among these is the presidential management model,

---

1. Mark Sauer, "Generals Opposing Iraq War Break With Military Tradition," *San Diego Union-Tribune*, September 23, 2007. Retrieved from http://legacy.utsandiego.com/news/ military/20070923-9999-1n23generals.html.

2. Robert Gates, *Duty: Memoirs of a Secretary at War* (New York, NY: Knopf, 2014).

3. See, for example, John P. Burke, *The Institutional Presidency* (Baltimore, MD: Johns Hopkins University Press, 1992); Colin Campbell, *Managing the Presidency* (Pittsburgh, PA: University of Pittsburgh Press, 1983); Alexander George, *Presidential Decisions in Foreign Policy* (Boulder, CO: Westview Press, 1980); John Hart, *The Presidential Branch: From Washington to Clinton,* 2nd edition (Chatham, NJ: Chatham House, 1995); Stephen Hess, *Organizing the Presidency,* 2nd edition (Washington, DC: Brookings Institution, 1998);

which posits that the management and decision-making styles presidents use can have a significant impact on their ability to lead and maintain control over individuals and agencies competing to dominate the policymaking process. Differences in management styles include the following:[4]

- The extent to which the president is involved in the intricacies and details of policymaking. Presidents Franklin Roosevelt, Lyndon Johnson, Jimmy Carter, and Bill Clinton preferred greater involvement, while Presidents Ronald Reagan, Dwight Eisenhower, and George W. Bush preferred to delegate.
- The president's preference for establishing hierarchies of authority versus more informal, ad hoc systems of policymaking. Presidents Harry Truman, Dwight Eisenhower, Richard Nixon, Ronald Reagan, and George W. Bush preferred the former, while Presidents Franklin Roosevelt, John Kennedy, and Barack Obama preferred the latter.
- The president's preference for verbal debate versus carrying out debates and briefings in writing. Presidents Franklin Roosevelt, Harry Truman, and Bill Clinton preferred the former; Presidents Richard Nixon and Jimmy Carter the latter.
- The president's preference for involvement in negotiations. Presidents Franklin Roosevelt and Lyndon Johnson preferred to negotiate, while presidents John Kennedy, Richard Nixon, and Jimmy Carter preferred to let others negotiate on their behalf.

Roger Porter, a noted political scientist, synthesized these characteristics into three general types of presidential management: centralized management,

---

Margaret G. Hermann and Thomas Preston, "Presidents, Advisors and Foreign Policy: The Effects of Leadership Style on Executive Arrangements," *Political Psychology* 15, 1 (1995), pp. 75–96; Terry M. Moe and William G. Howell, "Unilateral Action and Presidential Power: A Theory," *Presidential Studies Quarterly* 29, 4 (1999), pp. 850–872; William Newmann, "Causes of Change in National Security Processes: Carter, Reagan, and Bush Decision Making on Arms Control," *Presidential Studies Quarterly* 31, 1 (March 2001), pp. 69–103; Roger Porter, *Presidential Decision Making: The Economic Policy Board* (Cambridge, UK: Cambridge University Press, 1980); Robert J. Thompson, "Contrasting Models of White House Staff Organization: The Eisenhower, Ford and Carter Experiences," *Congress and the Presidency* 19 (Autumn 1992), pp. 113–36; and Shirley Anne Warshaw, *The Domestic Presidency: Policymaking in the White House* (Boston, MA: Allyn & Bacon, 1997).

4. Jack H. Watson, Jr. "The Clinton White House," *Presidential Studies Quarterly,* 23 (Summer 1993), p. 429; George C. Edwards, III and Stephen J. Wayne, *Presidential Leadership: Politics and Policymaking*, 5th edition (New York, NY: Worth/St. Martin's Press, 1999), p. 232.

characterized by a hierarchical and formal staff structure; adhocracy, in which decision making is flexible and informal; and multiple advocacy, in which key staff members are responsible for managing the system and making sure that all competing groups and individuals are represented in the policymaking process.[5]

The organization of the policymaking process within the executive branch tends to vary across issues, agencies, and over time throughout any given administration.[6] Consistent with the **adhocracy model** of policy management, Presidents Bill Clinton and George W. Bush both initially distributed assignments and selected whom to seek advice from and when, without making much use of regularized meetings or institutionalized patterns of providing policy advice.[7] This strategy has the advantage of being highly flexible, promoting creativity and "out-of-the-box" thinking, while enabling the president to maintain confidentiality regarding new policy initiatives by limiting the number of personally selected advisers involved in the process.[8] It is also attractive to newly elected presidents because it creates an image that the president is personally in command and actively involved in the policymaking process.

The adhocracy model is also often used for narrowly defined projects and those conducted over a short period of time. It may also be used to address politically sensitive issues. Because ad hoc working groups generally do not report directly to the president, he is somewhat buffered from controversy regarding their activities.

---

5. Porter, *Presidential Decision Making*. Other scholars emphasize the distinction between competitive management styles, hierarchical management styles, and collegial or "spoke of the wheel" management styles. See, for example, Bruce Buchanan, "Constrained Diversity: The Organizational Demands of the Presidency," *Presidential Studies Quarterly* 20 (1991), pp. 791–822; George, *Presidential Decision Making*; Richard Johnson, *Managing the White House* (New York, NY: Harper & Row, 1974); Thompson, "Contrasting Models of White House Staff Organization," pp. 113–136. In his study of the Carter and Reagan presidencies, Professor Colin Campbell evaluates the impact of a variety of additional characteristics, including the president's preference for centralized versus decentralized management, the president's relationships with his advisers, and the relationships among the president's advisers. See Campbell, *Managing the Presidency*. For a review of this literature, see Newmann, "Causes of Change," pp. 71–72.

6. See Thompson, "Contrasting Models of White House Staff Organization," pp. 113–136.

7. The turning point away from an adhocracy approach to a more centralized organization of policymaking came with a confluence of events after two years in office, including the Republican takeover of Congress and the appointment of Leon Panetta to the position of Chief of Staff. See Elizabeth Drew, *On the Edge: The Clinton Presidency* (New York, NY: Touchstone, 1994), pp. 347–349. For a discussion of the adhocracy approach, see Porter, *Presidential Decision Making*, pp. 25, 231–235.

8. Porter, *Presidential Decision Making*, p. 233.

Despite its attractiveness and prevalence in the early phases of new administrations, the adhocracy management style has several drawbacks.[9] One such drawback is that it promotes the creation of interagency groups to address particular aspects of broad policy initiatives without providing a clear view of, or mandate to address, the policy in its entirety. In such cases, responsibility for policy development is often diffuse or unclear, accountability is lacking, and access to the president is uncertain. Under such circumstances, the president's (and his principals') limited time and bandwidth are often wasted on resolving internal disputes and clarifying or defending his organization rather than on developing and promoting a particular policy. For example, during the adhocracy management period in the early Clinton administration, an interagency committee was established to analyze welfare reform. No clear mandate was given to the group, nor were the responsibilities or leadership roles within the group well-defined. As a result, Bruce Reed, who jointly directed the working group, sent memoranda directly to the president on several occasions merely to inform him of internal conflicts and seek his help in resolving disputes within the working committee—rather than using them to propose policy options or promote welfare reform itself. The group was frustrated and the welfare reform policy process stagnated. The lack of a mandate and designated responsibilities wasted time and meant that the process was transformed into a disciplinary mechanism rather than a tool for making good policy. As their administrations evolved, Presidents Bill Clinton and George W. Bush changed their organizational strategies to a hybrid combination of a **centralized management model** and a **multiple advocacy model**.[10] In contrast, President Barack Obama has generally pursued an increasingly centralized management model, with some instances of adhocracy. A strategy of centralized management is characterized by heavy reliance on the White House and Executive Office of the President's staff to filter ideas, policy proposals, and recommendations coming to the president from executive departments and agencies.[11] It emphasizes systematic

---

9. Porter, *Presidential Decision Making*, p. 235.

10. Porter, *Presidential Decision Making*, pp. 214–223, 235–252. See also: Alexander George, "The Case for Multiple Advocacy in Making Foreign Policy," *American Political Science Review* 66 (September 1972), pp. 751–785, and "The Devil's Advocate: Uses and Limitations," in U.S. Commission on the Organization of the Government for the Conduct of Foreign Policy, *Appendices* (Washington, D.C.: GPO, June 1975), volume 2, pp. 83–85; and George Edwards and Stephen Wayne, *Presidential Leadership: Politics and Policy Making* (New York, NY: St. Martin's/Worth Publishing, 1999), pp. 226–229.

11. Porter, *Presidential Decision Making*, p. 235.

evaluation of policy questions, with control vested in individuals solely responsible to the president who are often advocates of his views. Although executive branch departments and agencies have input in the policymaking process, their role is managed and controlled by the Executive Office and the president's personal staff. Information tends to flow vertically, and in most cases from the bottom to the top rather than vice versa. This organizational strategy has the benefits of clearly specifying who has the authority and responsibility for the development of specific policies and of enabling the president to manage a wide variety of issues, respond to change quickly, and minimize leaks (as long as the president's popularity is strong) by filtering actions through a personal staff.

The centralized management style also has drawbacks. In particular, it tends to focus responsibility for a particular policy in the hands of an individual or small group that is given preferential and often exclusive access to the president.[12] At worst this can promote a tendency known as **groupthink**, which can affect individuals in small, insulated, and cohesive decision-making groups that lack the procedures to guarantee an outside appraisal of their actions. Under such circumstances, decision makers in the group tend to evaluate and rationalize problems collectively, develop illusions of invulnerability and unanimity, view other groups and opponents as less capable, tolerate only self-censorship, and pressure internal dissenters to conform.[13] The group's assumptions and concerns are self-confirmed, and a desire for unanimity and support for the group's leader override the motivation for realistically appraising alternative actions. This dynamic may be exacerbated by presidents who discourage dissent and emphasize loyalty among their staff, as was the case for George W. Bush's decision to attack Iraq due to the conviction among several principal advisers that Saddam Hussein had an active weapons of mass destruction program. Even if the worst aspects of the groupthink dynamic do not appear, if

---

12. Elite theory emphasizes how the values and preferences of governing elites, which differ from those of the public at large, affect **public policy** development. The primary assumption of elite theory is that the values and preferences of the general public are less influential in shaping public policy than those of a smaller, unrepresentative group of people, or elites (Dye 2001; Dye and Zeigler 2012). These policy actors may be economic elites—foundations, wealthy people, corporate executives, oil companies, Wall Street investment bankers, and professionals such as physicians or attorneys. They may be cultural elites, such as celebrated actors, filmmakers, recording artists, or other media stars. Elected officials constitute an elite as well, as do other influential policy actors, such as scientists and policy analysts. Elite theory, then, focuses on the role of leaders and leadership in the development of public policy. See Michael Kraft and Scott Furlong, *Public Policy*, 4th edition (Washington, DC: CQ Press, 2013).

13. Irvin Janis, *Victims of Groupthink* (Boston, MA: Houghton Mifflin, 1972), p. 42.

other policymakers, departments, or agencies feel that this arrangement prevents them from voicing their concerns and having their policy proposal considered by the president, they are likely to become frustrated and attempt to influence the president by other means. In his memoir, former Secretary of Defense Robert Gates complained about micromanagement by the White House staff, arguing that the Obama administration "was by far the most centralized and controlling in national security of any I had seen since Richard Nixon and Henry Kissinger ruled the roost."[14] He and former Defense Secretary Leon Panetta were particularly incensed by attempts by NSC staff to become involved in operational activities by contacting combatant commanders directly.[15] In Gates's words, "The controlling nature of the White House and the NSS took micromanagement and operational meddling to a new level."[16]

This pattern is not unique to the Obama administration. As discussed in Chapter 15, even though public and congressional support for military action in Iraq was high in 1991, President George H. W. Bush's heavy reliance on a very small group of decision makers led a variety of senior officials to try influencing policy by operating outside of existing procedures and processes during Operations Desert Storm and Desert Shield in 1991. Although policymakers without access to the president or chief decision maker are not likely to be able to bring an alternative policy to fruition, they often have the capability to stall or disrupt the policymaking process. This pattern of policymaking played itself out vividly on the issue of health care reform during the first Clinton administration. President Clinton centered control and responsibility over health care reform in the First Lady's office. Doing so alienated a large number of individuals, agencies, and departments in the executive branch. Contrary to some media stories, most of these policymakers argued that they were not alienated because of the policy itself or the intensive involvement of Hillary Clinton. Rather, the process broke down because many policymakers who had a vested concern in health care reform felt that their concerns and policy suggestions were not being voiced or considered by the president.

Finally, centralized hierarchy can become bureaucratic and lead to duplicative efforts in many cases. Because information flows vertically, agencies can often duplicate each other's efforts without any awareness. Or just as problematic,

---

14. Gates, *Duty*, p. 586.

15. Richard Sisk, "Gates and Panetta Blast Obama for Micromanaging Military," *Military.com*, November 17, 2014, http://www.military.com/daily-news/2014/11/17/gates-and-panetta-blast-obama-for-micromanaging-military.html.

16. Gates, *Duty*, p. 587.

agencies can act in counter-purpose to each other unless the White House staff has the resources and time to intervene, which on most issues is not the case.

A system of multiple advocacy is designed specifically to overcome these limitations by exposing the president to stakeholders—individuals, agencies, and departments in the policymaking community with vested interests in the issues at hand that represent different viewpoints and concerns.[17] The president's or principal's role in this system is to be an honest broker and coordinator among departments and agencies that compete to promote their policy proposals. This competition exposes the president to a wide range of ideas. It also promotes quality control by guaranteeing that no single viewpoint dominates the decision-making process. This organizational strategy helps create opportunities for all parties to express their view about a given policy. Participation tends to enhance the perception of legitimacy and helps to bind participants to support a particular outcome. In its ideal form, the final stages of the decision-making process in this system involve a meeting between the president and multiple advisers, during which each is able to present and debate the tradeoffs of a final policy proposal.

The process of welfare reform policy formation during the second half of the Clinton administration represented a combination of centralized management and multiple advocacy (Chapter 12). In contrast to the jointly directed multiple-agency working group set up in 1992, Bruce Reed and the Domestic Policy Council (DPC) were given a mandate and specific responsibility for managing and developing a welfare reform policy beginning in 1994. From that point on, consistent with a centralized management model of organization, the DPC managed the process and acted as a conduit and advocate of presidential initiatives on welfare reform. In addition, however, the president and the DPC made an effort to address the concerns of key policymakers in the Department of Health and Human Services and other agencies and departments. For example, in the spirit of the multiple advocacy model, the final decision to sign the welfare reform legislation in 1996 was made after a meeting between President Clinton and senior advisers exploring some different positions in the welfare reform debate. His advisers disagreed and the president made his decision to sign the legislation after listening to each person in the room express his or her position regarding the proposed welfare reform.

Like the other management models, multiple advocacy has its weaknesses. First, it is not as time efficient for the decision maker as centralized hierarchy.

---

17. Alexander George, "The Case for Multiple Advocacy in Making Foreign Policy," *American Political Science Review* 66 (September 1972), pp. 751–785; and Porter, *Presidential Decision Making*, pp. 243–247.

Second, the roles of honest broker, coordinator, and accountability monitor of multiple stakeholders are difficult. As experienced by National Security Advisor Hadley, getting multiple agencies to evaluate their preferred strategies can require "breaking some china" to "unstick" the system. Third, although multiple advocacy promotes the idea that the consensus choice is the best policy, a consensus may not evolve. Furthermore, the president may decide that the consensus policy is not the best policy option.

POLICY CZARS AND WAR ROOMS

Since the 1980s, we have seen the rise in two trends in policy management: policy czars and war rooms. *Czar* is a term derived from *Caesar* that was first applied in the United States to business executives empowered to direct the industrial effort in the First and later the Second World War. Baseball's first commissioner in 1919 instantly became the baseball czar tasked with cleaning up the sport following the "Black Sox Scandal," and the New York Chamber of Commerce hired a milk czar in 1926 to sort out the city's milk delivery industry.[18]

One of the first "official" policy czars appointed in the early 1980s was the Director of the Office of National Drug Control Policy, more commonly called the "drug czar." Since then, presidents have increasingly utilized czars to give political focus to emergencies or policy issues that cut across agency programs. Unfortunately, these czars typically lack "line authority" or control over budget and spending allocations to actually impact policy or improve coordination on major issues. Furthermore, their growing use has raised issues of accountability, as most czars are not subject to Senate confirmation and are protected by executive privilege.

The concept of war rooms has also been around for a long time, but the term only became prevalent in the 1990s after President Clinton's campaign war room became famous during the 1992 election. The Clinton administration then tried to utilize the war room model on several policy campaigns, including the passage of the North American Free Trade Agreement (NAFTA) and health care reform. Experience has shown that as a policy management tool, war rooms are not effective if used over the long term, but as part of a policy campaign, they can be useful if the campaign has a clear goal and time limit.

CONCLUSION

As the centralized management model of policy management suggests, the Executive Office of the President (EOP) played a central role (at some point) in the Clinton, George W. Bush, and Obama administrations. Despite public

---

18. "Policy Tsars—Do They Ever Work?" *The Guardian,* June 5, 2013.

comments that they would decentralize the role of the White House and raise the profile of the cabinet, each of these presidents strengthened the role of the EOP in coordinating and leading the policy process. Each of these administrations also occasionally fell prey to some of the pitfalls of the centralized style of policy management. At the same time, consistent with the multiple advocacy approach, the EOP often gave President Clinton systematic exposure to and played the role of honest broker among policymakers with competing arguments and viewpoints. During the last year of the George W. Bush administration, the NSC dramatically expanded the scope and depth of the interagency process to encourage a reevaluation of U.S. strategy in Iraq. The Obama administration, similarly, used an extensive interagency process to develop the Trans Pacific Partnership and other trade deals.

Lessons from the successes and failures of policymaking during recent administrations that are explored in subsequent chapters suggest that although centralized management and the clear designation of authority and accountability can promote policy development and implementation, effective policymaking is contingent upon the decision-making unit's ability to also act as an honest broker and create a process that enables all stakeholders to express their voices in the policymaking process.

Key Terms

Adhocracy model

Centralized management model

Groupthink

Multiple advocacy model

Public policy

Review Questions

1. What presidential management styles are most likely to enhance procedural legitimacy? Why?
2. What is the difference between substantive and procedural legitimacy?
3. Why have policy czars become popular and what are the weaknesses commonly associated with this approach to policy management?

POLICYMAKING MEMORANDA

TOOLS OF THE TRADE

The unique constraints associated with policymaking in the executive branch make the decision-making process itself a critical component of all executive decisions. Following standard decision-making procedures and using the appropriate tools to initiate, analyze, and implement policy is critical because it provides continuity and structure that would otherwise be absent in a world that is often characterized by crisis management. Memoranda are key cogs in this system. Although the principals in the executive branch often develop informal means of communication, written memoranda are critical means of communicating and sharing ideas with others. They provide an essential means of framing action-forcing events, explaining the context in which the events are situated, and identifying salient facts the president or other decision makers need to know before making a policy decision, evaluating competing policy recommendations, and proposing how a chosen policy might be implemented. Adherence to the established format for writing memoranda is extremely important.[1] It enables all policymakers to use the tools of the policymaking process to voice their concerns and present their proposals in a coherent and systematic fashion. This is vital because a single memorandum on an important issue will likely be read by many. This increases the efficiency of the process and provides a sense of legitimacy

---

1. The Plain Writing Act of 2010 requires federal agencies to write "clear Government communication that the public can understand and use." Implementation of this Act is specified in Office of Management and Budget Memorandum M_11–15, "Final Guidance on Implementing the Plain Writing Act of 2010." For federal writing guidelines and other supporting materials, see http://www.dtic.mil/whs/directives/plainlanguage.html.

that enhances the commitment of all players to the policy outcome. Facilitating the input and exchange of ideas among multiple stakeholders also increases the likelihood that the president and his principals will be exposed to a broader range of opinions and information than would otherwise be the case.

The National Security Advisor may ask his deputies to write a memorandum that evaluates the effectiveness of current U.S. policy in Iraq. If they conclude that the answer is "not effective," then this will probably turn into a major political issue.[2] At that point, some parts of their memo(s) may be distributed to other stakeholders or incorporated into broader policy documents. The memo(s) might be consulted a third time when the special assistant responds to a criticism from the other stakeholders—in this case, the military leaders; a fourth time while drafting a rebuttal to the Department of State and Department of Defense; a fifth time when the *Washington Post* reports on disagreements among policymakers in the administration; and so on. This is what happened when National Security Advisor Hadley asked Meghan O'Sullivan and William Lutie to assess the situation in Iraq in 2006. As discussed in Chapter 16, their memos played critical roles in altering U.S. strategy. Their memoranda were effective, in part, because they were written in a systemic and persuasive manner that could be understood and utilized by a wide range of individuals throughout the policymaking process. Writing effective memoranda is, thus, a critical component of an effective policymaking process.

THE ROLE OF THE MEMORANDUM

In early 1993, a large number of presidential advisers sat in the Roosevelt Room in the heart of the West Wing of the White House. The purpose of the meeting was to discuss a decision memorandum to the president on whether to submit legislation to Congress that would create so-called Empowerment Zones— geographic zones in distressed areas that would receive special tax incentives and federal aid. The meeting with the president was tense because no consensus had been reached beforehand on whether to send Congress the Empowerment Zone legislation in its current form, and a decision memo had been drafted for the president with several options but no consensual recommendation.

---

2. The guidelines for writing a memorandum can be generalized outside of the executive branch. The examples of multiple stakeholders in the executive branch who may review memos regarding Iraq policy parallel those that are likely to appear in the legal and business arenas. See "Writing an Office Memorandum," http://faculty.law.lsu.edu/toddbruno/writing%20the%20memo.doc.

The meeting was an early test of the new decision-making system put into place by the Clinton White House in which unresolved policy issues of presidential importance would be submitted in a memo to the president containing all the options and views of the interested agencies.

Decision memoranda—specifically the decision-making memorandum, the **information memorandum**, and the **weekly report**—are among the most important tools in the policymaking process. The decision memoranda are the mechanisms by which ideas are presented, options are discussed, and resolutions on policy matters are reached. Without the ability to convey ideas concisely and clearly, a policymaker is effectively marginalized. This is bad for the individual policymaker and often has negative repercussions for the policymaking process. Following a consistent format for each type of memorandum standardizes the policymaking process and maximizes its effectiveness.

The required format for decision-making memoranda for the president of the United States as specified by the White House Staff Secretary's office is presented in Box 6-1. Despite its apparent simplicity, many people have difficulty writing effective memoranda. The most common error made by policymakers when writing decision memoranda is the tendency to alter the format of the memorandum to provide additional information. This problem is consistent across administrations. Although the reading tastes of different presidents or heads of agencies differ and they may prefer a slightly different format or set of procedures than those described in this chapter, the basic structure and purpose of the memoranda remain constant, as do the most common mistakes made by inexperienced staffers. As a basic rule, for example, no memorandum should be longer than five pages. There is often a desire on the part of staff to provide more information by attaching addenda to a memorandum. Memorandum writers often argue that an addendum is necessary because the additional information it contains must be made available to the president or agency head before they make their decision. Such an exercise is futile. Decision makers face severe time and informational constraints. Indeed, one of the most important roles of the memorandum is to compensate for those constraints by presenting only critically important information and doing so in a way that evaluates and suggests certain justifiable and coherent courses of action. If you know that your chief executive does not have time to read more than five pages of information, then why provide him or her with ten pages of addenda? It is a disservice to him or her and to the issue discussed in the memorandum.

The purpose of the memorandum is to enable the president to make a good decision under extreme information and time constraints. The memorandum must succinctly filter through the mass of data about a particular event, identify information that is critical for the decision maker to know, and make a series of recommendations about appropriate courses of action. Good memorandum writers must exhibit clear thinking based on a solid understanding of how the event in question evolved and how it is related to other ongoing domestic and international phenomena of importance to the executive. Long memoranda tend to indicate a lack of clear thinking, while concise memos are much more effective in conveying ideas and proposals. If the president or his senior advisers desire more information, they will mark "Discuss Further" on the memorandum and ask the relevant agencies or departments to provide it.

BOX 6-1   **Format for a Decision-Making Memorandum**

MEMORANDUM FOR THE PRESIDENT

DATE:

FROM:

SUBJECT:

I. Action-Forcing Event

Specify the nature of the event or question that merits a policy response, why the event or question matters to the president or to the United States, and why and when a response is needed.

II. Background

Provide a succinct assessment of material facts about the key issues, principal actors, and primary constituents affected by the action-forcing event so that the reader can make an informed, well-justified, and persuasive decision. Substantive and procedural information (about who, what, where, and when) may be relevant, but any information that will not affect the outcome is extraneous and should be excluded. All facts should be presented in an objective manner.

IV. Discussion/Analysis

Provide an analysis of potential responses to the action-forcing event based on an analysis of the material facts presented in the background section. The pros and

(Continued)

(Continued)

cons of potential policy options should be analyzed. A discussion of authorization and implementation options may also be presented.

III. Recommendation

Indicate single recommendation or list options. Identify and provide responses to the most important benefits and criticisms of the chosen option.

IV. Decision

❏ Approve   ❏ Approve as Amended   ❏ Reject   ❏ Discuss Further

---

Note: Legal and business memos use a similar structure. See "Writing an Office Memorandum," http://faculty.law.lsu.edu/toddbruno/writing%20the%20memo.doc. The Department of Defense provides an excellent guide for writing policy briefs. See Department of Defense, "Writing Style Guide and Preferred Usage for DoD Issuances," http://www.dtic.mil/whs/directives/corres/writing/Writing_Style_Guide.pdf. The guidelines for writing newspaper editorials and op-eds are also applicable. See http://www.cthealthpolicy.org/toolbox/opinion/op_eds_letters.htm.

This chapter will describe how to write decision and other types of memoranda for senior government officials. Using the formats developed by the Office of the White House Staff Secretary, readers will be guided through the memo-writing process and will learn to distinguish the form and purpose of decision memoranda, briefing memoranda, and information memoranda.

THE DECISION-MAKING MEMORANDUM

The decision-making memorandum plays a critical role in each of the three primary phases of the policymaking process: agenda setting, policy formation, and policy implementation. Of these three, the most important role of the decision-making memorandum is to set the agenda by identifying which events have sufficient importance to the Executive and to the United States of America to necessitate the policymaker's attention and bring that **action-forcing event** to his or her attention. The driving force behind a decision memorandum is, thus, the action-forcing event.

The Action-Forcing Event

An action-forcing event is a potential or existing situation that necessitates the need for presidential action and/or review. Examples of action-forcing events include military conflict, an upcoming vote on important legislation, or the issuing of an executive order by the president. The action-forcing event is the "hook." It explains to the decision maker why an issue matters and is worthy of a policy response. A well-written action-forcing event gives the decision maker a sense of the salience and urgency of the issue at hand.

The following is an action-forcing event:

> *In the past week the Justice Department released data showing that homicides in states with high unemployment rates have risen since the financial crisis. The Department's study indicates there is a strong correlation between these two factors.*

The following is not an action-forcing event:

> *Homicide rates have been rising all across America since the onset of the Great Recession. This growing problem is particularly trouble-some in states with very high unemployment rates and low economic activity. It is vital that you act to reverse this dangerous threat to the safety of the American people. After all, the security of its citizens must be the number one priority for its government.*

The difference between these two samples may seem subtle but are quite significant. The first pivots off a recent development. It is factual and it carries a sense of urgency. The second example does not cite a recent event. It describes a general trend, expresses an opinion, and then exhorts the decision maker to act.

If the memorandum is going to the president, the action-forcing event must be significant enough that senior advisers do not believe that they should respond without the president's specific consent. Of course, the threshold for taking action without specific presidential consent changes from administra-tion to administration. In some White Houses, presidents have relied heavily on the "cabinet government"—including cabinet secretaries and appointees such as the Chief of Staff, National Security Advisor, or other senior advisers—for advice and information. In administrations with this somewhat decentralized policymaking style, a lead adviser or agency is often empowered to make major decisions without specific consent on every situation and takes the lead role in promoting or implementing policy. The combination of the authority vested in their position as a commissioned officer to the president plus their relationship to the chief executive gives them considerable latitude to act on their own. In such instances, the principal of a policy council or agency may request a decision memorandum. The resulting memorandum may eventually go to the president, but it may also not go beyond the principal who requested it.

Decision-making memoranda must identify the salience of the action-forcing event for major stakeholders who are affected by it or will be affected by a proposed policy response. If the input of relevant agencies is not anticipated and considered, the neglected agencies will find alternative ways in which to move their views forward, such as circumventing the traditional policymaking apparatus. These could include direct contact with the president or other senior officers in the White House, such as the vice president, first lady, or chief of staff; communication with members of Congress; or the disclosure of information to the press. The potential for policy leakage in such cases is considerable. Indeed, approved **leaks** (information that is intentionally provided to the media in an informal manner in order to mobilize public support) and unapproved leaks (information that is provided to people outside of the formal decision-making apparatus without the knowledge or consent of the executive) take place on virtually every important issue. The authority of a presidency can be greatly damaged by the release of unapproved leaks (as opposed to strategic leaks designed to promote the president's agenda). Uncontrolled leaks weaken a presidency by making the internal control mechanisms seem irrelevant, thus promoting chaos within an administration. In addition, policy ideas that are delivered directly to the president from an agency head or outside source are not filtered by the established policy process and are, consequently, not likely to include other options or dissenting views, which can provide the president with more perspective before he makes his decision.

Because members of the policymaking community are most likely to go outside of the standard policymaking process when they feel that their view or concerns are not being presented to the president, one way that the White House staff can minimize leaks and other nonstandard practices is to make sure that the information and memoranda presented to the president are consensus documents. This does not mean that everyone in the policymaking process must agree that the action-forcing events are salient or that a particular set of policies are the most appropriate responses to those events, but there must be a consensus that the information presented to the president conveys the opposing views of all of the primary parties in the policymaking process.

Background

The background section provides a succinct assessment of material facts about the key issues and principal actors affected by the action-forcing event so that the reader has a sufficient command of the context to make an informed and well-justified decision. Although the action-forcing event section should be no more than a few sentences long, the background section can be anywhere from a couple of paragraphs to a page. This section must (1) provide a quick overview of the issue, including any specific, recent events that create the need for presidential action; (2) give the relevant historical or contextual background; and (3) provide essential information about the key issues, principal players, and the primary constituents affected by the crisis and by the various policy options so that an informed, well-justified, and persuasive decision can be made.

Although the amount of detail included in this section can be modified based on the familiarity of the president or agency head with the issue at hand, it is essential that this section meets two primary objectives. First, it must provide all material facts that affect the decision. This includes substantive and procedural information pertaining to the actors, events, and consequences of policy choices.[3] Second, it must not include any information that does not have a direct bearing on the decision at hand. All such information is a distraction and should be excluded.

Some memo writers divide the background section into two parts. The first part may be focused on the following issues:

- Review Current Policy: What are we (the nation, state, city, etc.) currently doing, why are we doing it this way, and what is the public's perception of the policy? The key is to assess how well the current policy is or is not working.
- Data Supporting the Necessity for Change: Identify the problem and the data that support its existence.
- History: Specify the relevant history surrounding the issue, including major historical policy successes or failures.

The second part may provide essential information about the actors affected by the current situation and those potentially impacted by the policy

---

3. See: "Writing an Office Memorandum," http://faculty.law.lsu.edu/toddbruno/writing%20the%20memo.doc.

response so that an informed, well-justified, and persuasive decision can be made. These may include the following:

- Elected officials in position of influence over the issue
- Interest groups
- Leading think tanks/academics
- Relevant administration officials
- International leaders
- Elites

Discussion/Analysis

This is the core of the memorandum. It should provide an analysis of potential responses to the action-forcing event based on an analysis of the material facts presented in the background section. If multiple options are presented, it is important that the author presents the proposals in this section as an honest broker and reserves his or her views until the recommendation section. To bias the analysis in favor of a particular outcome before competing views are presented would prejudice the decision maker. Presenting options as an honest broker helps to ensure that the decision memorandum serves as the sole deliverer of information on a given issue and that the participants in the decision process will not feel the need to undermine the resolution mechanism. Pros and cons related to both policy and political concerns need to be included.

The need to be fair and open to all options must also be weighed against the desire to provide the decision maker with concise, clear, relevant, and good choices. It is important that the decision memorandum not become a free-for-all forum for ideas that will confuse the decision maker and cloud the issues surrounding the action-forcing event. Therefore, it is vital that the author(s) of the memo work to build a consensus around those options that are consistent with the goals that the president and the executive branch feel are of vital interest to the United States. One way to limit the number of options while ensuring open discussion is for the author(s) to encourage agencies that disagree with the majority to unify behind one alternative option that would include some, but not necessarily all, of their views. Agencies that recognize the power of numbers will cooperate as long as they feel they will get something out of the process. However, there are simply instances where the participants in the decision process will feel—for ideological or political reasons—that they want to submit their own option to the decision maker. In these cases, the author(s) of the memo, after having exhausted all attempts at building a consensus, must include that option or face the reality that the process will be seen as illegitimate and may breakdown.

Recommendation

This is where the authors can stake out a policy position. If the author(s) of the decision memorandum make a policy recommendation that is not favored by a majority of stakeholders, they should not lead with it. Instead, the majority option should be given first billing. In addition, the authors need to be clear as to who supports and who challenges each option.

In considering what option to recommend, it is useful to do a reality check and think about the following:

- Does the recommendation resolve the problem raised by the action-forcing event?
- Is it actionable? Your recommendation should ideally be a stand-alone and not require another iteration of the process to figure out how to implement it.
- Is it politically sustainable? A policy that cannot be implemented or is not sustainable politically should not be recommended.

A sample decision-making memorandum is shown in Box 6-2.

BOX 6-2 Sample Decision-Making Memorandum to the President[4]

MEMORANDUM FOR THE PRESIDENT

FROM: Domestic Policy Council

SUBJECT: Executive order reducing the federal bureaucracy by at least 100,000 positions

I. Action-Forcing Event

You are tentatively scheduled to announce reductions in the federal bureaucracy on Wednesday, February 10, 1993.

(Continued)

---

4. Note that this is not a "perfect" example of a decision memo. It lacks a policy option section and mixes the policy analysis and background sections together. Nevertheless, it reflects the general style of writing typical of decision-making memoranda.

(Continued)

II. Background/Analysis

This executive order seeks to satisfy your campaign pledge to cut the federal bureaucracy by at least 100,000 positions through attrition, as a way to eliminate unnecessary layers of management and improve productivity.

One of every six dollars we spend on domestic programs goes to wages and benefits for federal workers—not counting administrative costs. Eliminating 100,000 positions in the bureaucracy would save $3 to $4 billion a year by FY1996.

This measure will reduce the government's civilian workforce of 2.2 million people by 4 percent over the next three years. It orders the Office of Management and Budget to issue detailed instructions directing the executive departments and agencies with more than 100 employees to achieve 25 percent of the cuts in FY 1993, 62.5 percent by the end of FY1994, and 100 percent by the end of FY1995. At least 10 percent of the reductions would come from management (Senior Executive Service, GS-14, and GS-15). Independent agencies are requested to make similar reductions voluntarily.

III. Recommendation

This action will help fulfill one of your most visible campaign promises. I recommend that you approve the proposed executive order.

IV. Decision

❐ Approve   ❐ Discuss Further   ❐ Reject

THE INFORMATION MEMORANDUM

The information memorandum is another important tool for policymakers. The key difference between the information memorandum and the decision-making memorandum is that the information memorandum should not raise issues for decision. The information memorandum serves two primary functions:

- It provides information that will be helpful on an issue/potential action item that will require a decision at a later date. For example, information memoranda of two to three pages can update the Executive on Commissions that are reviewing issues of large scope, such as Social Security reform, and strengthen his or her knowledge base prior to the delivery of a set of recommendations at the end of the Commission's study.

- It keeps the Executive informed of the progress or regression of an issue on which he or she has already made a decision. For example, Box 6-2 describes an executive order on reducing the size of government by a specific number, such as was issued by President Clinton in 1993. The White House staff would send an information memorandum to the president when certain benchmarks were reached, including the final target number.

The format of the information memorandum is shown in Box 6-3.

BOX 6-3	Format for an Information Memorandum

INFORMATION

MEMORANDUM FOR THE PRESIDENT

FROM:

SUBJECT:

I. Summary

Three sentences or less that state the subject and summarize the changes or provide an update on relevant information related to it.

II. Discussion

Highlight any problems or unresolved issues regarding the subject.

Summary Section

The summary section should quickly state the change or update in information. Using the executive order to reduce the size of government as an example, the summary would read as follows:

On June 17th, the Office of Personnel Management is prepared to report that we have met the goal stated in Executive Order (#) to reduce the size of the federal government through attrition by 100,000.

Discussion Section

The discussion section should highlight any problems or unresolved issues. Using the above reduction of the federal workforce as an example, the president's advisers may use the discussion section to underscore the fact that 60 percent of the reduction came from the Department of Defense and that this might open the administration up to criticism. However, not all discussion issues are by nature negative. The White House staff may, for example, also use the discussion section to report that the reductions in personnel will save more budget funds than previously estimated in the following years.

THE WEEKLY REPORT

An additional mechanism to provide the decision maker with timely information is the weekly report. The staff of each cabinet-level agency and White House office submits weekly reports to the president, vice president, White House Chief of Staff, and agency heads. The style of these reports depends, in part, on the objective of the writer.

Some agencies use weekly reports as a way to summarize the events of the prior week. For example, the report may be broken down into several sections. One section might describe speech and meeting activities with outside groups, such as interest groups, lobbyists, and elected officials. This section could also include important legislative activity. Another section of the report will focus on press activity. A fourth section describes the future schedule of important individuals in the administration or agency. Below in Box 6-4 is an example of what might be included in a typical weekly report from the EPA to the vice president:

BOX 6-4   **Potential Issues Raised in a Weekly Report**

WEEKLY REPORT

MEMORANDUM FOR VICE PRESIDENT GORE

FROM: Carol Browner, Environmental Protection Agency

SUBJECT: Weekly Report

I. Key Agency News

On 4/13 and 4/14 the administrator of the Environmental Protection Agency testified before the House Appropriations Subcommittee on the Veterans, HUD, and Independent Agencies on the administration's environmental budget.

II. Press Releases

On 12/3, the secretary will announce the Electricity Restructuring Bill, a new energy plan that uses resources more efficiently, cuts electric bills for consumers and businesses, and protects public health and the environment. The event will be open to press and questions will be taken at the end of the announcement.

III. Weekly Schedule

A list of the key event for each day of the coming week is attached.

Others may utilize the weekly report to pursue an ongoing dialogue with the decision maker on issues that are high on the decision maker's agenda. For example, the report can be used to respond to questions from the decision maker, provide timely information on an issue of importance, or seek guidance on an issue. Agencies may also use the weekly report as a way to subliminally suggest issues that they believe the decision maker should engage in. Below are two real examples from the weekly reports of the White House Domestic Policy Council:

> Health Care—Medicare Annual Cap on Rehabilitative Services: You recently asked about the $1500 annual cap on Medicare payments for outpatient physical therapy and other rehabilitative services. This cap was included in the Balanced Budget Act at Congressman Thomas' insistence; we had opposed it for fear that it would have had an adverse impact on chronically ill beneficiaries. Providers and advocates are now arguing that the cap has had just such an impact, pointing to a recent study showing that almost 13 percent of Medicare beneficiaries incur significant out-of-pocket expenditures as a result of the cap. Senator Grassley has proposed legislation that would allow Medicare beneficiaries to exceed the cap if they have an illness that clearly requires additional services. This proposal, however, may prove very costly; we are scoring it now as well as reviewing alternatives.

This paragraph underscores the weekly report's use as a way to respond to a question from the decision maker directly and a way to seek guidance indirectly. The last sentence is intentionally leading. It suggests that there may be some alternatives and subtly asks whether the decision maker wants to pursue them. And, in fact, President Clinton's written response was to encourage the development of alternatives.

> Tobacco—Oregon Verdict: A jury in Oregon last week ordered Philip Morris to pay $81 million in damages (including $79.5 million in punitives) to the family of a man who died of lung cancer after smoking for 40 years. The verdict was the largest ever against a tobacco company, exceeding the $51.5 million verdict awarded by a California jury against Philip Morris earlier this year. Shares of tobacco companies fell sharply this week as a result of the verdict.

This paragraph provides a classic example of the information power of the weekly report. It is simply a factual description of an important event from the week on a high-profile issue, yet because the information is timely and noted to be important, it raises the salience of the tobacco issue sufficiently to place it on the president's agenda.

CONCLUSION

The memorandum is one of the most important and influential tools in the decision-making process. It initiates the decision-making process by identifying an action-forcing event and bringing that event to the relevant decision maker's attention; it compensates for severe information and time constraints in the decision-making process by identifying the specific background information and analysis needed to make a decision; and it suggests an informed, balanced, well-justified, and strongly supported policy option. It is also one of the primary modes of communication among various stakeholders throughout the policymaking process.

To be effective, the memorandum must be well written. At the same time, it is important to remember that all decision memoranda, information memoranda, and weekly reports will be judged by the results they produce. What happens after a memorandum is written is even more important than the writing of the document itself. In particular, it is the action that a decision maker takes once he or she has read the memorandum that completes the decision-making process.

There are three actions that a decision maker can take in response to a memorandum. First, the decision maker can agree to a unanimous, consensus, or minority recommendation. This can set in motion several actions. If the memorandum calls for an executive action (which can include, e.g., the issuing of an executive order or a phone call to a head of state) or for new legislation (which requires congressional approval), the executive branch policy councils will direct the appropriate federal agency to begin drafting the recommended policy. These drafts will be developed jointly by the agency policy and legal counsel offices. Once completed, the legislation or executive order is submitted by the policy councils who, in coordination with the Office of Management and Budget, submit them for comment to other relevant agencies. The executive branch policy councils then are responsible for ensuring the action is completed, as are the relevant policy offices in each agency.

Second, the decision maker may want additional information, indicate some dislike for all the options presented, ask for input from other stakeholders, or feel an issue is not timely and decide to delay action on the matter. In these cases, the decision maker will check the "Discuss Further" option. If more information is required, the policy councils or the relevant offices in agencies will prepare additional materials, in coordination with the relevant agencies or any other persons from inside or outside of the executive branch that the decision maker requests information from, and resubmit a new memorandum. If the executive chooses to delay a decision, those same offices are responsible for raising the issue at a subsequent and more appropriate time.

Third, the decision maker may decide to reject the recommendations because the action-forcing event did not rise or no longer rises to a level at which he or she believes a decision must be made. This option is rarely exercised because although events may overtake the issues raised in the action-forcing event, a good policymaker should never submit a memo in which the action-forcing event is not action forcing.

Key Terms

Action-forcing event

Information memorandum

Leaks

Weekly report

Review Questions

1. What is the primary purpose of a decision-making memorandum? What role do decision memos play in the policymaking process?
2. What is the difference between a decision-making memorandum and an information memorandum?
3. What is the most common error made by policymakers when writing a decision memorandum?
4. What are the four actions the decision maker can take in response to a decision memorandum?
5. What constitutes an action-forcing event?
6. How do federal agencies utilize weekly reports?

THE STATE OF THE UNION AND THE BUDGET PROCESS

TIMING YOUR SWING: UNDERSTANDING INTERNAL WORKFLOWS IN THE EXECUTIVE BRANCH

Imagine you are a major league baseball player who has just struck out to lose the World Series. As you are walking back to the dugout, a teammate who had been watching the game from the bullpen informs you that he has figured out that the opposing team's pitcher telegraphs his pitches. You look at your teammate in disbelief and finally mutter the words, "Wish you had said something sooner."

As the scenario above underscores, information and ideas are only useful if shared at the appropriate juncture. The axiom "timing is everything" applies to policymakers and baseball players alike.

One of the biggest barriers to achieving policy success is timing. White House, EOP, and agency staff are under enormous time constraints. Most days their attention is reserved for the day-to-day responsibilities of governing, such as implementing existing laws and programs, negotiating with other agencies and offices, working with congressional staff or members of Congress, reviewing testimony and public statements on important issues, or arbitrating disputes among different offices and/or departments.

Those periods when policy staffs in the executive branch do focus on idea development are centered on a few key processes, the timing of which differs depending on whether the entity is in the EOP or a cabinet agency. Understanding when these periods occur is vital for policymakers.

STATE OF THE UNION

Two of these processes are annual occurrences. The first is the president's **State of the Union (SOTU)** address. The SOTU is an annual address presented by the president of the United States to the United States Congress. It reports on the condition of the nation and also allows the president to outline his legislative agenda and national priorities to Congress.[1] The SOTU is typically given before a joint session of the United States Congress and is held in the House of Representatives chamber at the United States Capitol.

From Jefferson to Taft, the SOTU was delivered in writing and was a report on the general condition of government and the nation at large. During the modern era, the SOTU transformed into a policy agenda for the president. It contains a list of recommendations that the chief executive requests Congress to act upon.

Work on the SOTU begins in earnest in mid to late summer, six months prior to the address, which usually occurs in late January. Typically, the EOP staff begins the process by organizing interagency working groups to develop recommendations for ideas to be included in the SOTU. Any ideas that are included are considered part of the president's agenda and are given priority by the White House for enactment, funding, and implementation.

The process of developing ideas for the SOTU lasts through the fall, in some cases into December. Initially a list of ideas from the agencies and EOP offices is compiled by the White House and analyzed and debated throughout the summer and early fall. If a consensus is not achieved, options are laid out in a decision memorandum at a principals' meeting of top White House and cabinet heads. Their recommendations (and any disagreements) are then sent to the president for his decision. Once a policy agenda is complete, the ideas are included in a document accompanying the SOTU that is sent to Congress, the press corps, and published for the public at large. The president's top priorities are referenced in the SOTU itself.

For a policy idea to become an administration priority, it must be inserted into the SOTU process at the beginning, around July or August. It is at this point that policy staff in government will be most receptive to ideas. Why? Because it is during this time that EOP staff have been directed to cast a wide net for new ideas, and they know that any idea will have adequate time to be vetted. Many of those inside and outside government mistakenly assume that they can submit ideas for the SOTU a month or two before the speech. In reality, that is much too late, particularly for ideas that have a budgetary impact. Policy ideas must go

---

1. "Ben's Guide to the U.S. Government," Government Printing Office, http://www.gpoac cess.gov/sou/index.html.

through many stages before they get to the president. This includes budget estimates, legal reviews, economic and policy impact assessments, political/legislative analysis, and sign-off from the appropriate agencies and EOP offices.

THE BUDGET

Like the SOTU, the Budget of the United States (colloquially referred to as "the president's budget") is also used as a tool by the administration to outline its policy and legislative agenda for the upcoming year. It is important to note that the president's budget is not a law, but rather a recommendation to the Congress required by law. In 1921, the Congress passed the Budget and Accounting Act of 1921. This law required the president to submit to Congress an annual budget for the entire federal government. The Act also created the Bureau of the Budget, now called the Office of Management and Budget (OMB), to review funding requests from government departments and assist the president in formulating the budget.[2] OMB plays a coordinating role in this process and provides policy guidelines through circulars, bulletins, and other detailed communications. OMB Circular No. A-11, available on OMB's web site, contains detailed instructions and schedules for submission of agency budget requests and other material to ensure that budget requests adhere to standardized conventions and formats.

OMB's budget process is based on policy and program goals within the broader framework of fiscal policy. The budget and policy questions OMB typically addresses with regard to policies and programs in its preparation of the budget include the following:

- Is it in line with the president's policy priorities?
- Is it well managed?
- Does it have definable goals, or is there evidence its goals are being met?
- Is it redundant?
- How do the costs measure up against the benefits?
- What is the impact of increasing or decreasing funding?
- Is it technically and administratively feasible?

Current law requires the president to submit a budget no earlier than the first Monday in January and no later than the first Monday in February.[3] Typically, presidents submit budgets on the first Monday in February, although a number of presidents have missed this deadline.

---

2. Daniel C. Desimone, "The Making of the Federal Budget," *Government Finance Review*, June 2002.

3. 31 U.S.C. 1105(a).

The president's budget request constitutes an extensive proposal of the administration's intended spending and revenue plans for the following fiscal year. The budget proposal includes volumes of supporting information intended to persuade Congress of the necessity and value of the budget provisions. In addition, each federal executive department and independent agency provides additional detail and supporting documentation to Congress on its own funding requests.

Initially envisioned as a way to help reign in deficits and improve the coordination of budget policymaking, the president's budget has become a tool of policymaking as well. As such, along with the SOTU, it is the primary annual process by which new ideas are submitted for consideration by the executive branch. However, unlike the SOTU, the budget process (see Box 7-1 below) is done on a much larger scale, and the opportunities for agencies to submit policy ideas (whether budget related or not for consideration) are greater than in the SOTU process.[4]

The budget process cycle can take almost two years. Roughly one year before publishing the president's budget, OMB issues its spring planning guidance to all executive branch agencies for the upcoming budget. This is the first window in the budget process for sharing new ideas, reforms, and so on. Often during this period, agencies will put together a memo on budget priorities that they will submit to OMB. Ideas included in this memo are a starting point in a larger discussion within the administration on which priorities will be funded and which will not. In tight budget environments, it is very important for new ideas to be included on priority lists as early as possible. Submitting ideas to agency program offices, budget offices, and to OMB divisions during this window is optimal.

In the summer, the second window for new ideas opens. This period coincides with the early stages of development of the president's SOTU policy agenda. During this time, agencies and OMB discuss budget options and issues, and OMB works closely with agencies in setting up their proposals for the director's review in the fall. During this period, White House and EOP offices often look for ideas to include in the budget that will later become part of the president's SOTU policy agenda. Often these ideas are in policy areas that the EOP feels have not been adequately addressed in the agency budgets.

Following this period, ideas are generally winnowed down. Policy proposals are often cast aside or cut back in order to meet budget targets, and any ideas that do not have a relevant sponsor (an agency, the White House staff, OMB)

---

4. Paul Weinstein, Jr., *Expanding Opportunities for Informed Participation in Public Policy* (Washington, DC: Science and Technology Institute, 2010).

BOX 7-1	**Major Steps in the Development of the President's Budget Within the Executive Branch**

Steps	Timeline
1. OMB issues spring planning guidance to executive branch agencies for the upcoming budget. The OMB director issues a letter to the head of each agency, providing policy guidance for the agency's unique budget request (absent more specific guidance, the out year estimates included in the previous budget serve as a starting point for the next budget).	Spring
2. OMB and the relevant executive branch agencies discuss budget issues and options. OMB works with the agencies to (1) identify major issues for the upcoming budget; (2) develop and analyze options for the upcoming Fall review; and (3) plan for the analysis of issues that will need decisions in the future.	Spring/Summer
3. OMB issues Circular A-11 to all federal agencies with official detailed instructions for submitting budget data and materials.	July
4. Executive branch agencies (except those that are exempt) make budget submissions to OMB.	September
5. Fiscal year begins.	October 1
6. OMB conducts its director reviews. During this process, OMB staff meet with senior agency representatives and analyze their proposals in light of presidential priorities, program performance, and budget constraints, often with input from White House and EOP offices and policy councils. During this process, issues and options are presented to the OMB director and other senior OMB officials for decision.	October/ November
7. OMB briefs the president and EOP advisors on proposed budget policies. The OMB director recommends a complete set of budget proposals to the president after OMB has reviewed all agency requests and considered overall budget policies.	Late November
8. **Passback** occurs. OMB usually informs all executive branch agencies at the same time about decisions on their budget requests.	Late November
9. Agencies may appeal to OMB and the president. An agency head may ask OMB to reverse or modify certain decisions. In most cases, OMB and the agency head resolve such issues, and, if not, they work together (and with White House staff) to present them to the president for a decision.	December
10. Agencies prepare and OMB reviews congressional budget justification materials. Agencies prepare these materials to explain their budget requests to the relevant congressional committees.	January
11. Transmission of the president's budget to the Congress.	First Monday in February

will not survive the budget knife. Finally, at the end of the process, OMB and the EOP offices often need to cut from elsewhere in the budget in order to finance the president's agenda. All these pressures mean government officials will be less inclined to consider new spending or tax ideas after the end of July.

CONCLUSION

The SOTU and the president's budget are the major vehicles by which new ideas are formulated, analyzed, debated, and put forward by the executive branch. As such, understanding the process for both is essential for policymakers. In addition to annual events like the SOTU and the president's budget, there are also unscheduled windows for putting forward new policy ideas, like emergencies (such as military conflicts or natural disasters) or unexpected events (like a dramatic decline in the stock market or a major spike in the crime rate). These periods are unpredictable and sometimes force policymakers to reevaluate existing policy. These periods can be challenging, but they also create great opportunities for policymakers who can develop well-thought-out ideas and know how to use the policymaking system to bring them to fruition.

Key Terms

Budget and Accounting Act of 1921

Budget of the United States

Passback

State of the Union (SOTU)

Review Questions

1. What roles do the State of the Union address and the president's budget submission play in the policymaking process?
2. Why are national emergencies such as natural disasters or military conflicts policy opportunities for the executive branch?
3. Describe the steps taken by OMB and the agencies in developing the president's budget submission.

POLICY IMPLEMENTATION TOOLS

IMPLEMENTATION TOOLS

Experts and stakeholders who are unfamiliar with the policymaking process often are disappointed when they provide groundbreaking insights, information, or data to the government but decision makers choose not to act upon it. Usually they blame politics, ideological differences, or bureaucratic inertia for the indifference. Certainly, each of these problems can and do occur. In some cases, however, the lack of progress is the result of something else: the failure of policymakers to turn their insights into real, usable policy. If experts and stakeholders want to maximize the likelihood that their ideas will be acted upon by government, they need to make sure they are not only talking to the right people at the right time, but also presenting their ideas in a format that can readily be understood and implemented by government. That requires understanding the policy process and the implementation tools available. To avoid unnecessary frustration, it is also important to understand what the government can and cannot do. This is a function of the policy tools that shape the scope and domain of government authority and its capacity to act.

AUTHORIZATION TOOLS

Policy authorization and policy implementation involve a variety of tools, including legislation, executive orders/authority, treaties, and legal precedents. Each of these tools has unique strengths and weaknesses. The nature of each legal process may dramatically change the nature and impact of the tool envisioned.

Policy authorization is needed to provide a legal basis for government action, but it is not sufficient and should not be confused with the **policy implementation tools** it authorizes. Although each may involve legislation, executive orders/executive authority, treaties, or legal precedents, the particular tool used may be different. For example, the creation of a new tax on gasoline will probably require the enactment of legislation, whereas implementing a decision to buy more fuel-efficient cars for government agencies might be accomplished through an executive order from the president.

Policy authorization tools such as legislation and executive orders have unique strengths and weaknesses. The nature of each legal process may dramatically change the nature and impact of the tool envisioned.

Legislation

Although the president cannot submit legislation or compel Congress to vote on a bill, he nevertheless has an important role in the legislative process. The president can direct his administration to draft bills, convince allies in Congress to introduce legislation, and use the powers and trappings of his office (including the threat of veto or the promise of support for legislation) to get laws enacted.

Despite these sources of influence, using the legislative process to gain enactment of laws is not without its drawbacks. Bills must be negotiated through Congress and most bills never make it into law. Furthermore, those bills that do become law are often quite different from what the president and his administration may have first envisioned. Finally, the legislative process is usually long and time consuming. Only in the gravest emergencies are bills enacted in an expeditious manner.

Even with its drawbacks, legislation has several advantages over other authorizing tools. First, some policy tools, such as the creation of a tax incentive or a grant program, cannot be implemented without a new law or a change in an existing one. Second, the passage of legislation is often perceived by the public as being more legitimate than an executive order or a policy change caused by a court decision. Finally, the difficulty Congress has in enacting laws means that once a bill is passed, it is more likely to remain in place than an executive order, which can be overturned by a future administration with the signature of the president.

Executive Orders

Executive orders are often perceived to be a fast and expedient alternative to legislation. An executive order in the United States is an order issued by the president as the head of the executive branch of the federal government. In other countries, similar edicts may be known as decrees or orders-in-council.

Executive orders do have the full force of law because issuances are typically made pursuant to existing statutes (some of which specifically delegate to the president some degree of discretionary power) or are based in a power inherently granted to the executive branch by the Constitution. At the same time, they are limited in scope by the source of their legal authority (the Constitution and existing statutes). Furthermore, subsequent administrations can override an executive order just as easily as it was put into force, and Congress could withhold the necessary funding needed to implement the president's directive.

Despite their sometimes controversial nature and limited range of authority, executive orders have increased in use by presidents. The primary reason for this is that they can be put into effect without congressional approval. This is especially relevant for presidents who have low approval ratings, are in the last year of their final term of office, or are interacting with a Congress (or one of the two chambers) controlled by an opposition party. Policy analysts hoping to influence an administration should keep these circumstances in mind when suggesting a legislative process or executive order as the best way to put a policy idea in effect.

Treaties and Legal Precedent

Treaties are ratified by Congress and are legal documents. Consequently they also have the same strengths and weaknesses as an authorizing tool as legislation. Treaties typically only need to be ratified by the Senate. There are exceptions, however, such as agreements involving commerce and revenue, that require ratification by the House of Representatives. U.S. courts may also cite domestic legal precedent as a means of authorizing or implementing specific policies.

RECOMMENDING THE RIGHT POLICY TOOL

Policy implementation tools are the means by which governments apply the policy. The government has at its disposal a set of policy tools that effectively fall into three broad categories that Bemelmans-Videc, Rist, and Vedung have named **carrots**, sticks, and sermons.[1] Any of the instruments in these three categories may vary among criteria like resource intensiveness, targeting

---

1. Marie-Louise Bemelmans-Videc, Ray C. Rist, and Evert Vedung (eds.), *Carrots, Sticks, and Sermons* (London, UK: Transactions, 2007).

(precision and selectivity), or political risk (the legitimacy criterion).[2] Box 8-1 discusses some of the types of implementation tools that are available to policy makers.[3]

BOX 8-1	**Policy Implementation Tools**			
Tool	**Examples**	**Carrot**	**Stick**	**Sermon**
Subsidize	Direct payments, loans, price supports, tax incentives	x		
Ration	Medicare coverage limitations, airline slots at airports, housing voucher eligibility limits		x	
Tax	Raise or lower income tax rates, impose tax on specific good like gasoline or tobacco to influence behavior/use	x	x	
Privatize	Sell or transfer government assets to private sector, such as the Postal Service or Amtrak	x	x	
Contract	Contract out for government services (managing web pages) or to buy products for government agencies (defense weapons or IT)	x		
Regulate	Licensing, inspection, enforcement of standards in a broad range of areas including the environment, financial services, health care, food safety, worker safety, etc.		x	
Conduct Research	National Science Foundation support for academic studies, National Institute for Health support for medical research and innovation	x		
Educate	Public campaigns led by senior officials such as president, First Lady, vice president on an important issue (fighting obesity, "don't do drugs," etc.)			x

2. Bemelmans-Videc et al., *Carrots, Sticks, and Sermons.*

3. Paul Weinstein, Jr., *Expanding Opportunities for Informed Participation in Public Policy* (Washington, DC: Science and Technology Policy Institute, 2010).

Each policy tool will produce different outcomes depending on their effectiveness, efficiency, equity, impact upon liberty/freedom, administrative and technical feasibility, political viability, and social acceptability. Policymakers must decide what policy tool or mix of tools will ensure the optimal outcome. Box 8-2 provides a set of criteria for making these decisions.[4]

Carrots are often popular with elected officials because they can be used to change behavior through incentives rather than penalties. Some carrots, such as grants, vouchers (food stamps), or refundable **tax credits** (Earned Income Tax Credit) are direct subsidies that provide a specified amount to the beneficiary. Other subsidies attempt to leverage resources from the beneficiary or a third party. These include loans, matching grants, and insurance.

Carrots can be effective policy tools, but their success can often be curtailed by a lack of resources or poor design. Poor design can often lead to unintended consequences. For example, some have argued that subsidized student loans have enabled colleges and universities to raise prices without a reduction in market demand, thus undermining the program's goal of making college more affordable.[5] Subsidies can also be subject to error and fraud. For example, it has been estimated that the Earned Income Tax Credit is subject to improper payments of possibly 24 percent.[6]

Sticks include a number of policy tools, including monetary penalties (fines), nonmonetary penalties, targeted taxes or fees, bans or restrictions, disclosure, and military force. Sticks can be very effective policy tools, particularly when applied to behavior that is clearly defined. But sticks have a number of weaknesses. First, sticks require enforcement and resources to ensure adequate supervision. Often elected officials will enact laws to regulate an industry or individual behavior without providing the resources or the authority to ensure that the law is being adhered to. Second, sticks are typically unpopular if applied to a large population, making them difficult to enforce in some instances. Finally, sticks can be poorly designed, leading to unintended consequences in which the behavior being restricted actually worsens. For example, the Clinton administration in 1993 ended the tax deduction for executive

---

4. Weinstein, *Expanding Opportunities.*

5. See work by Sara Goldrick-Rab for an interesting discussion of the impact of the student loan program on the cost of college.

6. Some believe this estimate is too high. See the General Accounting Office and its work on improper payments for more information on this topic.

BOX 8-2	**Criteria for Evaluating Policy Tools and Proposals**

Criterion	Definition	Limitations	Uses
Effectiveness	Probability of success	Agreement on definition of success, future uncertainty	Most policy proposals
Efficiency	Achievement of goals in terms of lowest possible cost	Measuring in terms of cost benefits is not always easy or possible. Sometimes other factors are more important	Tax, regulatory, budget, monetary policy
Equity	Fairness in distribution of policy's costs and benefits to all strata of society	Hard to measure. Disagreements on how to define equity	Access to health care and education, civil rights, issues involving those with disabilities
Liberty/ Freedom	Extent to which policy restricts privacy and rights/choices	Often entangled in ideological debate	Gun and property rights, restrictions on Internet use, abortion
Administrative/ Technical Feasibility	The ability of government to implement a policy as intended, given technical and administrative limitations	Policies are often proposed and enacted without feasibility studies or test trials	Most policy proposals
Political Viability	Likelihood of political support	Hard to determine. Political support or opposition can change quickly because of events	Most policy proposals. The more controversial, the more relevant
Social Acceptability	The extent to which the public will accept a proposal	Difficult to analyze or determine, even when using technical measures like polling, focus groups, etc. Some measures are more scientific than others. Interpreting data is subjective	Most policy proposals

compensation over $1 million as a way to dampen the rise in CEO pay. Yet, performance-based pay, in the form of stock options, was exempted in order to encourage the development of new companies and entrepreneurs in the technology sector. Although well intentioned, this "loophole" led to an explosion in compensation in the form of stock options that may or may not have exacerbated the spread between executive pay and the income of typical working Americans.

Sermons can be effective implementation tools if their limitations are understood. Examples of sermon policy tools include public campaign such as the "war on drugs"; First Lady Michelle Obama's campaign to fight childhood obesity, otherwise known as "Let's Move"; or diplomacy by a head of state or his or her representative.[7]

Campaigns are most effective if they are headed by a high-profile individual with a positive approval rating, are time limited, and focus on a societal problem that is best addressed through individual, personal action rather than government intervention. Although sermons are often cheaper to implement than carrots or sticks, they do require resources. And with regard to diplomacy, the threat (direct or indirect) of possible military force can often make the difference between a successful diplomatic endeavor and an unsuccessful one.

Over the years, the number and complexity of policy tools outlined in Box 8-2 has grown dramatically. This has occurred in part because the lack of resources (money) due to structural deficits (except for a few brief periods such as the late 1990s) forced policymakers to be more creative and target benefits more narrowly. It is also the result of the growing number of areas in which government is now involved. As a result, many of today's policy implementation tools have become increasingly more complex. Policymakers need to be cognizant of the growing catalog of policy tools available to those in government. For example, according to the Congressional Research Service, there are more than 100 major tax incentives and the cost is more than $1.1 trillion annually.[8] These tax incentives come in several forms: deductions, credits, deferral, rebates, and expensing (see Box 8-3).[9] In many instances, different tax incentives exist to

---

7. For more information, visit the Let's Move web site: http://www.letsmove.gov.

8. Chuck Marr, Chye-Ching Huang, & Joel Friedman, *Tax Expenditure Reform: An Essential Ingredient of Needed Deficit Reduction* (Washington, DC: Center on Budget and Policy Priorities, 2013).

9. Weinstein, *Expanding Opportunities*.

BOX 8-3	**Primary Types of Targeted Tax Incentives**

Type	Explanation
Deduction	An expense or an amount of money that lowers your taxable income. It is subtracted from the amount of money you made throughout the year (your gross income). Once all deductions are subtracted, the remainder is known as your *adjusted gross income*, or *AGI*. Examples of deductions include contributions to a traditional IRA, student loan interest that was paid during the year, tuition and expenses, alimony paid, and classroom-related costs for teachers. There are also deductions that are related to self-employment income. The *standard* or *itemized deductions* are subtracted from the AGI, yielding your taxable income. This is the number that determines the amount of tax that you owe.
Credit	Dollar-for-dollar reductions that are subtracted from your tax liability. Let's say, for instance, that you qualify for a $100 tax credit. The government is, in essence, saying to you, "We are giving you credit for having already paid $100 in tax." Therefore, $100 is subtracted directly from the amount of tax that you owe. There are tax credits for college expenses, for retirement savings, even for adopting children. Some well-known tax credits include the American Opportunity education credit, the Earned Income Credit, and the Child Tax Credit. There are many more special-interest, business, or investment credits as well.
Deferral	Allows taxpayers to delay paying taxes to some future period. In theory, the net taxes paid should be the same. In practice, due to the time value of money, paying taxes in future can be preferable (for the taxpayer) to paying them now. Taxes can sometimes be deferred indefinitely, or they may be taxed at a lower rate in the future, particularly for deferral of income taxes. It is a general fact of taxation that when taxpayers can choose when to pay taxes, the total amount paid in tax will likely be lower. By deferring taxes on the returns of an investment, the investor benefits in two ways. The first benefit is tax-free growth: instead of paying tax on the returns of an investment, tax is paid only at a later date, leaving the investment to grow unhindered. The second benefit of tax deferral is that investments are usually made when a person is earning higher income and is taxed at a higher tax rate. Withdrawals are made from an investment account when a person is earning little or no income and is taxed at a lower rate.
Expensing and Accelerated Depreciation	Schemes that allow business firms to write off assets faster than true economic depreciation are referred to as *accelerated depreciation*. At the extreme of accelerated depreciation, the firm expenses—that is, deducts from taxable income—the asset's full cost of acquisition. The result can be a dramatic reduction in tax liability.

encourage similar behavior. For example, there are five incentives to help students and parents pay for college at the time of enrollment or after graduation.[10] In addition, there are several other incentives to help parents and relatives save for a dependent's college tuition.[11]

As this example suggests, different tax incentives have different strengths and weaknesses. Tax credits can be made refundable to provide a financial benefit to lower-income families at the same level as higher-income families. But such credits can also be subject to abuse. Deferral of taxes may encourage people to save, but it can also create unintended economic distortions, such as too much savings during recessionary periods when more spending might be a more desirable societal goal. Furthermore, although providing subsidies through the tax code can be less bureaucratic than providing support through agency-specific programs, and therefore more effective in terms of take-up rates, almost all tax incentives that are targeted make the code more complex and may be a factor in the underreporting of taxable income.

CONCLUSION

Policymakers do not have the luxury of responding to policy challenges in a vacuum. Government officials are restrained by the specific types of policy authorizing and implementation tools they have at their disposal. Such tools, like the policies themselves, have strengths and weaknesses that need to be understood if the best result is to be attained.

Key Terms

Carrots

Policy authorization tool

Policy implementation tool

Tax credit

Tax deduction

---

10. Government Accountability Office, *Improved Tax Information Could Help Families Pay for College* (Washington, DC: GAO, May 2012).

11. Government Accountability Office, *Improved Tax Information*.

Review Questions

1. What is the difference between policy authorization and policy implementation tools?
2. What is a weakness of the effectiveness measurement criterion for evaluating policy tools and proposals?
3. What are the advantages of legislation versus executive orders as a policy authorization tool?
4. What are some of the reasons for the rise in the number of targeted tax incentives?

LEGISLATIVE CLEARANCE AND COORDINATION

SAPs, LRMs, and Other Policy Acronyms

LEGISLATIVE CLEARANCE AND COORDINATION

You are a new employee in federal agency trying to find your way through a bureaucracy of almost two million. How do you make an impact early? Get yourself on the Office of Management and Budget's (OMB) Legislative Referral Distribution List, and soon every official statement, testimony, and other documents will come across your desk. Getting your name on the OMB distribution list is like getting on the "A" party list. Now you can get past the bouncer at the door. What you do at the party is a whole other story.

In this chapter, we will discuss how administration policy is cleared through the executive branch. In particular, we will highlight the influential role that OMB plays by overseeing policy and legislative proposals to be adopted as **administration policy**. OMB provides accountability to the executive branch by routinely monitoring day-to-day activities of the entire government. It has the power to clear legislation and major regulations. It also has the authority to issue administration positions on policy matters. In this chapter, we will explain and evaluate how the formal oversight process run by OMB— called the **legislative referral memorandum (LRM)** process—and OMB's preparation of **statements of administration policy (SAP)** affect the policy-making process.

Like decision memoranda, LRMs and SAPs enable everyone to engage in the policymaking process in a more fair, coordinated, and centralized manner than would otherwise be the case. Specifically, they provide a means for OMB to communicate executive policy positions and solicit input from all agencies and departments on every policy proposal being considered by executive branch. The appropriate use of these tools thus provides a conduit for the exchange of ideas with the chief decision maker. As a result, it enhances the perceived legitimacy of the system. This, in turn, tends to increase the commitment among policymakers to support the resulting policy. It also makes the policy outcomes better, to the extent that they tend to reflect a wider range of inputs than they would if these channels did not exist.

LEGISLATIVE RESPONSIBILITY IN THE EXECUTIVE BRANCH

The president's legislative responsibilities are founded in his or her constitutional duties and powers to perform the following:

- Require the opinion, in writing, of the principal officer in each of the executive departments;
- Take care that the laws are faithfully executed;
- Give the Congress information on the State of the Union;
- Recommend to the Congress such measures as he judges necessary;
- Approve or disapprove bills passed by the Congress;
- Convene either or both Houses of the Congress.

In order to fulfill these duties, the president presides as the chief executive officer in charge of a vast policymaking and coordinating body called the Executive Office of the President (EOP). The EOP consists of approximately 2,000 employees who work in congressionally mandated (established by statute) executive agencies with specific programmatic responsibilities or who are members of the president's personal staff. Congressionally mandated agencies include organizations like OMB, the U.S. Trade Representative, the Council of Economic Advisers, and the Council on Environmental Quality. The president's personal staff, in turn, includes both people who maintain the White House residence (taking care of the First Family meals, cleaning, laundry, etc.) and the people who serve on executive policy councils such as the Domestic Policy Council, the National Economic Council, and the National Security Council, which are charged with managing policy decisions for the president.

BOX 9-1	The White House Office and the Executive Office of the President

Executive Office of the President

Council of Economic Advisers
Council on Environmental Quality
Executive Residence
National Security Staff
Office of Administration
Office of Management and Budget
Office of National Drug Control Policy
Office of Science and Technology Policy
Office of the United States Trade Representative
Office of the Vice President
White House Office

The White House Office

Domestic Policy Council
    Office of National AIDS Policy
    Office of Faith-Based and Neighborhood Partnerships
    Office of Social Innovation and Civic Participation
    White House Rural Council
National Security Advisor
National Economic Council
Office of Cabinet Affairs
Office of the Chief of Staff
Office of Communications
    Office of the Press Secretary
    Media Affairs
    Research
    Speechwriting
Office of Digital Strategy
Office of the First Lady
    Office of the Social Secretary
Office of Legislative Affairs

(Continued)

(Continued)

Office of Management and Administration
    White House Personnel
    White House Operations
    Telephone Office
    Visitors Office
Oval Office Operations
Office of Presidential Personnel
Office of Public Engagement and Intergovernmental Affairs
    Office of Public Engagement
    Council on Women and Girls
    Office of Intergovernmental Affairs
    Office of Urban Affairs
Office of Scheduling and Advance
Office of the Staff Secretary
    Presidential Correspondence
    Executive Clerk
    Records Management
Office of the White House Counsel

Given the large cadre of employees within the EOP, the task of coordinating policy and responding to legislation between the EOP and the executive branch of government—cabinet departments and smaller agencies—can be very complicated. Coordination of the policymaking and legislative processes within the EOP takes place at two levels. At the highest level, major policy decisions and major legislation are controlled by the White House policy councils, which develop and implement major policy decisions using the decision-making memoranda we discussed in Chapter 6. The resulting decisions are then run through a formal clearance process conducted by OMB called the LRM process.

Most legislative issues and other policy matters, such as executive orders and presidential decrees, however, do not necessitate presidential involvement. These issues, such as clearing congressional testimony or providing the views of the administration on a particular legislative bill, are handled primarily by OMB itself through the LRM clearance process and do not necessarily involve the White House policy councils directly. When the White House policy councils are not involved, OMB plays the lead role in resolving policy conflicts and guaranteeing that resulting legislation or actions are consistent with the policies and objectives of the president.

This power is one that is closely guarded by OMB and is often a point of contention between the various agencies in the executive branch, which often believe OMB does not always act as an honest broker and forces decisions based solely on budgetary concerns (how much will it cost) and not on the broader policy goals of the administration. OMB counters by arguing that budgetary concerns should have a high priority regarding any policy decision and that discussions over the cost of proposals lead to more precise and well-thought-out policy proposals. As we discussed in Chapter 3, the debate over OMB's role has in part led to the ever-growing role of the White House policy councils. Despite the growing role of the policy councils, the sheer number of decisions that must be reviewed necessitates that OMB, with its larger bureaucracy, runs the day-to-day clearance process.

THE CLEARANCE PROCESS

OMB's LRM clearance process is intended to do the following:[1]

- Permit the coordinated development, review, and approval of legislative proposals needed to carry out the president's agenda;
- Help the agencies develop draft bills that are consistent with and that carry out the president's policy objectives;
- Clearly identify for Congress those bills that are part of the president's program and the relationship of other bills to that program;
- Assure that Congress receives coordinated and informative agency views on legislation that it has under consideration;
- Assure that bills and position statements submitted to Congress by one agency properly take into account the interests and concerns of all affected agencies;
- Provide a means whereby divergent agency views can be reconciled.

OMB Circular A-19 sets forth the basic guidelines and procedures for carrying out its clearance process. The LRM clearance function covers agency

---

1. Memorandum from Acting OMB Director Jeff Zients to Department and Agency Heads, April 15, 2013, "Legislative Coordination and Clearance," https://www.whitehouse.gov/sites/default/files/omb/memoranda/2013/m-13-12.pdf.

legislative proposals, agency reports and testimony on pending legislation, SAPs, and enrolled bills. These procedures have been substantially the same for more than fifty years. An example of a LRM is included in Box 9-2.

BOX 9-2	**Legislative Referral Memorandum**

LRM ID: JAB342

EXECUTIVE OFFICE OF THE PRESIDENT

OFFICE OF MANAGEMENT AND BUDGET

Washington, D.C. 20503–0001

Tuesday, September 17, 2002

LEGISLATIVE REFERRAL MEMORANDUM

TO:	Legislative Liaison Officer—See Distribution below
FROM:	Richard E. Green (for) Assistant Director for Legislative Reference
OMB CONTACT:	James A. Brown
PHONE:	(202)395–3473 FAX: (202)395–3109
SUBJECT:	REVISED TRANSPORTATION Final Version, Draft Bill on to revise, codify, and enact certain maritime laws as part of title 46, United States Code, "Shipping."
DEADLINE:	10:00 A.M. Tuesday, October 1, 2002

In accordance with OMB Circular A-19, OMB requests the views of your agency on the above subject before advising on its relationship to the program of the president. Please advise us if this item will affect direct spending or receipts for purposes of the "Pay-As-You-Go" provisions of Title XIII of the Omnibus Budget Reconciliation Act of 1990.

COMMENTS: This draft recodification has been circulated to you twice before, via LRMs JAB1 (January 17, 2001) and JAB148 (January 23, 2002). We are circulating this to you now for final review and signoff. Personnel or units with which DOT has worked in resolving issues identified in previous versions include: Defense: Dwight Moore (Transcom); Justice: Debra Kossow (Torts); INS (definitions: of "U.S. citizen" and "consular officer"); Federal Maritime Commission: Amy Larson; Commerce, Bernard Cody (NOAA)). IF WE DO NOT HEAR FROM

YOU BY THE DEADLINE (EITHER IN THE FORM OF A COMMENT OR NOTIFICATION THAT A COMMENT WILL BE FORTHCOMING SHORTLY), WE WILL ASSUME THAT YOU HAVE NO OBJECTION TO CLEARANCE OF THIS FINAL VERSION.

DISTRIBUTION LIST

AGENCIES:

   114-STATE—Nicole Petrosino—(202) 647–1794

   044-Federal Maritime Commission—Amy W. Larson—(202) 523–5740

   061-JUSTICE—Daniel Bryant—(202) 514–2141

   118-TREASURY—Thomas M. McGivern—(202) 622–2317

   117 & 340-TRANSPORTATION—Tom Herlihy—(202) 366–4687

   025-COMMERCE—Michael A. Levitt—(202) 482–3151

   029-DEFENSE—Samuel T. Brick Jr.—(703) 697–1305

EOP:

Jennifer S. Kron

   LRM ID: JAB342 SUBJECT: REVISED TRANSPORTATION Draft Bill on to revise, codify, and enact certain maritime laws as part of title 46, United States Code, "Shipping."

RESPONSE TO LEGISLATIVE REFERRAL MEMORANDUM

   If your response to this request for views is short (e.g., concur/no comment), we prefer that you respond by e-mail or by faxing us this response sheet. If the response is short and you prefer to call, please call the branch-wide line shown below (NOT the analyst's line) to leave a message with a legislative assistant.
   You may also respond by:

   (1) Calling the analyst/attorney's direct line (you will be connected to voice mail if the analyst does not answer); or

   (2) Sending us a memo or letter. Please include the LRM number shown above, and the subject shown below.

TO: James A. Brown Phone: 395–3473 Fax: 395–3109

Office of Management and Budget

Branch-Wide Line (to reach legislative assistant): 395–3454

(Continued)

(Continued)

FROM: _____ (Date)

_____ (Name)

_____ (Agency)

_____ (Telephone)

The following is the response of our agency to your request for views on the above-captioned subject:

_____Concur

_____No Objection

_____No Comment

_____See proposed edits on pages _____

_____Other: _____

_____FAX RETURN of _____ pages, attached to this response sheet

LRM ID REJ42

Source: Legislative Referral Memorandum, September 17, 2002, http://www.mlaus.org/download/619a.txt.

Legislative Proposals

All legislative proposals that agencies in the EOP wish to transmit to the Congress must be sent to OMB for clearance. OMB circulates the bills to other affected agencies and appropriate EOP staff. The EOP agencies or staff may favor it or have no objection. They may also propose substantive or technical amendments or perhaps a complete substitute. Divergent views can be reconciled via telephone, letters, or interagency meetings called by OMB.

After review, analysis, resolution of issues, and obtaining policy guidance from the relevant EOP agencies, OMB may offer the proposing agency positive feedback by advising it that (1) there is "no objection" from the standpoint of the administration's program to the submission of the proposed draft bill to the Congress, or (2) the proposed bill is "in accord with the president's program," if it implements a presidential proposal. This "advice" is conveyed then by the submitting agency to the Congress in its transmittal letter. Major legislation is sometimes transmitted personally by the president. On the other hand, if OMB decides that the proposed bill conflicts with an important administration objective, or it is not in accordance with the president's program, it can stop the bill from being transmitted to the Congress. In such cases, disagreements between OMB and executive agencies must be resolved before the bill can be transmitted.

CLEARANCE OF AGENCY TESTIMONY AND REPORTS ON PENDING LEGISLATION

If a congressional committee asks an agency in the EOP to report or testify on pending legislation, or if an EOP agency wishes to volunteer a report on an issue being considered by a congressional committee, similar clearance procedures are followed. Congressional testimony is a useful means for an EOP agency to convey the administration's views on legislation or other congressional matters without directly involving the president. Indeed, the White House often prefers that an EOP agency takes the lead on noncritical or controversial issues or legislation. The strategy of allowing **agency-owned issues** enables the president to stay above the fray, and it protects him or her from potentially contentious debates on issues or legislative proposals that are not of major importance to the country as a whole. In such instances, the LRM process allows the White House staff to oversee and coordinate these "agency-owned" issues without direct presidential involvement and without expending a scarce resource known as "presidential prestige."

Statement of Administration Policy (SAP)

OMB also prepares a SAP for major bills scheduled for House or Senate floor action as well as those to be considered by major congressional committees such as the House Rules Committee. SAPs are also prepared for so-called non-controversial bills considered in the House under suspension of the rules—bills that are voted on without the opportunity to offer amendments.

The SAP process coordinates, systematizes, and rationalizes the administration and formulation of the president's policy. SAPs are important because they provide a direct and authoritative way for the administration to let the Congress and, via the press, the American people know the views of the president on a particular bill or legislative issue. The SAP may be used to indicate support for legislation by the administration and the president. It may also be used to clarify the president's position in support of the whole bill or specific components of the legislation. Alternatively, the SAP may be used to indicate the administration and the president's disapproval of all or part of a particular bill. When the disapproval is strong enough, the SAP may contain a veto threat from the president. There are three levels of veto threats used in SAPs. These are, in order of strength, "The president will veto"; "Senior advisers will recommend to the president that he should veto this legislation"; and "The secretary of treasury (or the relevant agency) will recommend to the president that he should veto this legislation."

An example of a SAP is included in Box 9-3.

BOX 9-3   Statement of Administration Policy

EXECUTIVE OFFICE OF THE PRESIDENT

OFFICE OF MANAGEMENT AND BUDGET

WASHINGTON, D.C. 20503

December 11, 2014

(House)

STATEMENT OF ADMINISTRATION POLICY

H.R. 83—Consolidated and Further Continuing Appropriations Act, 2015

(Rep. Rogers, R-KY)

The administration supports House passage of H.R. 83, making appropriations for fiscal year (FY) 2015, and for other purposes. The administration appreciates the bipartisan effort to include full-year appropriations legislation for most Government functions that allows for planning and provides certainty, while making progress toward appropriately investing in economic growth and opportunity, and adequately funding national security requirements. The administration also appreciates the authorities and funding provided to enhance the U.S. Government's response to the Ebola epidemic, and to implement the administration's strategy to counter the Islamic State of Iraq and the Levant, as well as investments for the president's early education agenda, Pell Grants, the bipartisan, Manufacturing Institutes initiative, and extension of the Trade Adjustment Assistance program. However, the administration objects to the inclusion of ideological and special interest riders in the House bill. In particular, the administration is opposed to the inclusion of a rider that would amend the Dodd-Frank Wall Street Reform and Consumer Protection Act and weaken a critical component of financial system reform aimed at reducing taxpayer risk. Additionally, the administration is opposed to inclusion of a rider that would amend the Federal Election Campaign Act to allow individual donors to contribute to national political party committee accounts for conventions, buildings and recounts in amounts that are dramatically higher than what the law currently permits.

Furthermore, the administration is disappointed that the bill would fund the Department of Homeland Security through February 27, 2015, at last year's levels. Short-term continuing resolution funding measures are disruptive, create uncertainty, and impede efficient resource planning and execution. The administration urges the Congress to enact comprehensive full-year appropriations legislation for all Government functions free of provisions that have no place in annual appropriations bills.

Source: Executive Office of the president, Office of Management and Budget, https://www .whitehouse.gov/sites/default/files/omb/legislative/sap/113/saphr83h_20141211.pdf.

OMB prepares SAPs in coordination with the agency or agencies principally concerned and other relevant EOP units. Once the SAP has passed through the clearance process, it is sent to Congress by OMB's Legislative Affairs.

Enrolled Bills

At the end of the legislative process, after Congress has voted and passed a particular bill, it is enrolled (i.e., sent to the president for his approval or disapproval). The Constitution provides that the president shall take action within ten days after receipt of the bill, not including Sundays.

To assist the president in deciding his course of action on a bill, a review process, which is similar to the LRM process for bills submitted to Congress by the president, is set into motion in which OMB requests that each interested agency submit its analysis and recommendation to OMB within 48 hours. These **views letters** are signed by the head of the agency or a presidential appointee. OMB prepares a memorandum to the president on the enrolled bill, which transmits these views letters and summarizes the bill, significant issues, and various agency and OMB recommendations. If an agency recommends disapproval or a signing statement, it is responsible for preparing a draft of an appropriate statement for the president's consideration.

CONCLUSION

In this chapter, we discussed how administration policy is cleared through the executive branch. We highlighted the influential role that OMB plays by overseeing and clearing policy and legislative proposals. Through the LRM process and the preparation of SAPs, OMB provides accountability to governmental actions, guarantees that positions taken by the EOP are consistent with the president's policies and agenda, and provides Congress and the American public with a direct and authoritative statement about the president's position on important policies and legislation. These tools enable everyone to engage in the policymaking process in a more fair, coordinated, and centralized manner than would otherwise be the case. As a result, when used effectively, they can enhance the perceived legitimacy of the system. This, in turn, tends to increase the commitment among policymakers to support the resulting policy. To the extent that the resulting policy outcome reflects a wider range of inputs, it is also likely to be better balanced and satisfy more concerns than would otherwise be the case.

Key Terms

Administration policy

Agency-owned issues

Legislative referral memorandum (LRM)

Statement of administration policy (SAP)

Views letters

Review Questions

1. When does a policy become "administration policy?"
2. What are the executive branch's legislative responsibilities?
3. What is the purpose of the LRM clearance process?
4. Describe the three levels of veto threats in a SAP.
5. What is the role of OMB in the legislative clearance process?
6. Under what circumstances does the White House encourage or approve of agency-owned issues?

POLLING AND THE POLICYMAKING PROCESS

POLLING AND POLICYMAKING: MYTHS AND REALITIES

Political pundits, editorial pages, and politicians looking for a campaign issue have publicly debated the use of polling by policymakers in the executive branch. Some critics of polling argue that truly great leaders should ignore polls, that polls are untrustworthy, and that polling is somehow undemocratic. Others suggest that the use of polling indicates that the executive branch is permanently campaigning and avoiding tough or unpopular decisions.[1] National politicians have inadvertently fanned the public's anxieties about polling by deriding its use. President George W. Bush denounced polling and prided himself on making decisions that went against public opinion. To separate himself from polling, he required his principal pollster, Jan van Lohuizen, to report to his Deputy Chief of Staff and Senior Adviser Karl Rove rather than to him.[2] President Obama asserted that he, too, would lead, "not by polls, but by principle."[3] Echoing President Bush, President

---

1. Shoon K. Murray and P. Howard, "Variation in White House Polling Operations: Carter to Clinton," *Public Opinion Quarterly* 66 (2002), pp. 527–558; Kathryn D. Tenpas and James A. McCann, "Testing the Permanence of the Permanent Campaign: An Analysis of Presidential Polling Expenditures, 1977–2002," *Public Opinion Quarterly* 71, 3 (2007), pp. 349–366.

2. Tenpas and McCann, "Testing the Permanence," p. 356; Kathryn D. Tenpas, "Words vs. Deeds: President George W. Bush and Polling," *Brookings Review* 21, 3 (2003), pp. 32–35.

3. Ben Smith, "Meet Obama's Pollsters," *POLITICO* (April 3, 2009), http://www.politico.com/news/stories/0409/20852.html.

Obama argued, "I've got my own pollsters. But I wasn't elected just to do what's popular. I was elected to do what was right."[4]

Despite such proclamations, polling is an important component of the modern executive branch and the policy process.[5] Pollsters hired by the Democratic National Committee and Republican National Committee, in particular, play important roles in political campaigns and in the policy-making process once the president has been elected. President Obama has relied heavily on pollsters Joel Benenson, Paul Harstad, and David Binder; President George W. Bush relied on pollsters Jan van Lohuizen and Fred Steeper; President Clinton relied on pollsters Stanley Greenberg, Doug Schoen, and Mark Penn; President Reagan relied on pollster Dick Wirthlin; President Carter relied on pollster Patrick Caddell; and Presidents Nixon, Ford, and George H. W. Bush relied on pollster Robert Teeter.[6] Presidents Reagan, Clinton, and Obama used polling more extensively than Presidents Carter, George H. W. Bush, and George W. Bush;[7] nonetheless, polling has clearly come to serve the "mutual needs of all presidents."[8]

Contrary to the exhortations of its critics and the reluctance of presidents to advertise their use of polling, we argue that polling can enhance the democratic nature of policymaking by providing a conduit through which information about constituents' concerns are channeled to policymakers. Polling helps to clarify the public's values and attitudes. It also reveals how they perceive specific policy initiatives. This information enables the president, the president's staff, and other stakeholders to be more responsive and accountable to their constituents.[9] "Going public" also increases the president's "power to persuade" his constituents, policymakers in the White House and Congress, as well as other

---

4. Sam Stein, "Obama Mocks Polls But Spends More on Them ($4.4 M) than Bush Did," *Huffington Post* (July 29, 2010), http://www.huffingtonpost.com/2010/07/29/obama-mocks-polls-but-spe_n_663553.html.

5. Lawrence Jacobs and Robert Shapiro, "The Rise of Presidential Polling: The Nixon White House in Historical Perspective," *Public Opinion Quarterly* 59 (1996), pp. 163–195.

6. Smith, "Meet Obama's Pollsters."

7. Murray and Howard, "Variation in White House Polling Operations," pp. 527–558.

8. Diane Heith, "Staffing the White House Public Opinion Apparatus, 1979–1988." *Public Opinion Quarterly* 62 (1998), p. 186, cited in Murray and Howard, "Variation in White House Polling Operations," pp. 527–558; Stein, "Obama Mocks Polls."

9. Lawrence Jacobs, "The Recoil Effect: Public Opinion and Policymaking in the U.S. and Britain," *Comparative Politics* 24, 3 (1992), pp. 199–217.

potential critics.[10] In Chapter 1, we argued that the tools, techniques, and processes of policymaking enable and enhance the president's ability to lead the policymaking process by promoting the president's agenda, acting as an honest broker among competing stakeholders, and incubating new ideas. By providing a channel for the public to express their viewpoints on policy initiatives at various stages in development, polling enhances these functions and makes the policymaking process more effective.

This chapter introduces the basics of polling in the executive branch. It provides rebuttals to common criticisms of polling in the executive branch, reviews polling basics, and specifies who does the polling in the White House.

REBUTTALS TO COMMON CRITICISMS

There are many popular criticisms about polling and politics. Separating the kernels of truth within them from fiction is a useful way to begin.

> *Criticism:* Polling is damaging to the democratic process. Elections provide the appropriate means for the public as a whole to voice its concerns. Polling undermines the importance of elections by enabling the small group of people interviewed to circumvent the electoral process and exercise a substantial amount of influence.

> *Rebuttal:* The reality is that polling can help strengthen the democratic process by providing an additional channel through which a diverse set of constituents can express their views and concerns to executive and congressional decision makers. If polling is done correctly, it often provides a better indicator of what the "American people" as a whole feel about a particular set of issues than do elections or even referenda on those same issues. Polling also facilitates communication with the public by informing politicians about how particular policies are being interpreted by the public.

Scholars Kathryn Tenpas and James McCann argue that although the ability of presidents to poll became institutionalized in the White House during the Nixon administration, the use of polling varies across administrations as a matter of leadership style.[11] President Ronald Reagan and President William J.

---

10. Tenpas and McCann, "Testing the Permanence," pp. 349–366; Sam Kernell, *Going Public: New Strategies of Presidential Leadership* (Washington, DC: Congressional Quarterly Press, 1997).

11. Tenpas and McCann, "Testing the Permanence," pp. 349–366.

Clinton are famous for their extensive use of polling and direct interaction with pollsters. At the other end of the spectrum, President George H. W. Bush is known for his sparing use of polling and his very limited contact with pollsters. Indeed, the experiences of his administration provide a cautionary tale about the dangers operating without accurate information about public's perceptions and sentiments. Robert Teeter, the chief pollster for the George H. W. Bush administration, lamented that "one of the political downfalls of the administration was that no one was paying any attention to the public."[12] Perhaps lulled by President Bush's high levels of popularity following the end of the first Gulf War, the administration reportedly did not commission a poll between January and December of 1991, less than a year before the next election.[13] Scholars Shoon Murray and Peter Howard assess the consequences of failing to use polling bluntly:[14]

> As a result, President [George H. W.] Bush and his top aides did not have the type of current, in-depth information that would allow them to follow how daily events affected the president's image and standing with particular segments of the public, to know how the public responded to breaking events and thereby craft their spin, to pretest policy initiatives and spot potentially controversial issues, or to test the public's response to phrases in order to craft successful speeches.

Criticism: Politicians use polling to decide their position on issues.

Rebuttal: The reality of policymaking is that ideas are usually developed first, then they are polled to see how broadly they will be supported and how to best market them. As President Clinton's Domestic Policy Adviser Bruce Reed points out,[15]

> We sometimes get accused of having an agenda of poll-driven ideas . . . I think it was actually the other way around. We would

---

12. Murray and Howard, "Variation in White House Polling Operations," p. 543.

13. David Moore, *The Super Pollsters: How They Measure and Manipulate Public Opinion in America.* (New York, NY: Four Walls Eight Windows, 1995), p. 361, cited in Murray and Howard, "Variation in White House Polling Operations," p. 543.

14. Murray and Howard, "Variation in White House Polling Operations," p. 543.

15. Bradley H. Patterson, Jr., "The White House Staff: Inside the West Wing and Beyond," (Washington, DC: Brookings Institution Press, 2000).

come up with a host of ideas and we'd use whatever channels we could to convince people around here to do them. It wouldn't hurt if something was popular, but that wasn't where we got the idea in the first place . . . I think the president had always been interested in the use of public opinion to figure out what are public feelings, not to make the policy decisions.

Joel Benenson, chief pollster and senior strategist for President Barack Obama, expressed similar sentiments about the role of pollsters working for the president:[16]

Our job isn't to tell [the president] what to do. Our job is to help him figure out if he can strengthen his message and persuade more people to his side. The starting point is where he is and then you try to help strengthen the message and his reasons for doing something.

Polling is most often used to help market policy proposals that have already been developed. It empowers the president to bring a policy to fruition by testing public reactions to key phrases and expressions used in public pronouncements and speeches, highlighting what the public understands and might misinterpret, and helping the president frame a chosen policy in ways that resonate with the public. In 1997, at the request of the president and the vice president, the DPC and the NEC began developing ideas to address the issue of urban sprawl. The working group produced a range of ideas. One proposal that was developed was the Better America Bond program. Under this proposal, the Treasury Department would authorize state and local communities to issue bonds, the proceeds of which would be used to purchase open spaces, park land, and to clean up so-called brownfields—contaminated former industrial sites.

After developing the proposal, the idea was evaluated by the president's pollster Mark Penn. Penn included questions about the basic idea, to provide communities with funds to purchase open spaces to save for future generations, in one of his weekly surveys. His firm also tested potential names for the program. The polling data found at least 70 percent support for the basic idea. "Better America Bonds" was the name chosen over "Green Bonds" and "Better

---

16. Michael D. Shear, "Polling Helps Obama Frame Message in Health-Care Debate: Data Shape Fight Against Insurers," *Washington Post* (July 31, 2009), http://www.washingtonpost.com/wp-dyn/content/article/2009/07/30/AR2009073001547.html.

Community Bonds." In this case, the polling data provided additional support for sending the Better America Bond legislation to Congress. Polling was also used to help decide how to "spin" or market the proposal.

Of course, polling does not end when the policy proposal is sent to Congress or an executive order is issued. If a proposal is in play—if, for example, the idea is being debated by a congressional committee—then polling will continue to see whether public opinion has been altered by the congressional debate.

> *Criticism:* Presidents are constantly campaigning.

> *Rebuttal:* There is a big difference in the role of a pollster during a campaign and once the campaign is over. As Joel Benenson argues: [17]

> When you're in a campaign, there are a lot of moving strategic pieces. You have one Election Day and your job is to get to 51 percent of the vote. When you're working for an office holder, on the other hand, your focus becomes whatever their focus is. . . . Whether you're debating immigration or tax policy, deficits or gun control issues, you have to have a clear argument. You need to find the most persuasive argument you can make to get the greatest number of people to agree with you. So it becomes . . . proactive in a different way. You have different goals and . . . how you define winning changes. You're not focused on 51 percent on Election Day anymore. Outside a campaign, winning is ultimately about persuading the greatest number of people to your side of the argument.

The White House often uses polling to identify the relationship between the presidential favorability ratings and particular policies or political issues. Box 10-1 lists such a chart compiled by White House consultant Dick Morris. Many of the issues and related policies, like welfare-to-work, were first raised by Clinton's 1992 presidential campaign committee and then were refined by the policy development staff in the White House. They were then tested against the president's popularity ratings.

---

17. Matthew Smith, "Polling and Policy: Pollster Joel Benenson Discusses the Role of Polling in Setting Presidential Agendas," *Chicago Policy Review* (April 15, 2013), http://chicagopoli cyreview.org/2013/04/15/polling-and-policy-pollster-joel-benenson-discusses-the-role-of-polling-in-setting-presidential-agendas.

| BOX 10-1 | 1992 Campaign Poll |

Issues for President's Speech, Train Trip, Gore Speech

In this poll, we ranked every issue we are thinking of using by their likelihood of making people vote for Clinton and then tested them for their feasibility in accomplishing their goals. The numbers indicate percentage of respondents that chose *more likely* [and] the percentage of those that chose *less likely*.

These 44 proposals all test above 60% and all but two test with feasibility over 50%.

Issue	Likelihood of support for Clinton	Feasibility
Welfare to work	80–17	51–43 (cumulative)
Welfare/work in neighborhoods	79–20	51–43 (cumulative)
College tax credit	78–28	75–20
Cop killer bullet ban	78–18	70–24
Track sex crimes	76–20	68–24
No guns for felons	74–23	57–40
Clean drinking water	74–21	68–26 (cumulative)
Enviro crimes/lien	73–22	64–30 (cumulative)
Adult college tax credit	73–24	77–18
Trigger locks	72–23	68–27
100,000 cops	72–23	71–24
3 hours educational TV	72–22	76–21
Enviro right to know	72–24	70–25 (cumulative)
Ban racial preference in adoption	72–19	76–16
75% cleanup toxic waste	71–25	54–45
Welfare employee tax credit	71–25	51–43 (cumulative)
Education savings bonds	71–22	68–26
IRS deadbeat dads	71–27	74–21
School health clinics meet	medical needs of kids	70–28
State standardized test for promotion	68–27	70–26

(Continued)

(Continued)

Issue	Likelihood of support for Clinton	Feasibility
No tax deductions for deadbeat dads	72–22	69–28
Brady bill dom violence misdems	68–27	57–36
State standardized test graduation	68–28	71–22
Fed govt. standardized test/ promotion	68–29	74–21
Welfare/placement bonus	68–27	51–43 (cumulative)
No guns under 21	68–24	53–43
Iran/Libya sanctions	68–25	49–45
50,000 literacy teachers	67–31	73–23
Welfare-staffed child care	67–30	51–43
HMO notification/alt treatment	67–26	
TV family hour	65–26	68–25
6 yr bal budget plan	65–29	61–33
Violence on kids TV	64–28	71–25
Ban cig ads at kids	64–31	59–36
Mandatory adoption if abuse	64–26	66–26
Targeted tax cuts	64–26	62–30
Health Ins for Unemployed	63–33	
No firing of HMO Doctor	63–26	
Penalize drug countries	62–31	44–48
Teen gangs RICO	61–33	50–43
No cap gains on home sale	61–33	50–43
Adopt after 1 year foster care	60–27	68–24
Ban meth (drug)	58–33	52–34

Source: Dick Morris, *Behind the Oval Office* (Los Angeles, CA: Renaissance Books 1999), pp. 627–628.

Criticism: Pollsters manipulate data.

Rebuttal: Unquestionably, pollsters can alter survey results by changing the way that questions are asked and polls are conducted. Indeed, there are many intentional and unintentional ways that polling can be biased. In practice, however, intentional manipulation of polls by professional pollsters is more limited than one might imagine. Why? In short, manipulating polls is bad for business.

A pollster who is continually tilting questions or the interpretation of the responses to achieve results that he or she wants to see (or believes that his or her clients want to see) will soon be viewed as unreliable and ineffective. Biasing results denies policymakers the information that makes polling such a powerful tool. Rather than enhancing the policymaking process and empowering decision makers, biased polling can misdirect decision makers and undermine the policymaking process by encouraging them to promote unpopular or unsupported policies. As a result, regardless of their particular viewpoints or the answer they "want" the results to support, politicians quickly lose patience with pollsters whose data or analyses they believe are inaccurate or misleading.

In addition, biased polling opens politicians to criticisms that they are trying to shape public opinion, hide bad information from the public, are being deceptive, or worse, that they are disconnected from the world their constituents live in. Regardless of who is right or wrong, raising such concerns is often counterproductive and costly.

Benenson sums up the value of polling and the danger of doing it poorly as follows:[18]

> You have to understand what is beneath the surface that is shaping the opinions, beliefs, and attitudes of the American voters to persuade them. So you have to consider both policy and politics; you have to look through the voter's prism, from their perspective, to understand them. You're not going to persuade them if you're not addressing what they're bringing to the table. So you poll with both in mind, and try not only to take the public's temperature, but to really understand their opinions on some deeper level. You can do that by asking meaningful questions and trying to quantify the

18. Smith, "Polling and Policy."

answers, but you have to be sure that what you learned quantitatively is backed up by accurate data analysis. Your most persuasive arguments should be well informed by that.

Criticism: Polling has become a substitute for leadership.

Rebuttal: Certainly some politicians shift their policy positions when polls indicate that those positions are no longer supported. Responding to polling data does not, however, necessarily reflect a lack of leadership. Nearly all politicians use polling data to evaluate their policy decisions and most, appropriately, weigh public opinion in their analysis of the policy's success. More than an evaluation tool, however, polling can be used to promote and empower leadership. The best politicians use polling to help them sell ideas they believe are in the best interest of the country. Polling is most effective when used as a way to market positions already taken both to the public at large and to critics in the policymaking process itself. In his book, *Behind the Oval Office,* Dick Morris points out that President Clinton used polling to support positions he believed were right for the country, but unpopular:[19]

Clinton had decided to oppose a constitutional amendment to allow school prayer, but polls showed that the public supported the amendment. Deadlock? No. Our polling identified the specific religion, spiritual, and moral activities the public wanted in schools, activities that had been subsumed under the rubric of "school prayer." But we found that prayer itself was not that high on the list: people really wanted schools to teach values, ethics, and morals. Armed with this information, Clinton explained that the First Amendment did not limit the teaching of any of these subjects and that there was no justification for tinkering with it. The demand of school prayer abated.

In an interview at the *Chicago Policy Review,* Obama pollster Joel Benenson argues that the job of a pollster working for sitting policymakers is to build support for the positions they choose:[20]

---

19. Dick Morris, *Behind the Oval Office* (Los Angeles, CA: Renaissance Books 1999), p. 338.
20. Smith, "Polling and Policy."

I'll never tell anybody what position to take on an issue; that's their decision. My job as the pollster is to tell them how to persuade the greatest number of people to their side of the argument . . . Whether you're debating immigration or tax policy, deficits or gun control issues, you have to have a clear argument. You need to find the most persuasive argument you can to get the greatest number of people to agree with you.

POLLING BASICS

Polling is an important and useful tool of policymaking. At a minimum, it democratizes the policymaking process by providing policymakers with a source of information about the views of the public at large while giving the public a de facto means of bolstering support for popular initiatives and undermining support for unpopular ones; it enables policymakers to test new ideas and determine how best to market them; and it can enhance political leadership on popular issues by giving the executive branch an additional justification for promoting widely supported proposals. The beauty of polling is that by sampling a small number of randomly chosen citizens, a well-designed survey can provide a good approximation of the general public's likely response to a potential policy initiative or their likely choice in an upcoming election. Polls can be captivating, and the statistics, graphs, tables, and charts created from them can appear authoritative and compelling—yet they can also be deceptive.

In order to use polls effectively, it is important to know their strengths and limitations. The bottom line is that polls and the statistics they generate can never speak for themselves, and two equally intelligent and honest people can legitimately interpret the same polling questions and the survey results they generate differently. The phrasing of a polling question, the people being asked to answer the questions, and the techniques used in analyzing and presenting the results can all affect how the results are interpreted and, consequently, how they are used.

Does this suggest that all surveys yield "Lies, Damn Lies, and Statistics"?[21] No. But it does suggest that polls and the statistics they produce are powerful tools that can easily be misused. To gain the most out of using them and to

---

21. See Darrell Huff, *How to Lie With Statistics* (New York, NY: W. W. Norton, 1982).

avoid being seduced or misdirected by them, it is important to identify what you want to know. Then follow four simple guidelines:[22]

1. Ask the right questions;
2. Ask the right people;
3. Use the right techniques to analyze the results;
4. Interpret and present the results effectively.

To begin with, pollsters must ask the right questions. The way that questions are phrased and the context in which they are asked can have a profound impact on how people interpret and respond to them. For example, one of the most important policy issues in the 2000 presidential election involved the role of government, with claims and counterclaims exchanged regarding the dangers of "big government" versus the benefits of "smaller government" and putting power in the hands of "the people." Polls regarding the public's impression of Vice President Gore's and Governor Bush's policies on the role of the government varied considerably, depending how the question was asked. ABC News results showed, for example, that Governor Bush had a big edge in "holding down the size of government"—but that likely voters by a 2–1 margin said "providing needed services" is more important.[23] Asking the "right" questions means asking questions that are valid—that is, do the questions address the specific issue you are interested in? The results of the ABC News poll suggest that although the public supported Bush's anti–"big government" initiative, it did not support a reduction in government-provided services. This type of nuance would not be clear if the survey only asked people whether they supported Bush's plan to reduce "big government." A **valid question** is one that unambiguously refers to the specific issue that the pollster wants to evaluate. It is important to recognize that any single policy may have multiple social, political, or economic dimensions to it. As a consequence, no single question will be able to provide a valid

---

22. A variety of useful sources provide information on polling and statistical analyses. These include "About Polling," www.publicagenda.org/aboutpubopinion/aboutpubop1.htm; Earl Babbie, *The Practice of Social Research* (Belmont, CA: Wadsworth, 1995); Damodar Gujarati, *Basic Econometrics* (New York, NY: McGraw-Hill, 1995); David Freedman, Robert Pisani, and Roger Purves, *Statistics* (New York, NY: W. W. Norton, 1998); Jeffrey Katzer, Kenneth Cook, and Wayne Crouch, *Evaluating Information: A Guide for Users of Social Science Research* (Reading, MA: Addison-Wesley, 1998); and G. King, R. O. Keohane, and S. Verba, *Designing Social Inquiry* (Princeton University Press, 1994).

23. See *ABC News*, http://www.abcnews.go.com/sections/politics/DailyNews/trackingpoll_001025.html.

indication of public opinion on all of those dimensions. Instead, one must ask a number of questions focused on the various dimensions of a policy to get a clear picture of the public perception of the policy as a whole.

The right question must also be reliable. A **reliable question** is one that is asked in a way that is likely to be interpreted similarly by people with different backgrounds, at different times, and in different contexts. Will "big government" be interpreted differently by teenagers who do not rely heavily on government services than by elderly people on Medicare? A reliable question is one that is likely to be interpreted the same way regardless of who is responding the survey and when. Unfortunately, this may be more difficult than it first appears because voters' responses are also often affected by events outside of the survey itself, such as their most recent experiences or the last thing they heard about a particular issue. For example, polls taken after major news events can be distorted. As a consequence, it would be a mistake to interpret a poll on public support for gun control taken the day after a gun shooting at a school as a good indicator of general public support for gun control. In order to increase their reliability, polls are often taken over several days. Polls conducted during the week generally produce more representative samples than those conducted over weekends, when many people are not at home. A single-night poll, say one that occurs on Thursday, is less representative of the voting population because it misses everyone who works on Thursday night.

In addition to misinterpreting the meaning of a question, a respondent's answer can be affected by how or when a question is asked. If, for example, a poll asks if you agree or disagree with a plan to reduce aid for textbooks for school children, few would concur. But if a poll asks if you agree or disagree with a plan to shift money from textbooks to computers, the response might be different. How questions are ordered can also impact the results of a poll. For example, people are more likely to respond positively to a question regarding increased government spending on public services if the question preceding it on the survey asked them who should get the most credit for eight years of growth and rising national incomes, than they are if the question preceding it on the survey asked them to evaluate new tax policy. Effective pollsters can lead or avoid leading respondents to particular answers by altering the wording or the order of the questions asked. If this is a concern, multiple polls are conducted using slightly different questions or with the questions in a different order to test for this type of bias.

Once valid and reliable variables are chosen and your survey is designed to avoid potential unintended biases, it is important to ask the "right" people to answer the questions.[24] One of the great strengths of surveys is the ability of the pollsters to infer what the "American people" think about a particular set of issues by surveying a small sample of them. Due to the beauty of **statistical inference**, a small sample of people can provide a reasonably accurate picture of a population of several tens of millions. The key to this capability, however, rests on the ability of the pollster to select the survey respondents randomly. To be randomly selected, everyone in the population must have an equal or known non-zero probability of being chosen as a potential respondent. If the distribution of people in the sample reflects—or can be weighted to reflect—the distribution of people in the population at large, then variations in responses within the sample will tend to parallel those in the population at large. This remarkable phenomenon is known as the **central limit theorem**. With this in mind, polling "the American public" means that people from urban neighborhoods in North Philadelphia must have an equal chance of being selected as those from Ames, Iowa, or Corpus Christi, Texas. If people in all of these areas do not have an equal chance of being chosen, but it is possible to determine the probability that they would be missed, then the survey results can be weighted accordingly so that their views are given the weight that they would have had if they were all counted. If everyone in the population does not have an equal or known probability of being selected for a poll, then the sample is not considered to be a **random sample** and will be biased—that is, its results will reflect the distribution of people who responded to the poll but will not reflect those of the overall population of the United States.

One common polling technique is to have a computer randomly dial telephone numbers of potential respondents. This works fairly well in randomly selecting people with telephones, but it will tend to reflect the views of people with more than one phone more heavily than those who have only one or those who do not have access to a phone of their own. To correct for this problem, the results of telephone surveys should be weighted so that the responses from households with multiple phones are discounted proportionately based on the increased probability that they would be selected for the survey.[25]

In addition to polling the entire country, policymakers are often interested in distinct subsets of the American population. For example, because currently registered voters are more likely to vote in upcoming elections than unregistered

24. For a good review of the practice of using surveys and the problems of sampling, see Freedman et al., *Statistics*, pp. 333–437.

25. Freedman et al., *Statistics*, pp. 346–348.

voters, policymakers may be particularly interested in finding out what registered voters think about a particular policy initiative. If all registered voters had an equal chance of being polled or a known likelihood of being excluded, then the sample of respondents could be considered random, and inferences about all registered voters could be made from the results of the sample. Such a survey would, however, provide no information about what non-registered voters think about the issues at hand. Focused surveys like this can be taken for groups designated by race, gender, religion, income level, union membership, party affiliation, or any other common characteristic that can be used to identify the group one is interested in. For purposes of cost or efficiency, pollsters use different kinds of random sampling techniques, including simple random samples, stratified random samples, clustered random samples, and even multistage sampling, which combines two or more of the other strategies. Each represents a variety of random or probability samples.[26]

Generally, the greater the sample size, the more likely the results from the poll will accurately reflect the views of the public at large. All polls have a sampling error. The sampling error is a measure of how likely it is the poll actually reflects public opinion. Increasing sample size can help reduce the error. The bigger the sample, the smaller the error, but once you get past a certain point—say, a sample size of 800 or 1,000—the improvement is very small. The results of a survey of 300 people will likely be correct within 6 percentage points, while a survey of 1,000 will be correct within 3 percentage points. But that is where the dramatic differences end. When a sample is increased to 2,000 respondents, the error drops only slightly, to 2 percentage points.[27]

In addition to reporting the statistical significance of particular survey results, polling results are often presented with a **confidence interval** to give an indication of their accuracy. For example, polling statistics may report that 59 percent of the American public supports tougher gun control, with a 95 percent confidence interval of plus or minus 3 percent. The confidence interval reflects the degree of confidence that the survey results reflect those in the broader population. The results found that 59 percent of the respondents in the survey support tougher gun control, but that the actual number in the population at

---

26. Jeffrey Katzer, Kenneth Cook, and Wayne Crouch, *Evaluating Information: A Guide for Users of Social Science Research*, 3rd edition (New York, NY: McGraw-Hill, 1991), p. 180, and, more generally, pp. 175–187.

27. For a review of polling and statistical sampling, see "About Polling," http://www.publicagenda.org/aboutpubopinion/aboutpubop1.htm, and Freedman et al., *Statistics*, pp. 333–437; as well as the literature cited in note 4 in this chapter.

large is unlikely to be exactly 59 percent. To compensate, the research provides a confidence interval around the result. If pollsters ran the survey a second time, the results would differ slightly because the composition of respondents to the survey would be slightly different. If the survey was repeated multiple additional times and a 95 percent confidence interval was estimated each time, 95 percent of the confidence intervals would contain the actual level of support in the population at large.[28] Consequently, estimating a confidence interval provides an indication of the pollster's confidence that survey results reflect the attitudes of the population at large.

The second commonly used type of polling is known as the **focus group** or **dial group**. A focus or dial group is a group of individuals with specific similar characteristics who are asked to view or listen to a speech, commercial, or policy statement while holding an opinion "dial," which allows the participants to state the degree of approval or disapproval of certain phrases, words, or proposals. The information is then analyzed to identify the degree of approval or disapproval of the material that is being tested.[29] For example, when figuring out how best to frame its response to the financial crisis of 2008, the Obama administration reportedly used this method to find out that the public responded more favorably when its economy-enhancing policies were referred to as "recovery" or "reinvestment" policies rather than as part of a "stimulus" program.[30] Like a targeted sample, polls taken from a focus group will be biased toward the feelings of a particular group rather than the general public. As a result, generalizations based on the polling results will be biased in favor of the opinions of the specific focus group and may not reflect those of the larger subset of the population they are intended to represent.

A third commonly used technique is the **mall intercept method**. In this approach, space is set up at mall, shopping center, or storefront. Passers-by are asked to review clips of speeches, commercials, or rebuttals to ads or attack statements. The viewing is followed by a questionnaire in which opinions are solicited and evaluated by the consultants.[31] Although potentially useful, this

---

28. For a detailed discussion of confidence intervals, see David M. Lane, "Confidence Intervals Introduction," *Statistics Education: An Interactive Multimedia Course of Study,* University of Houston Clear Lake and Tufts University, http://onlinestatbook.com/2/estimation/confidence.html.

29. Katzer et al., *Evaluating Information* 3rd ed., p. 215.

30. Smith, "Meet Obama's Pollsters."

31. Patterson, "The White House Staff," p. 215.

technique is the least accurate of the three discussed. Its respondents may appear to be "random" to the extent that they are not chosen by the interviewer, but it is not truly random because only people shopping at the mall who walk past the interviewer have a chance of being selected. As a consequence, the results from such a poll will be biased and will tend to reflect the views of a narrow set of people who likely have the average income of the people in the shopping center and who like to shop at the time of day and at the location where the interview took place. Such a sample is not scientific because it suffers from multiple biases that make its findings highly suspect.

Once the sample has been chosen and the polls taken, it is important that the analyst uses the appropriate techniques for analyzing and interpreting the data. Although our goal here is not to introduce and evaluate different statistical measures of association or the concept of statistical significance, it is vitally important that all consumers of polling data recognize that regardless of how definitive the results look, they are approximations. Equally important, even if the results are very precise and show a strong, positive, and statistically significant relationship between two variables, the statistical result does not "prove" that the two variables are causally related. It merely shows that for whatever reasons (and there may be several), variations in the two variables coincide with one another. For example, although religion, race, and party identification are often highly correlated, one's religion does not determine one's race, and neither religion nor race determines one's political party identification. Cause and effect, like beauty, are in the eye of the beholder.

Finally, once the data have been analyzed, they must be presented to be useful. Presentation matters. Simple techniques such as changing the scale on the side of a graph can make small changes in trends look dramatic or large changes in trends look insignificant. Big bullet points and colorful graphs grab people's attention and can easily direct them toward (or away from) the issues at hand. Masters of presentation, like Ross Perot, can effectively use graphs and tables to give the sense of authority and decisiveness in response to complex and nuanced problems. Once the table or graph is presented, the audience will focus on it—not on where it came from, whether it was the best or most appropriate means for presenting the results, or whether it really gets to the heart of the problem or left out something important.[32] Box 10-2 lists the ten steps that result in a good poll.

---

32. "About Polling" provides a useful reference for people interested in conducting polls. http://www.publicagenda.org/aboutpubopinion/aboutpubop1.htm.

BOX 10-2	Ten Steps to Making a Good Poll

1. **Ask the right questions.** Be sure that the questions asked are valid so that they ask about precisely what you want to know, and reliable and nonleading so that different people at different times will interpret the question the same way. How the questions are worded is key. The wording of questions can affect a response. For example, if a poll asks whether you agree or disagree with a plan to reduce aid for textbooks for school children, few would concur. But if a poll asks whether you agree or disagree with a plan to shift money from textbooks to computers, the response might be different.

2. **Order the questions correctly.** How questions are ordered can impact the results of a poll. If you ask, for example, whether you support tax cuts and then ask a question about a spending proposal, you might impact the results of the poll.

3. **Time the polling well.** The most reliable polls are taken over several days. Polls conducted during the week generally produce more representative samples than those conducted over weekends, when many people are not at home. A single-night poll, say one that occurs on Thursday, is less representative of the voting population because it misses everyone who works on Thursday night.

4. **Check the evening news.** Check to see what events are occurring during the polling. Voter's responses often are based on the last thing they hear reported about the campaigns. Polls taken after major news events can be distorted. For example, a poll on gun control taken right after a gun shooting at a school might be distorted.

5. **Ask the right people.** If and only if people from the population are selected randomly, such that everyone in the population has an equal or known probability of being interviewed, can the responses of everyone in the population be inferred from the results of a poll of a small sample of that population. If not, the results will be biased in favor of those who were included in the sample. The samples in some "quickie" polls that are conducted overnight and surveys in which people vote on the Internet, such as Dick Morris's "Vote.com," are neither random nor necessarily representative of the voting population.

6. **Ask enough people.** Generally, the greater the sample size, the more likely the results accurately reflect the views of the public at large. As we mentioned earlier, good national samples should consist of at least 1,000 individuals.

7. **Identify the respondents.** Who is included in the sample? Is the poll surveying all adults, registered voters, likely voters, urban dwellers, or suburbanites? Politicians are often most interested in the opinions of likely voters because only about a half of all adults and two-thirds of registered voters actually cast ballots in presidential races. Regardless of the subset of the population one is interested in, everyone in that group must have an equal chance of being chosen to take the poll. If not the results will be biased and invalid.

(Continued)

8. **Use the appropriate techniques to analyze the results**. Standards of statistical analyses should be followed and maintained at all times to minimize biases in the data and misinterpretation of the results.

9. **Estimate an acceptable confidence interval.** All polls have sampling errors. Estimating a confidence interval around the data provides a good assessment of the accuracy of the data.

10. **Interpret and present the results effectively.** The results should be presented in an easily assessable manner that highlights their implications for the policy issues at hand.

WHO POLLS FOR THE WHITE HOUSE?

Contrary to popular belief, there is no official pollster within the White House. In fact, it is the national political parties—the Democratic National Committee (DNC) and the Republican National Committee (RNC)—who hire the pollsters that work for the president. These pollsters are paid by dollars raised from DNC or RNC supporters, not taxpayer funds. Consequently, scholars often estimate the amount of polling in the executive branch by tracking the amount of money on polling that the DNC and RNC report to the Federal Election Commission.[33] Because the president is the head of his or her respective national party, he or she chooses which pollster works for DNC or the RNC. Thus, in effect, the pollster works for the president but not the White House. The president, in turn, may interact with the pollster through an intermediary. In the George W. Bush White House, Karl Rove, senior adviser, deputy chief of staff, and the director of the Office of Strategic Initiatives, and Matthew Dowb, senior adviser for the RNC in 2002 and chief strategist for the Bush re-election campaign in 2004, served as the points of contact for pollsters Jan van Lohuizen and Fred Steeper.[34] In the Obama White House, David Axelrod, senior adviser to the president, maintained regular contact with pollsters and collected their findings for the president.[35] In the prelude to the 2012 elections, David Simas, assistant to the president and strategic director

---

33. For total annual payments to White House pollsters for survey research only from 1977 through 2000, see Murray and Howard, "Variation in White House Polling Operations," pp. 554–555. For expenditures by the DNC and RNC since 2000 to specific polling organizations, see the Center for Responsive Politics, http://www.opensecrets.org/parties/expend.php.

34. Tenpas, "Words vs. Deeds," pp. 32–35.

35. Smith, "Meet Obama's Pollsters."

of the White House Office of Political Strategy and Research, assumed this role. Simas managed multiple pollsters for president Obama:[36]

- John Anzalone and Jeff Liszt, Anzalone Liszt Research
- Joel Benenson, Benenson Strategy Group
- David Binder, David Binder Research
- Cornell Belcher, Brilliant Corners Research & Strategies
- Diane Feldman, The Feldman Group
- Lisa Grove, Grove Strategic Insight
- Paul Harstad, Harstad Strategic Research

The pollster is a political consultant and not a government official. Therefore, his or her interaction with White House staff is limited and controlled by ethics laws. For example, political meetings can only be held in a few designated areas within the White House complex: the family residence atop the White House; the ceremonial office of the vice president in the Eisenhower Executive Office Building; and the Ward Room located in the basement of the West Wing, next to the White House Mess and around the corner from the Situation Room. The Ward Room is one of the few places where political meetings can take place. Polling questions are crafted by employees of the polling firm rather than the White House. However, White House staffers talk often with pollsters when they are preparing the questions to make certain that the questions are factually correct.

The reason for the legal separation of pollsters from the White House lies in the Hatch Act of 1939.[37] The Hatch Act was designed to "ensure that federal programs are administered in a nonpartisan fashion, to protect federal employees from political coercion in the workplace, and to ensure that federal employees are advanced based on merit and not based on political affiliation."[38] On December 28, 2012, President Obama signed S. 2170, the Hatch Act Modernization Act of 2012, into law.[39] This revision modified penalties under the Hatch Act and clarified its

---

36. Chris Cillizza, "Inside President Obama's Campaign Team." *Washington* Post (August 8, 2012), http://www.washingtonpost.com/blogs/the-fix/post/president-obama-settles-on-campaign-team/2012/08/08/6fa3c9a0-e181-11e1-a25e-15067bb31849_blog.html. For a review of David Simas, see Michael Shear, "Obama's New Political Chief Tries to Reassure Democrats," *New York Times* (March 1, 2014), http://www.nytimes.com/2014/03/02/us/politics/obamas-new-political-chief-tries-to-reassure-democrats.html.

37. Scott Blocht, "The Judgment of History: Faction: Political Machines, and the Hatch Act," *University of Pennsylvania Journal of Labor and Employment Law* 72, 2 (2005), pp. 225–277.

38. United States Office of Special Council. https://osc.gov/pages/hatchact.aspx.

39. White House Office of the Press Secretary, December 28, 2012, https://www.whitehouse.

applicability to state and local governments. One of the core implications of the Hatch Act is that it limits the ability of employees in the executive branch—other than a few designated persons including the president and vice president—from engaging in political activities. Disputes about potential violations of these restrictions are managed through the United States Office of Special Counsel.[40]

Within the White House, the Office of Political Affairs has traditionally served as the principal point of contact for pollsters and the political consultants. In January of 2011, President Obama closed the OPA. He shifted responsibility for the presidential re-election campaign to new headquarters in Chicago and relocated deputies in the OPA to the Democratic National Committee.[41] Within the White House, David Plouffe was brought in to serve with Valerie Jarrett as senior adviser to the president and assistant to the president for public engagement and intergovernmental affairs, as one of the president's chief strategists.[42] In January of 2014, President Obama reinstituted OPA. Under the direction of Assistant to the President David Simas, the Office of Political Strategy and Outreach (OPSO) is also intended to "provide the president and senior staff with information about the political environment to help advance the president's agenda and coordinates constituent outreach efforts on behalf of the president."[43] It was designed to signal the importance that the president placed on the election of fellow Democrats by serving as the "one-stop shop for all things midterms."[44]

In contrast to the pollsters and related political consultants, the OPSO is like all members of the White House staff. People working in the OPSO are federal employees and are subject to ethics, conflict of interest, and financial disclosure rules.[45] Nonetheless, concern about the overlap of electoral politics

---

gov/the-press-office/2012/12/28/statement-press-secretary-hj-res-122-hr-3477-hr-3783-hr-3870-hr-3912-hr- (Accessed May 29, 2015).

40. United States Office of Special Counsel, https://osc.gov/.

41. Jeff Zeleny, "Obama Will Move Political Operations to Chicago," *International New York Times* (January 20, 2011), http://www.nytimes.com/2011/01/21/us/politics/21obama.html.

42. Chris Good, "David Plouffe: The Man Who Will Re-Make the White House," *The Atlantic* (January 27, 2011), http://www.theatlantic.com/politics/archive/2011/01/david-plouffe-the-man-who-will-re-make-the-white-house/70368/; John Heilemann, "The West Wing, Season II," *New York Times* (January 23, 2011), http://nymag.com/news/politics/70829/.

43. The White House, https://www.whitehouse.gov/about/internships/departments.

44. Edward-Isaac Douvere, "White House to Launch New Political Office," POLITICO (January 24, 2014), http://www.politico.com/story/2014/01/white-house-office-of-political-strategy-outreach-102582.html.

45. Patterson, "The White House Staff," p. 205.

and policymaking in the executive branch are commonly raised. Early in 2014, for example, Representative Darrell Issa (R-CA) complained that the OPSO was acting as a campaign arm of the Democratic Party. After an investigation, the allegations were dismissed. U.S. Special Counsel Carolyn Lerner argued in July of 2014,[46]

> It appears that the White House adhered to OSC guidance in determining the scope of activity for OPSO. To the extent that OPSO's activities are limited to those described in the White House correspondence, OPSO appears to be operating in a manner that is consistent with Hatch Act restrictions.

The Hatch Act has been legislatively revised and upheld by the Supreme Court multiple times. It has also repeatedly addressed complaints against Republican and Democratic candidates in local, state, and national elections.[47] Consequently, the balancing act of polling as a tool for winning elections and promoting the policymaking process of sitting presidents continues.

CONCLUSION

Presidents often attempt to distance themselves from pollsters and downplay their use of polling. These actions hide the fact that polling plays a central role in getting the president elected and helping him or her lead and manage the policymaking process once in office. As reflected in spending on pollsters reported to the Federal Election Commission by the Democratic and Republican National Committees, polling is used extensively in the modern executive branch. Presidents, like George H. W. Bush, who do not take advantage of the insights about the public's values and sentiments that polling provides operate with an unnecessary informational constraint. Most important, polling provides an essential conduit and channel for those opinions to be heard and thereby enables the executive branch to respond to public demands and recognize a need to educate the public on its activities. This enhances both the democratic process and the ability of the executive branch to be responsive to public concerns.

---

46. Loren French, "Watchdog Clears White House of Hatch Act Violations," POLITICO (July 24, 2014), http://www.politico.com/story/2014/07/white-house-hatch-act-109364.html#ixzz3X8bUe6uX.

47. Blocht, "The Judgment of History," pp. 225–277.

In summary, polling can be used to test the public's receptiveness to particular policy proposals. Once the proposals have been implemented, polling can be used to test the public's awareness of the links between various policy initiatives and its economic, political, and social well-being. By doing so, polling helps policy makers determine how to best market the policies and inform the public of these benefits. In addition, polling helps keep executive branch and Congress informed about public values and sentiments. Consequently, it makes the policymaking process more responsive to the concerns of their multiple constituents. By providing these functions, polling can add legitimacy to the policymaking process in the executive branch, making it more efficient, more effective, and more likely to be supported by decision makers in Congress and the public at large.

Key Terms

Central limit theorem

Confidence interval

Dial group

Focus group

Mall intercept method

Random sample

Reliable question

Statistical inference

Valid question

Review Questions

1. Name four guidelines that pollsters should follow.
2. What is a dial or focus group? How does this commonly used polling technique differ from the mall intercept and random dial methods? What are the strengths and limitations of these techniques?
3. What are the ten steps to conducting a useful poll?
4. Who drafts polling questions for the White House?
5. At what points in the policymaking process is it useful to take polls? Why?

COMMUNICATING AND MARKETING POLICY

THE IMPORTANCE OF COMMUNICATING AND MARKETING POLICY

Throughout the policymaking process, and particularly once the policy proposal is near completion, it is critical to communicate and market the policy initiative to policymakers outside of the executive branch and to the public at large. A policy proposal that fails to gain the public's attention or fails to convince the public of its merits cannot be sustained over the long term. Ironically, the advent of the Internet and 24-hour coverage of political events by the media has increased, rather than decreased, the importance of clear and effective communication and marketing of government policies to the public. The increase in the availability of instantaneous information has raised the public's awareness of political issues, but it also has dramatically increased the likelihood that the public will be bombarded by a cacophony of disparate bits of information that can easily be misunderstood. In the face of an information overload, people unconsciously tend to relate new information to their preconceived notions of what they expect to see (**cognitive bias**) or what they want to see (**motivated bias**).[1] In such circumstances sound bites can be very appealing, though they are also easily misinterpreted. Furthermore, if people fail to see the relevance of a particular policy to their own needs, they may lose interest and ignore the new information all together. If this happens, public support for a particular policy proposal will remain weak. To gain public and congressional support, policymakers must

---

1. For a discussion of the impact of cognitive and motivated biases on perceptions and decision making, see Robert Jervis, Richard Ned Lebow, and Janice Gross Stein, *Psychology and Deterrence* (Baltimore, MD: Johns Hopkins University Press, 1985), pp 18–33.

provide a clear and persuasive means to interpret the policy under consideration and recognize its merits and deficiencies. If that support does not materialize, the policy will not likely gain the legitimacy needed for successful implementation.

In this chapter, we analyze several of the most important tools that policymakers use to communicate and market policy proposals. These include fact sheets and press sheets, question and answer documents, and speeches. We will focus on how these materials are written and when and why these tools are used. We will also specify how policymakers interact with the three offices situated in the White House and the other federal agencies that are responsible for managing the press and directing and implementing a communications strategy. The relevant White House offices are the Speechwriting Office, the Communications Office, and the Press Office.

- The Speechwriting Office is charged with preparing all remarks, radio addresses, and public speeches for the presidents or agency heads. It alone produces approximately 2,500 pages of public statements each year.
- The Communications Office is responsible for developing a media strategy that emphasizes the policy and legislative strategies of each executive agency involved in the policy process.
- The Press Office is responsible for day-to-day contact with the media, including the management of press logistics and scheduling and the provision of immediate answers to real-time questions or concerns.

Policymakers in the White House and federal agencies interact with all three offices on a daily, and sometimes hourly, basis. The relationship between policymakers and these offices is occasionally adversarial, often complex, and always important.

The hierarchy among these offices changes from administration to administration. Some administrations elevated both the Press and Communications Office to the same level, with each reporting to the chief of staff. Others have positioned Communications on top and had Press and Speechwriting report to the communications director. The Obama administration adopted such a model, but also gave the press secretary direct access to the president and his chief of staff, thus complicating the lines of authority (see Box 11-1). This contrasts to the Bush administration prior to the arrival of Tony Snow, which subjugated the Press Office under Communications.

BOX 11-1	**Structure of Obama White House Communications and Press Operations**

Office of Communications
Office of the Press Secretary
Media Affairs
Research
Speechwriting
Office of Digital Strategy

Some argue that good policies speak for themselves. Others believe that effective marketing can sell any policy, good or bad. We argue that the truth lies somewhere in between. A good policy that cannot be articulated in an accessible manner is not likely to gain wide support. That is why it is important that policymakers keep in mind how they will market their ideas throughout the policymaking process.

SPEECHWRITING

Before the advent of the Internet and 24-hour cable news, the speech was the primary tool by which leaders conveyed a policy to the public. These modern venues are very good sources of raw information about a policy initiative; however, speeches remain unique and important tools to communicate with the public because they provide a forum for policymakers to present, explain, and market a policy to a focused audience. For example, speeches are often used to frame debates at the start of a policy campaign. They enable policymakers to set the agenda for the discussion against which their opponents will have to fight. The first public speech on a particular issue is like a shot across the bow of other ships in the policy arena. If a policy speech is not successful, it can set back an effort to pass legislation, open up criticism on a proposed regulation or executive order.

The relationship between speechwriting and policymaking is complicated yet complementary. Speechwriters are the translators of the intricacies of policies to the public, yet speechwriters do not participate formally in the policymaking process and they often disdain the involvement of policy staff in the writing of speeches. Typically the policymaking staff provides a summary of the policy to the speechwriters before a speech is written, yet policy speeches generally contain only a few lines of detailed information about the policy itself. Based on the policy summary, the speechwriters will produce a draft about three days before the actual speech (one exception to this time frame is the State of the Union address where speechwriters begin working on a first draft weeks ahead of the address). After the draft is completed, it is circulated to policy staff for their factual review. Policy staffers are asked to correct any "technical" errors and return the draft to the speechwriters.

The **fact checking** of a speech is critical and often more complicated than it first appears. Sometimes a factual discrepancy may be incredibly subtle. What appears to be accurate to a speechwriter may in fact be a major error to a policymaker. For example, during the 2000 election, Vice President Al Gore was criticized for supposedly exaggerating the administration's record on community policing when he claimed the Clinton-Gore administration had put 100,000 more police officers on our streets. Although the Clinton-Gore administration had made enough grants to communities to enable them to place 100,000 more cops on the beat, the communities had not yet spent all the funds and hired all the police. What seemed an innocuous discrepancy—but a more artful description of a policy achievement to a speechwriter—was a faux pas from a policy perspective, and created some political problems for candidate Gore in the 2000 election. The mistake mentioned above underscores the importance of the quality and level of communication between speechwriters and policy staff. The more involved policy staffers are in the editing and rewriting of a particular speech, the lower the number of factual errors. At the same time, it is important for policy staff to understand that the more they try to clarify a speech with details and information, the duller and less effective the speech will be in marketing a policy proposal.

Speechwriters are often called on to draft opinion/advocacy pieces in order to help build support for policy initiatives. Although policymakers provide speechwriters with a specific proposal to defend as well as detailed information about the pros and cons of the policy they will be writing about, the advocacy component of the speechwriting process is similar to the opinion and editorial (op-ed) writing process used in major newspapers. John Timpane, the former op-ed editor of the *Philadelphia Inquirer,* provides potential op-ed writers with an excellent set of guidelines for writing advocacy statements that may be used by op-ed and speechwriters alike. Timpane argues that the first thing a good commentary or advocacy piece should do is express an opinion. He writes that he receives scores of pieces in which the authors write "about" something that interests him or her, but they fail to advocate a particular position on the issue at hand. As a result, their writing may be informative, but it is not persuasive and, consequently, will not be accepted as an op-ed.[2]

A good opinion piece should state an opinion within the first two or three sentences. The most common way to assert a position in an op-ed piece is to argue that "Something is or is not so," "something is or is not worthy of attention," "something should or should not be done," or "something will or will not happen unless action is taken." In the policy world, the parallels could be: "It's true/not true that welfare programs create a culture of dependency"; "The new Senate bill requiring each family of four or more to own a computer is an affront to the Constitution"; "Philadelphia should/should not ban guns in public places and public safety will improve"; and "If we pass the new tax-cut bill, our gross national product will plummet." In addition, a good op-ed should be linked to the current concerns of its readership. In the policy realm, this suggests that policy proposals should be designed to clearly address the concerns of constituents. Finally, op-eds and policy proposals alike will be stronger if they include concrete evidence to support to their propositions and undermine potential counter proposals.

Likewise, there are guidelines to follow when preparing a speech announcing a new policy or set of policies. In order for a speech to effectively convey and sell a policy, the speech should accomplish the following:[3]

1. Explain the policy in simple terms. In fact, one can argue that any policy that cannot be described clearly and coherently may not be an effective policy because the people it is designed to help will not understand how to take advantage of the proposal. If you need a whole speech to explain all the nuances of a particular proposal, then you probably are going to have a great deal of difficulty in garnering support for an idea. This does not mean that the proposal itself cannot be detailed and sophisticated,

2. John Timpane, *Philadelphia Inquirer*, http://www.philly.com/philly/blogs/inq_ed_board/About_The_Inquirer_Editorial_Board.html. Other online guidelines include the *New York Times* online, http://www.nytimes.com/2004/02/01/opinion/and-now-a-word-from-op-ed.html; The Health Advocacy Toolbox, http://www.cthealthpolicy.org/toolbox/opinion/op_eds_letters.htm; the *Thoreau Institute* online, http://www.ti.org/howtooped.html; and DePaul University online, http://newsroom.depaul.edu/facultyresources/OPEDTips/index.html.

3. Thanks to Jim Kestler, a former speechwriter for Senator Charles Schumer, for his suggestions on this section.

but the basic goal of the policy and how it will be achieved must be clear and easily explained.

2. Define a specific problem of public concern that the policy is going to address and make a persuasive argument that the policy is needed and is the appropriate solution to the problem at hand. A speech is a linear form of communication. If the problem is underspecified or vague, then the purpose of the speech will remain unclear and support for the policy will be weak.

3. Use evidence to show that the problem exists and that the proposed solutions will address it.

4. Persuade the audience to agree with the problem and the solution—the policy proposal—that you have developed.

COMMUNICATIONS

The Communications Office is charged with long-term message planning and coordination. One way to think about the difference between the Communications and Press Offices is to compare them to their counterparts in the corporate world: marketing and public affairs. Like corporate marketing offices, Communications is focused on message development, message coordination (among all parts of the U.S. government), and message amplification, whereas the Press Office is focused on media relations and day-to-day interactions with reporters.

The Communications Office is responsible for developing the broad themes that provide a recognizable framework for the president's (or chief decision maker's) ideas and policies. It focuses on how public events are staged, and how they will look and sound to the audience. It works closely with the scheduling offices and often serves as the intermediary between scheduling offices and the policy offices and staff. Coordination between the policy offices and the Communications Office is critical. Coordinating activities can, however, be difficult because the two groups have potentially competing objectives. In particular, in contrast to the policy staff, the Communications staff is far less concerned with the policy itself and what the policy is intended to do, than how the proposal fits into the theme of the moment. As a result, the Communications Office is much more likely to actively promote, rather than discourage, the announcement of a new education policy when education policy fits into the theme that the office is currently promoting. To avoid conflict and maximize synergy, the policy staff will often try to coordinate the public announcement of its proposals with the

Communication Office's message calendar and use this timing of an event as a deadline for preparing any proposals under development on education policy. Thus, for example, if the Communications Office is planning on emphasizing the president's education agenda around the time that students are going back to school, the policy councils will use that date as a deadline for completing policy proposals related to education.

Once an event is scheduled, the policy offices are charged with helping the Communications Office produce the public materials that will be disseminated at the event. In advance of the event, the Communication Office and policy offices will develop a fact sheet and press paper (these are sometimes the same, or are differentiated by the inclusion of a message component in the press paper). If appropriate, they may also prepare a report on the proposal and its state-by-state impact, background information on the site and why it was chosen, background information on the people or events highlighted in the event as examples of beneficiaries of the policy, and whatever charts or graphs are needed to support the points being made in the event. The involvement of the policy offices from the White House and other executive agencies is required to guarantee that the policies are portrayed accurately.

Unlike speeches, fact sheets and press papers are often first developed by the policy staff. The Communications Office staff only begins to edit the material after a draft is completed by the policy councils. Thus, press sheets tend to be more detailed and specific than speeches. As a consequence, reporters and others who are interested in more detailed information about a particular issue or policy tend to rely on fact sheets rather than speeches as the primary source of information. Press or fact sheets have become increasingly important with the advent of the Internet because they provide a credible and direct on-line source of information about the administration's policy.

One of the primary objectives of writing a strong fact sheet or press paper is to control the information that is made available to the public. A well-written fact sheet can also relieve the pressure on the Press Office, Communications Office, and the policy agencies to comment on the details of policies with which they are not familiar. A strong fact sheet or press paper should contain enough facts so the majority of reporters can write their stories without having to interview policy staff in an Agency or at the White House. This is important because most policy staffers do not have clearance to talk with the press. This restriction is generally imposed both as a way of controlling leaks and, more important, as a means of reducing the chance that policy staff could provide policy details that could either cause the reporter to lose interest in writing the story or direct the reporter's attention toward details that distract the reporter from the message objective.

A second objective of a fact sheet or press paper is to drive home the message that the Communications staff wants the public to receive from the event. Box 11-2 is an example of a typical press/fact sheet prepared by the policy and press offices. It provides considerable detail of the gun buyback plan announced by the Clinton administration including cost, numbers of guns to be purchased, and how many committees are already participating in the program. It also highlights the administration's overall theme of using so-called commonsense gun measures focusing on keeping guns away from criminals as a way of reducing gun violence. This theme is underscored in the headings describing different aspects of the program in the announcement.

BOX 11-2   **Gun BuyBack Fact Sheet**

President Clinton Announces Gun Buyback Partnership With the District of Columbia, April 28, 2000

Today, President Clinton, joined by District of Columbia Mayor Williams, Metropolitan Police Chief Ramsey, and Housing Secretary Cuomo, will announce a new gun buyback partnership between the District of Columbia and the Department of Housing and Urban Development. Under the initiative—the largest ever in D.C. and one of the largest ever in the country—a total of $350,000 will be made available to purchase an estimated 7,000 guns through a local gun buyback program jointly administered by the Washington Public Housing Authority and the Metropolitan Police Department. In addition, the Bureau of Alcohol, Tobacco and Firearms will trace all guns recovered in the buyback. A total of 85 communities across the country are now participating in the first round of HUD's BuyBack America program to launch similar local gun buyback programs and to take tens of thousands of unwanted guns out of circulation. Today's initiative is part of a comprehensive effort by the Clinton administration to provide more tools for communities to reduce gun violence, and to advance common sense gun safety legislation to keep guns out of the wrong hands.

Taking Thousands of Guns out of Circulation in Washington

In the wake of the recent shooting at the National Zoo, President Clinton today will announce a major partnership between the federal government and the District of Columbia to fund the largest gun buyback in the city's history. Under

(Continued)

(Continued)

today's partnership, HUD's BuyBack America program will provide $100,000 and the Metropolitan Police Department will provide $250,000 to fund the buyback, which will be held June 23rd and 24th. The District of Columbia Public Housing Authority will partner with the Metropolitan Police Department to conduct the buyback, which will fund the purchase of an estimated 7,000 guns and take them off the street and out of circulation permanently. Last August, the Metropolitan Police Department conducted two successful buybacks. The first, funded in part by HUD, yielded 600 guns; the second, 2,300 guns. According to an ATF report on the buybacks, the vast majority of firearms recovered (2,200) were handguns, and far exceeded the District's average annual recovery rate of 2,105 crime guns. Among the firearms frequently recovered were the types of guns often used in crimes and illegally trafficked by unlicensed dealers.

Providing Resources to Fund Buybacks Across the Country

A recent study released by HUD shows that people living in public housing are more than twice as likely to suffer from gun-related victimization as the general population. And while gun crime is down by 35 percent since 1992, nearly 12 children are still killed every day by gunfire. To help reduce the toll of gun violence, President Clinton last September unveiled a $15 million HUD gun buyback initiative—the largest gun buyback program in history. Under the first round of the BuyBack America Initiative, HUD is providing funding to a total of 85 communities to enable Public Housing Authorities (PHAs) to partner with local law enforcement agencies to conduct local gun buyback programs. By reducing the number of firearms in circulation, buyback programs can help prevent accidental shootings, gun suicides, gun crime and unauthorized gun use. The HUD buyback program encourages a cap of $50 for each working gun, and encourages PHAs to provide the awards in the form of gift certificates for goods or services rather than cash. Every HUD-sponsored buyback must be run by a local police department—with no amnesty given for any crimes committed with returned firearms. And to ensure permanent removal from circulation, all guns are destroyed unless they are relevant to an ongoing law enforcement investigation, or they have been stolen from their lawful owner.

Working With D.C. Law Enforcement to Combat Gun Crime

Today's initiative is another example of efforts by the federal government and the District of Columbia to work together to combat gun crime. Under innovative programs such as Operation Cease fire, which has received nearly $1 million in federal funding since 1995, local police are partnering with the U.S. Attorney and the ATF to increase gun enforcement and gun crime prevention programs. Also, through the administration's Youth Crime Gun Interdiction Initiative, local police are working with the ATF to trace all crime guns recovered in the District to crack down on illegal gun traffickers that supply guns to juveniles and criminals.

Keeping up Pressure to Enact Common Sense Gun Legislation

In addition to announcing these new tools to combat gun violence, the president will again emphasize the importance of common sense gun measures that can reduce gun violence by keeping guns out of the wrong hands. Noting that the Congress missed an opportunity to pass gun safety legislation by the April 20th anniversary of the Columbine shootings, the president will urge Congress to complete work on juvenile crime legislation and pass a final bill that closes the gun show loophole, requires child safety locks for handguns, bars the importation of large capacity ammunition clips, and bans violent juveniles from owning guns for life.

Source: http://clinton4.nara.gov/WH/New/html/20000428.html.

PRESS OFFICE

The primary responsibilities of the Press Office are to interact with the media on a daily basis, to respond to public inquiries of the day regarding governmental activities, and to implement the communications strategy. Implementing the communications strategy includes "spinning" the message of the day, managing the release of information and executive messages to the public, and preparing briefings by policy experts in the administration.

It is important to note that although the term *spin* has become a value-laden term often used by the media to refer to efforts by politicians to evade questions or mislead others into thinking that policy actions benefit them, it is not a derogatory term. In policy circles, *spin* refers to the marketing efforts used to promote support for a particular policy. Policy spin is factual evidence presented in a way to support a proposal or position. It is not meant to mislead but rather to inform the public in a way that puts a proposal in the best light.

When most people think of the White House Press Office, they typically focus on its relationship with the White House Press Corps. The Press Corps is mainly comprised of national reporters for major media outlets. But the Press Office also interacts on a daily basis with other types of media. These include specialty press outlets, regional press media, and social media. Specialty press outlets are typically centered on certain common demographic groups, such as the elderly, Asian-Americans, or women. These press outlets can also be operated by certain industries or groups, such as the banking sector or unions.

Regional press media include local television affiliates, papers in mid-sized cities such as the *Louisville Courier Journal,* and drive time radio shows. Social media is the fastest growing media sector. The Obama administration has revolutionized how the presidency interacts with social media—going beyond just maintaining a web page to establishing blogs, Twitter handles, and a Facebook page. One reason for the major focus on social media is that it allows the White House to avoid the filter of a reporter and directly connect to constituents. For these types of media, like the other media outlets, the Press Office becomes involved after policy is made, not before. It generally becomes engaged in the process the day before a policy is scheduled to be presented to the public. Once engaged, the Press Office works in tandem with the policy staff in preparing the information to be used to support press inquiries. These include fact sheets and press papers, and question and answer sheets.

When an event will highlight a new or significant policy, the Press Office generally holds briefings with members of the policy staff who are likely to entertain questions from the press corps. In certain high-profile agencies and the White House, the Press Office may hold as many as two regular briefings every day. These briefings include a morning briefing by the Press Secretary's Office, which is "on the record," but not on camera. The morning briefing usually focuses on breaking morning news and policy announcements that will take place later in the day. The afternoon briefing is "on camera" and is based on prepared question and answer (Q&A) sheets (see Box 11-3). Each day the policy staff prepare Q&A sheets on hot topics or on the policy announcement of the day.

BOX 11-3   **Gun Buyback Event, Q&A, April 28, 2000**

Q: Critics say that gun buybacks don't actually take guns out of the hands of criminals. Is there any evidence to suggest that gun buybacks actually reduce gun crime?

A: Every time we take a gun out of circulation through a buyback program, we help reduce the incidence of gun violence—not only gun crime, but also gun-related accidents, suicides, and other unintentional uses of guns. For instance, people living in a home with a gun have a suicide risk that is five times greater than those who live in a home without a gun. We also know that of the nearly 12 young people who are killed every day by gunfire, more than a third are by gun suicides and accidents. And many of the firearms obtained through buybacks are the types of guns frequently used in crimes.

Unfortunately, there haven't been any truly comprehensive studies of buyback programs, and there certainly has never been a program of the magnitude of the HUD $15 million program—which could help communities to buy back tens of thousands of guns. That is why HUD will make money available from the initiative to study the effects of buybacks, and identify promising practices to help make the programs more effective. However, it is also important to note that another important element of gun buyback programs is the impact they have on communities and their citizens. Gun buybacks give people an opportunity to get involved with law enforcement in local efforts to reduce violence, and they give residents hope that they can change their communities for the better.

Q: Weren't the guns retrieved in the last D.C. buybacks older guns and guns that wouldn't have been used in crimes?

A: The ATF reviewed the two gun buybacks conducted by the District last year and found that among the firearms most recovered were types of guns that are frequently used in crimes, illegally trafficked, or recovered by law enforcement agencies. This includes three of the most commonly recovered crime guns in America (the Raven .25 pistol, the Davis .380 pistol, and the Jennings .22 pistol). These same types of firearms are also consistently among the most frequently recovered firearms used in crimes in the District. In addition, handguns account for over 80% of all crime gun traces conducted nationally by the ATF, and 2,200 of the 2,912 guns turned into the District's buybacks were handguns. It only makes sense that by taking these types of weapons out of our nation's communities, we are reducing the likelihood of countless gun-related tragedies.

Q: Isn't it highly unlikely that a gun buyback would have prevented a tragic incident like this week's shooting at the zoo?

A: Well, there is an ongoing investigation into the zoo shooting and I believe that authorities do not yet have the gun used in that incident. Of course we may never know if one single action could have prevented the shooting. Still, this week's tragic incident serves as further proof that we must do more to keep guns out of the wrong hands—kids especially. Gun buybacks are just one way we can address this problem—and they work hand-in-hand with child safety locks for handguns, smart gun technology, and cracking down on illegal traffickers who supply guns to youth—are other ways which the president has also proposed. The president believes we must take action on all fronts in order to address the problem of gun violence in this nation. Today's announcement is simply one more tool the president wants to give local communities to support their gun violence reduction efforts.

(Continued)

(Continued)

Q: Do you really think removing even a few hundred thousand guns from circulation through the HUD program will make a difference when there are over 200 million guns privately owned guns in America?

A: We believe it will make a difference, although we agree that it certainly isn't a solution on its own. HUD's buyback program is just one more tool that we are giving communities and law enforcement to improve public safety and reduce gun violence. But Congress has an important opportunity to give communities even more tools to reduce gun violence, which is why they should pass common sense gun legislation that requires Brady background checks at gun shows, bans the importation of large capacity ammunition clips, and requires child safety locks for guns.

Q: If the HUD program is a $15 million initiative, why are only 85 communities participating? Why is so little money being spent out of the initiative so far ($2.7 million)?

A: These communities represent the first round of funding. Last week, HUD announced that Public Housing Authorities can use FY 2000 funds toward buybacks and we expect many more communities to seek funding in the second round. HUD has already begun to receive applications for the second round of buybacks.

Q: What HUD program is funding the buybacks?

A: Housing authorities commit HUD Public Housing Drug Elimination Grant (DEG) funds to the buyback and HUD provides 43 cents in additional funds for every dollar of DEG money committed to the buyback. For the District of Columbia, this breaks down to $70,000 in DEG funds and $30,000 in matching funds. Buybacks must be carried out in cooperation with local police or sheriffs and the guns must be destroyed unless it turns out they were stolen or are needed for a criminal investigation.

Source: Domestic Policy Council, the White House.

Several points about the Q&A in Box 11-3 should be noted. In the second Q&A exchange, the answer clearly responds to the question asked in the first two sentences. It states what types of guns were bought back, and that these guns are commonly used in crimes. Sometimes, however, the data needed to support a response like this are not available. When data are not available, the respondent must be prepared to provide a qualified response and should not avoid answering the question. For example, in the first Q&A exchange, the respondent does not have the data needed to respond to the question directly. He or she provides anecdotal evidence in response to the question, but then acknowledges that the actual data are not available.

In addition to answering the question and either specifying data to support the case or acknowledging the need for additional information, the answers are short and concise. In Box 11-3, there are some good examples of concise responses, and several examples of overly detailed responses. The fifth Q&A exchange is most concisely written response to the question. It is short, factual, and to the point. The first Q&A, approximately 350 words, is simply too long and runs the risk that an administration spokesman may forget or confuse part of the response when he or she is asked to repeat the administration's position. Although some of the facts are useful, adding in too much information can create confusion and could potentially open up additional lines of questioning. Finally, most of the responses to the questions are written in a style that is not laden with policy jargon and is generally approachable to a large audience.

In sum, there are four keys to writing good Q&A sheets:

1. Make certain the answer to the question is in the first two sentences;
2. Provide evidence to support the answer;
3. Answers should be short, concise, and to the point. Anything over 200 words should be condensed;
4. Answers need to be written in terms that the general public can understand.

As the Q&A regarding the gun buyback policy shows, the questions asked can make it difficult to prepare good responses in terms of these criteria. Nonetheless, following these guidelines as precisely as possible can promote clarity in communicating an idea, while minimizing the risks of being misdirected and not getting the primary message across.

CONCLUSION

A policy proposal that cannot be effectively marketed to the public and the press cannot be sustained over the long term. With the advent of the Internet and 24-hour cable television, the relationship between policymaking and communications/media strategy and tactics has never been more important. In this chapter we have outlined some of the tools that policymakers and communications staffers use to present proposals. These tools are simple in concept, yet their importance cannot be underestimated. Over time and as the relationship between media and policy continues to evolve, new tools will be developed to manage it. Despite ongoing advances in information and media technology, however, the role of speeches, fact sheets and press papers, and question and answer sessions will remain relevant.

Some argue that good policies speak for themselves while others believe that effective marketing can sell any policy, good or bad. We argue that the complexities of most policies make even those that are likely to achieve their objectives very difficult to understand without guidance. That is why it is important that policymakers communicate and market their ideas throughout the policymaking process. Such an approach will help ensure that proposals can be explained to the constituents they were intended to serve. This will increase the perception that the policy and the process are legitimate and that they both reflect the concerns of their constituents. If a policy cannot be explained and its benefits are not clear, it will not be supported. This does not mean the proposal would have produced an unpopular result, as some critics might argue, but it does mean the proposal is less likely to survive the political process and come to fruition.

Key Terms

Cognitive bias

Fact checking

Motivated bias

Spin

Review Questions

1. What does John Timpane argue is the first thing a good commentary or advocacy piece should do?
2. Describe the four rules to follow when preparing a speech announcing a new policy or set of policies.
3. What is the primary objective of a press paper or fact sheet? Who develops the first draft of a press paper or fact sheet?
4. What are the four keys to writing good Q&A sheets for government officials announcing new policy?
5. Name the three offices in the White House and federal agencies most involved in communicating and marketing policy. How do their roles differ?

SOCIAL POLICYMAKING

Welfare Reform During the Clinton Administration

WELFARE REFORM AND THE POLITICAL PROCESS

In the previous chapters, you learned about some of the primary tools, techniques, and processes used by policymakers in the executive branch of the U.S. government. This chapter and those that follow will present case studies that show how these tools, techniques, and processes are used in the real life policymaking process. This chapter explains how the tools, techniques, and processes were utilized by members of the Clinton administration to transform welfare reform from a campaign slogan to a fully developed policy proposal and eventually a law.

On August 22, 1996, President Clinton fulfilled his campaign promise to "end welfare as we know it," by signing the Personal Responsibility and Work Opportunity Reconciliation Act into law. Shortly after its passage, he also succeeded in restoring benefits to legal immigrants, thereby correcting what he saw as its primary limitation. Welfare caseloads fell by 51% between 1993 and 1999, and 1.3 million welfare recipients moved from welfare to work between 1997 and 1998 alone.[1] The transformation of welfare reform from a campaign slogan into a successful policy was, however, much less efficient than the convergence between the final policy outcome and President Clinton's campaign promises suggests. Indeed, the effectiveness of the policymaking process used to create a welfare reform policy varied substantially over time. The purpose of

---

1. "Clinton-Gore Accomplishments Reforming Welfare by Promoting Work and Responsibility," White House press release, February 7, 1999, p. 2.

this chapter is to review how the tools and techniques used in the policymaking process were utilized and to identify the conditions under which the policy process worked most efficiently. The impact of the welfare reform on the recipients, states, or national government will not be assessed.

Early in its term, the Clinton administration gave health care reform, the economic plan, the crime bill, and other policy initiatives priority over welfare reform. As a result, welfare reform did not receive a clear mandate by the president. Instead of placing control of the policy process with a White House policy council, as he had with the economic plan and the crime bill, President Clinton delegated the development of welfare reform to a jointly led inter-agency committee whose members often disagreed about how to interpret, and whether to implement, the president's campaign promises. In part because of its status as a low priority initiative and a lack of interagency coordination, little progress was made on welfare reform until congressional Republicans gave it political salience by including it as part of their 1994 Contract with America. From that point on, the president shifted authority, responsibility, and direct accountability for welfare reform policy exclusively to the Domestic Policy Council (DPC). The president and senior White House staff also became actively involved in sparring with Congress, and the administration used its wide ranging capabilities to successfully modify the congressional proposals to make them conform to its welfare reform goals.

One of the primary policy lessons to be learned from the welfare reform experience is that policy initiatives which do not receive sufficient leadership from the White House, or are organized without a specific unit being given decision-making authority and accountability, are likely to stall. This is particularly likely when there is not a clear mandate from the president and disagreements exist among the policy development team members regarding the president's objectives and the appropriate means to achieve those objectives.

The tools and techniques we described in earlier chapters were used throughout the entire welfare reform policymaking process. Decision-making memoranda, polling, SAPs and LRMs, and communications strategy played a critical role throughout. However, their roles and effectiveness varied significantly between the period prior to 1994—when there was no clear mandate from President Clinton, the management of the policy process was decentralized, and authority over the working group was dispersed inside and outside of the White House—and the period after 1994 when welfare reform became a clear priority for the president and management and control of the policy process was brought back to the White House. These differences are the focus of this chapter.

THE EARLY PHASE: DECENTRALIZATION, DEBATE, AND DEADLOCK

The degree of welfare reform proposed during the presidential campaign marked a significant and uncharted change from the past. Although everyone understood president-elect Clinton's desire "to change welfare as we know it," the Clinton team did not agree about the urgency of welfare reform relative to health care reform and other policy initiatives. Once in office, these debates expanded to include disagreements between members of Clinton's campaign team and his newly appointed advisors over how to interpret—and whether to implement—the president's campaign promises regarding welfare reform. These internal debates resulted in several actions early in the administration that undermined the potential for any early success at welfare reform. In particular, no financial support was provided for welfare reform and the responsibility for policy development was delegated to a jointly administered interagency task force which was given the minimal directive of "studying" the problem.

The welfare reform process got off to a weak start early in 1992, when Secretary of the Treasury Lloyd Bentsen presented President Clinton with a five-year budget proposal that did not include any money for welfare or health care reform. The budget proposal required both policy initiatives to be self-financing. This financial constraint greatly complicated efforts to reach a consensus regarding the form welfare should take, and it undermined the desire on the part of some members of the administration to make welfare reform a priority early in President Clinton's term. The resulting ambivalence toward welfare reform by some in the executive branch was reinforced by a belief that welfare reform would not be supported by the majority of Democrats in Congress—with the strong exception of Senator Moynihan, who strongly advocated pursuing welfare reform before health care reform.

These factors were compounded further by disagreements within the executive branch over how to interpret the president's objectives. For example, some people, including the Assistant Secretary for Planning and Evaluation of the U.S. Department of Health and Human Services David Ellwood, argued that welfare reform should be tested in a small number of states before pursuing a comprehensive change on a national scale. Others, such as HUD Secretary Henry Cisneros, opposed placing time limits on welfare recipients. In order to resolve these and other issues, the president appointed a twenty-seven-member interagency task force to develop a welfare plan. The task force was jointly managed by the Deputy Assistant to the President for Domestic Policy Bruce Reed and David Ellwood, in collaboration with Assistant Secretary for the Administration for Children and Families at the Department of HHS, Mary Jo Bane. Bruce Reed was the leading advocate of comprehensive reform in the administration. In contrast, both David Ellwood and Mary Jo Bane preferred a go-slow approach.

Between 1993 and 1994, there were disagreements between the DPC, the HHS, and the Department of Labor regarding fundamental issues such as how to interpret the president's objectives regarding the form and scope of welfare reform, the degree of federal oversight versus freedom of states, the issue of granting states waivers, the rights of legal immigrants, whether to begin with a centrist or left-of-center policy, and whether, how, and when to implement the policy changes. In general, HHS pushed for a more liberal reform with relatively more centralized control in the federal government, while the DPC preferred a "new democrat" policy that granted states somewhat more authority. Two of the most contentious issues involved the imposition of time limits on welfare recipients and the grant of waivers to states that would allow them to pursue welfare reform independently of federal action. The HHS wanted to maintain oversight over state welfare policies and argued that waivers should be used sparingly only after careful study. Some members of HHS criticized the White House staff as driven by expediency and politics, a desire for very quick access to information, and a bias toward giving increasing power to states. The White House staff, in comparison, wanted to use the waivers as a safety valve and saw them as a means to let states implement welfare reform even if no policy change was made formally.

After welfare reform became more of a priority issue for the administration in 1994, granting waivers took on the added strategic role of challenging Congress into action by demonstrating the administration's ability and willingness to implement welfare reform at the state level regardless of whether or not Congress enacted legislation. Before federal welfare reform was passed in 1996, forty-five states and the District of Columbia had received federally approved welfare demonstration waivers. As a result, though their success varied, many of these states were actively engaged in limited welfare reform long before the national bill was passed.

Unlike the NEC, which called formal meetings to resolve outstanding issues, disagreements among members of the welfare reform task force were generally resolved informally. When this failed, the chief of staff and sometimes the president played the role of arbiter to settle differences. Using the limited contact time with the chief of staff and the president to settle minor issues as well as major disagreements among task force members caused the process to grind down to a halt. Most of these issues could have been resolved within the working group if leadership and accountability had been placed under the leadership of one entity instead of two. The irony of the joint-leadership is that it increased the perception on the part of the participants that their views were not being given a fair hearing by the president. As a result, group cohesion and effectiveness declined.

It is important to recognize that even when disagreements regarding a specific policy initiative exist, one of the primary goals of a policymaking committee like this task force is to develop a consensus proposal—that is, to write a proposal that the participants agree brings their viewpoints to the president's attention. Bruce Reed, for example, commonly used information memoranda to inform the president about progress on the welfare reform initiatives, appraise him of disputes, and to seek clarification on the president's objectives and position.

When a consensus document is not created, or particular parties feel that their viewpoints are not given a fair hearing before the president, the excluded parties often strike back by raising public doubts or mobilizing public support against the policy in question. One way of doing so is to leak information to the press. For example, members of the executive branch who felt that their opinions were not being addressed leaked information about a Cabinet meeting on January 5, 1994, to the *New York Times.* In the article, they argued that the president was trying to devise a strategy to make it appear as though he were pushing for change in the welfare system, even while delaying action on the bill until health care reform had a chance to clear Congress.[2] The negative publicity created by this leak was compounded by published statements by Senator Moynihan who was upset that administration had placed a priority on health care reform rather than welfare reform. Jason DeParle of the *New York Times* reported that Senator Moynihan criticized President Clinton for raising the subject of welfare reform to appease the public "whenever he gets into trouble," while, at the same time, "appointing people who had no intention of doing it."[3]

---

2. Jason DeParle, "Clinton Puzzle: How to Delay Welfare Reform Yet Seem to Pursue It," *New York Times* (January 5, 1995), p. A13.

3. Jason DeParle, "Moynihan Says President Is Insincere About Reforming the Welfare System," *New York Times,* (January 8, 1994) S1, p. 8.

In response to the publication of these leaks and criticisms that the administration was not acting on its welfare reform promises, Bruce Reed used a memorandum to appraise the president of the situation (including identifying reporters who are likely to write unfavorably and favorably about welfare reform), highlight the danger of leaks—especially as related to new studies by the OMB and HHS regarding cost and financing estimates of the welfare reform plan—and suggest ways to present and promote the president's plan. He specifically suggested that the administration emphasize that primary questions involving welfare reform "including where to find the money, how to get the states to come on board, and how to make the program work" turn on the issue of how quickly the reform is phased-in. He argued that the forthcoming reports from the HHS and OMB would likely be leaked and that it was, therefore, essential that the administration present a good story to the press before additional negative stories are published. He even suggests that a specific reporter, Ronald Brownstein, be contacted. Three days later, Brownstein wrote a story for the *Los Angeles Times* that outlined and supported the administration's phase-in plan and highlighted the costs associated with a congressional GOP alternative (without specifying the cost of the administration's proposal).[4] The resulting exchange of leaks, memoranda, and responses demonstrate how policy can be presented to the public with a negative "spin" to raise doubts and undermine support or with a positive "spin" to increase or regain support for a specific initiative.

After extensive negotiations within the administration, President Clinton unveiled the Work and Responsibility Act on June 14, 1994. Most significantly, the administration's welfare reform proposal called for a mandatory work requirement after two years of welfare on the Aid to Families with Dependent Children (AFDC) program for people born after 1971. People who could not find work were to be placed in federally subsidized jobs. To achieve this objective, the program called for $9.3 billion in additional federal funding over five years, and it strengthened regulations regarding paternity and child support. All but $2.1 billion in funding for this proposal would come from reductions in other federal entitlements. The Clinton welfare bill was introduced in the Senate as S224 and in the House of Representatives as HR 4605 on June 24, 1993. The administration, however, did not push the bill through Congress and Congress did not act on it.

---

4. Ronald Brownstein, "New Welfare Limits Could Be Aimed First at the Young," *Los Angeles Times* (February 20, 1994), p. A1.

Despite finally producing a bill, the welfare reform process stalled. It stalled, in part, because of the ad hoc organization of the policymaking process during the early Clinton administration. This case study highlights how the president's own indecisiveness about welfare reform led to the creation of a modified policy process, which created a final product that was discarded in the legislative wasteland. In sharp contrast, once the president decided to make welfare reform a priority, the situation changed. In 1994, he applied the hybrid organizational model that combined centralized management and multiple advocacy to welfare reform policy. As a result, the Clinton administration managed to take the welfare reform initiative away from Congress and secure passage of a bill that ultimately met most of its concerns.

PHASE II: ACTION, RESPONSE, AND RESOLUTION

The second phase of the welfare reform process began on November 8, 1998, when Republicans won a majority in both houses of Congress. As part of their campaign pledges, the newly elected members of Congress promised to fulfill the "Contract with America" by bringing action on the House and Senate floors on a variety of issues, including a conservative welfare reform proposal entitled the Personal Responsibility Act. The Republican victory served as an important catalyst for welfare reform in the Clinton administration in at least two ways. First, in post-elections polls run by *The Wall Street Journal*, voters cited welfare reform as their number one policy priority, surpassing other issues including health care reform, a balanced budget, and term limits.[5] Furthermore, the polls revealed that voters linked the existing AFDC welfare system to broader social problems—including the creation of an urban underclass, crime, social decay, loss of family values, the rise of children having children, etc. This outcome and the popular sentiment in support of welfare reform forced the Clinton administration to reassess the relative priority it had given to welfare reform. The post-1994 Clinton administration shifted its priorities from health care back to welfare reform and was forced to choose between introducing a new welfare reform proposal or rejecting or trying to modify the congressional proposal.

Second, the Personal Responsibility Act included in the Republican "Contract with America" gave the Clinton administration a foil to fight against. The Personal Responsibility Act was far more disturbing to Democrats in the Congress than Clinton's earlier proposal—it cut off all AFDC and housing

---

5. Mickey Kaus, "They Blew It," *The New Republic* (December 5, 1994), pp. 14–18.

benefits for illegitimate children whose mothers are under 18 and barred the children from ADFC for life; recipients must work after two years and are permanently denied AFDC for life after five years; AFDC, housing and the Supplemental Security Income program are stripped of their entitlement status and placed under spending caps; and virtually all benefits for legal immigrants are denied. Having recognized its mistake in not making welfare reform a priority, the severity of the Republican alternative gave the Clinton administration a target which the president could justify vetoing or driving toward the center. With renewed vigor, the Clinton administration initiated a strategy to exploit differences among the Republican ranks between moderates and conservatives and between the National Governors Association and Congress, and regain the lead in welfare reform. The Republican bill was approved as H.R. 4 by the House of Representatives in a 234–119 vote on March 24, 1995. The next day President Clinton used his weekly radio address to denounce the bill and begin the administration's attack.

The White House strategy had several components to it. First, Bruce Reed of the DPC was given direct responsibility for welfare reform. This shift in authority to the DPC was unrelated to, but helped by the departure of David Ellwood, who had to return to his academic responsibilities in order to maintain his university tenure. The resulting power shift was important because it meant that debate within the welfare reform task force could move beyond the question of what the president intended welfare reform to be, to questions of strategy and how best to promote the president's agenda. It also meant that welfare reform was now run out of the White House.

The involvement of particular agencies and departments in this task force tended to shift over time as the welfare reform process evolved. Initially, welfare reform was centered in the DPC, HHS, and the INS. As the policy evolved, and particularly after it became law in 1996, the group was expanded to include the Department of the Treasury, the Department of Housing and Urban Development, and the Department of Transportation. The inclusion of these additional participants served two purposes. From a functional standpoint, this change reflected the expansion of issues involved in the welfare reform. In addition, however, the inclusion of additional parties helped the White House spread information about its agenda and, thereby, facilitate the implementation of its objectives.

The Office of Management and Budget played an important management and evaluation role in the welfare reform process. Although the A-19

Clearance Process (discussed in Chapter 9) was used only when legislation was involved, the OMB played an active role in reviewing both administration and congressional proposals. It paid particular attention to policies regarding legal immigrants and the impact of the proposals on children in poverty. For example, in November of 1995 it reported that the proposed policy changes that resulted from a House and Senate compromise between the Personal Responsibility Act approved by the House of Representatives (H.R. 4) on March 4, and the Welfare Reform Act approved by the Senate on September 18 (which included more than forty amendments to H.R. 4) would result in one million more children living under poverty. As a result of this assessment, President Clinton vowed to veto the budget reconciliation bill which contained the welfare reform provisions.

It is important to recognize that OMB's role in making sure that the resulting bill was consistent with the president's agenda included both the policy formation phase and oversight of policy implementation. On February 28, 1996, HHS Secretary Donna Shalala testified before the Senate Finance Committee and announced that the president could not support the National Governors Association welfare proposal in its current form. She used this venue to present the president's request that the proposal be modified to provide vouchers for children of parents terminated from assistance, to retain the entitlement status of child welfare services and food stamps, and to promote fundamental revision of the immigration section. On April 26, HHS Assistant Secretary Mary Jo Bane presented the newly proposed White House welfare reform bill to Congress, arguing that it will promote work, encourage parental responsibility and provide a safety net for children.

The process of policymaking was generally informal, but the policy councils served as a focal point for organizing key issues and bringing various agencies and departments together. For example, rather than having the Department of Labor and the HHS discuss a particular issue regarding welfare reform with one another, the DPC would call a deputies meeting that included both Labor and HHS to discuss the issues at hand. Meetings were held weekly when necessary, but were stopped when they were not considered necessary. Participants in the process considered communication between the various parties to be open and congenial, ironically more so than when there was joint control.

Second, the administration began a strategic effort to increase its role in, and take control of, the welfare reform debate. This effort began with the organization of a working session on welfare on January 28, 1995, that brought the president and the White House welfare reform task force together with members of the National Governors Association, the House of Representatives, the Senate, mayors, county officials, and others in a forum to build a bipartisan partnership to develop a welfare program. The goal of the forum was to develop a means of promoting local control while not putting states at financial risk. The president also actively took part in the National Governors Association summer meeting where, on July 31, he announced his support for a compromise welfare proposal presented by Senate Majority Leader Robert Dole. He also announced that he had directed the HHS to provide "fast-track demonstration approval" to states with certain waiver requests. As discussed above, the granting of waiver requests became part of a strategy to enable the administration to promote welfare reform regardless of congressional action and, thereby, force Congress to respond to its initiatives.

Divisions between moderates and conservatives in the Senate made it difficult for Senator Dole to push the welfare bill through Congress. He did not succeed in doing so until September 19, and it was not until mid-October that House and Senate conferees convened to resolve the differences in the House and Senate Bills. In that time, support for the bill by President Clinton and congressional Democrats began to fade. The decline in support was accelerated by a report presented by OMB on November 8, which suggested that the Welfare Reform Act would result in one million more children living in poverty. It was crushed when Congress linked the welfare reform proposal to the increasingly contentious budget negotiations that ultimately led to a government shutdown. President Clinton vetoed the budget reconciliation bill containing the welfare provisions. In an attempt to embarrass the president, the House and Senate resubmitted the welfare reform bill on its own. He vetoed the bill on January 9, 1996. He justified doing so by arguing that an acceptable bill must provide more funding for child care, health coverage for low income families, requirements for state funding, and additional funding during times of economic downturn.

Box 12-1 is an information memorandum used during this period to inform the chief of staff about the policy debate in December of 1995. It underscores the political thinking of some of the president's key advisors at that time. It is an excellent example of a well-written information memorandum except that it breaks the rule that information memoranda should not provide policy recommendations.

BOX 12-1	Memorandum to the Chief of Staff Regarding the Status of Welfare Reform

December 18, 1995

MEMORANDUM FOR THE CHIEF OF STAFF

FROM: Bruce Reed

         Rahm Emanuel

SUBJECT: Welfare Reform Update

The Republicans have reached virtual agreement on a new welfare reform conference report. Their current plan is to bring it to the House floor on Wednesday and the Senate on Thursday. Unless Senate Democrats mount a filibuster or we find a way to engage in bipartisan negotiations, it could end up on the president's desk for veto before Christmas.

I. Summary

This latest conference report is designed to cause us maximum possible discomfort. It's not good enough to sign, but not enough to make it easy to explain our veto. It is actually better than the Senate bill on a few of our priorities (like child care), and because of add-backs and changes in the CBO baseline, the overall level of budget savings is lower than the Senate bill. But the new conference report still contains some obscure but important structural changes that we have strongly opposed, like two-tiered SSI benefits for disabled children and a block grant of certain foster care programs, as well as deep cuts in food stamps and benefits for legal immigrants.

So far, most congressional Democrats are with us in opposing the current conference report. But the Blue Dogs may feel compelled to vote for it, and many Senate Democrats are concerned about how we make our case against the bill. Since the conference report has not yet been filed, Breaux is meeting with Roth tomorrow in a last-ditch effort to force bipartisan negotiations, and the Blue Dogs are meeting with Kasich and Shaw to insist on further improvements on welfare reform as part of the budget talks.

A. Overall Budget Savings: The original House bill saved $91 billion over 7 years, and the Senate bill $66 billion. The original conference report (vetoed as part of the reconciliation bill) was scored at $77 billion. The latest conference report saves $58 billion. Part of this reduction ($10 billion) is due to CBO's re-estimate of the baseline; most of the rest is due to add-backs in childcare, child

(Continued)

(Continued)

nutrition, child welfare, and SSI kids. In terms of budget cuts, the latest version is better than the Senate bill in some areas and worse in others—but because the overall number is lower, Republicans will argue that this bill is better than the Senate bill we endorsed. (CBO now estimates that the AFDC block grant in the conference bill will provide at least as much money over the 7 years as the entitlement.)

By comparison, the Coalition budget saves $46 billion on welfare, the administration's Dec. 7th budget plan saves $39 billion, and the rough consensus from Democratic-wide negotiations this weekend was a savings target of $43 billion.

B. Child Care: The latest conference report is $1 billion better than the Senate bill on child care. That is still not as much as we think is necessary—the Coalition budget calls for $3+ billion—but we can no longer argue that the Republicans are cutting child care.

C. Child Nutrition: Lugar and Goodling agreed not to block grant school lunch, only to allow seven statewide demonstrations around the country. The level of child nutrition cuts in the conference report is now the same as in the administration's budget.

D. Child Welfare: The conference report preserves the entitlement for maintenance payments, and no longer includes any big dollar cuts in child welfare. It does block grant foster care and adoption assistance (while maintaining baseline levels of spending), which we oppose—but they've made it harder for us to get much traction.

E. SSI Kids: This is the biggest political vulnerability of the new bill. It cuts SSI benefits by 25% for all but the most severely disabled kids—a cut of $3 billion more than the Senate (although $1 billion is returned to the states in a services block grant).

F. Food Stamps: The conference report cuts $26 billion, compared to $21 billion in the Senate and $19 billion in our current budget proposal. The state option to block grant food stamps is better than the Senate bill, but not as good as the original House proposal.

G. Immigrants: Again, the conference report cuts much more deeply than we would like—$15 billion on SSI for legal immigrants, compared to about $5 billion in our proposal and the Coalition's. Unfortunately, the administration is almost alone among Democrats in fighting hard to reduce the size of the cuts in benefits for legal immigrants and in food stamps.

H. Medicaid: A recent version of the conference report ended the guarantee of health coverage for welfare mothers. If that provision remains in the bill, it may be our best argument for vetoing the bill. But the Republicans know that, and will probably fix it.

II. Strategy

The difference between our position and theirs is not enormous in budget terms—$58 billion vs. $43 billion. Our greatest challenge is persuading the Republicans that the long-term benefit of a bill becoming law outweighs the short-term advantage of forcing a veto. Breaux and the Coalition will approach the Republicans tomorrow with that message, as well as with the attached list of fixes which would force a bipartisan discussion and address most of our problems. If that effort fails, we should veto the bill on the grounds that Republicans are just playing budget politics rather than making a serious bipartisan effort at real reform.

Source: Domestic Policy Council, the White House.

In the Spring of 1996, the administration pursued a strategy of taking over the welfare reform initiative while emphasizing the inability of the 104th Congress to accomplish any significant policy goals. To demonstrate executive action, President Clinton used a meeting with the National Association of Counties in March as a platform to announce that he had approved waivers for fifty-three different welfare reform projects in thirty-seven states, covering nearly 75 percent of all welfare recipients. The waivers were significant because they enabled states to act immediately, regardless of congressional action. Ultimately, waivers were granted to forty-five states. In addition, the administration announced a series of executive actions to promote welfare reform. For example, on May 4, President Clinton announced executive actions urging states to tighten eligibility of mothers on welfare, and on June 18, he announced actions to strengthen child support enforcement through the implementation of a new federal system to track delinquent parents across state lines, he took executive action on teen pregnancy, and he took executive action on the earned income tax credit.

Second, the administration used speaking engagements by senior members of the administration, radio addresses by the president, and the State of the Union Address as bully pulpits to publicize its actions and specify its position. For example, in the State of the Union Address on January 23, President Clinton put the onus on Congress to send him a bipartisan bill and promised to "sign it immediately."[6] Health and Human Services Secretary Donna Shalala spelled out

---

6. Jeffrey Katz, "Clinton's Changing Welfare Views," *Congressional Quarterly* (1996), p. 2116.

the administration's priorities while testifying before the Senate Finance Committee on February 28, 1996. She argued that the president would not support NGA welfare proposals unless they were modified to provide vouchers for children of parents removed from assistance, retained the entitlement status of child welfare services and food stamps, and included a fundamental revision of the issue of legal immigrants. On April 26, HHS Assistant Secretary Mary Jo Bane presented a new welfare bill from the administration to Congress, which she argued would promote work, encourage parental responsibility, and provide a safety net for children, all while saving $48 billion in seven years. Congressional Republicans responded by introducing a welfare reform bill modeled on the NGA proposal that made concessions to the president by promoting federal control of child protection and adoption programs and allowing legal immigrants who are not yet citizens to be eligible for cash welfare. In addition to these concessions, however, the congressional Republicans tied a bill that would give states control over Medicaid to the welfare plan. President Clinton responded by calling the link to Medicaid a "poison pill," but then surprised his Republican critics on May 18 by using his radio address to praise a newly proposed welfare plan from Wisconsin that went beyond what they anticipated he would support. In an ironic twist of events, this action spurred the House of Representatives to take the unusual step of promoting a waiver by approving the "Wisconsin Only Bill," to allow Wisconsin to put its plan into place, thus furthering the administration's goal of enabling states to take further action without a successful bill moving through Congress.

The White House strategy succeeded. Freshman congressmen urged their leadership to delink welfare from Medicaid, and on July 11, the Senate and House leadership announced their decision to split welfare and Medicaid reform bills. White House Spokesman Mike McCurry announced that, "We now stand on the verge of having a welfare proposal that can get bipartisan support and the president's signature," and that although the president would seek some changes, they were not insurmountable.[7] On July 16, as negotiations on the budget reconciliation package containing the Personal Responsibility and Work Opportunity Act began, President Clinton encouraged the process by announcing, "I think we have now reached a turning point, a breakthrough on welfare reform."[8] And, by August 1, the House and Senate conferees had passed the final version of the bill.

---

7. Katz, "Clinton's Changing Welfare Views," p. 2116.

8. Katz, "Clinton's Changing Welfare Views," p. 2116.

The question at hand following the passage of the bill was whether the president would sign it. As it stood, the bill cut off welfare, Social Security, and food stamps to legal immigrants, and did not provide childcare necessities to mothers who had been on welfare and were cut off. The president valued all of these items highly. Bruce Reed fought hard to persuade the president to sign the bill, arguing that welfare reform was a process, not just a single piece of legislation and that it could be modified once passed. Dick Morris also pushed the president to sign the bill by citing recent polling results in which two identical samples of respondents were asked the same series of questions about how much spending on poor people and inner cities they would support. In the first sample, the questions were asked without any bias, in the second sample, the question was asked with the caveat, "Please assume that Congress has passed and the president has signed a welfare reform bill requiring welfare recipients to work and setting up time limits for how long people can stay on welfare." The survey found that 65 percent of people who assumed welfare reform had passed supported spending on inner cities, while only half of those of the others supported such spending.[9] Another public opinion survey indicated that vetoing the bill would transform a fifteen-point win for the president into a three-point loss in a race with Dole for the presidency.[10] These polls clearly indicated strong public support for signing the bill. Liberal Democrats in the administration tried to counter the impact of these polls in a last-ditch appeal to convince the president to veto the bill.

In order to make his decision, President Clinton called in his senior advisers who did not support the bill, including Leon Panetta, George Stephanopoulos, and Donna Shalala, and those who did, including Hillary Clinton and Bruce Reed. He asked each person in the room to voice his or her concerns, he listened to them, and then made his decision. On August 22, he signed the Personal Responsibility and Work Opportunity Act of 1996 into law and promised to seek changes to correct its greatest flaws. Not all members of the policymaking team supported his decision to sign the bill. In protest, Assistant Secretary for HHS's Administration for Children and Families Mary Jo Bane and Acting Assistant Secretary of HHS Planning and Evaluation Peter Edelman resigned, citing concerns about the new welfare reform law.

After signing the bill, President Clinton began a strategy of publicizing the need for additional modification to the welfare policy and spurring Congress

---

9. Dick Morris, *Behind the Oval Office: Getting Reelected Against All Odds* (Los Angeles, CA: Renaissance Books, 1999), p. 303.

10. Morris, *Behind the Oval Office*, p. 300.

into action. These efforts began with the administration's use of the president's State of the Union address on February 4, 1997, to stress the importance of overturning the ban on aid to legal immigrants. President Clinton argued that, "To do otherwise is simply unworthy of a great nation of immigrants," and he called for an increase in spending arguing that "no one can walk out of this chamber with a clear conscience unless you are prepared to finish the job."[11] He then used the fiscal 1998 budget proposal as a means of promoting an increase in spending to alter the restrictions regarding legal immigrants, Medicaid, food stamps, and the welfare-to-work component in the welfare reform law.

Borrowing strategy from the Republican Congress, President Clinton insisted that any budget deal would need to restore some welfare cuts. In contrast to the congressional failure to use a similar linkage to its advantage earlier and largely because of the failure of Congress to negotiate a successful budget without closing down the government a year earlier, linking welfare reform to the increasingly bipartisan talks on balancing the budget helped to promote an agreement. The budget deal that was announced on May 2 restored $9.7 billion over five years for SSI and Medicaid benefits to two-thirds of the legal immigrants who would have lost them, added $1.5 billion over five years to the food stamp program, and provided $3 billion for state welfare-to-work programs.[12] Once the blueprint was established, budget reconciliation bills were negotiated by the House Ways and Means Committee, the House Education and the Workforce Committee, and the Senate Finance Committee, as well as the House and Senate Agricultural committees which addressed food stamps provisions.

As the reconciliation bills were negotiated, the Clinton administration continued to use both its bully pulpit and executive orders to shape the outcome. In particular, Vice President Al Gore joined Senate Majority Leader Tom Daschle in publically criticizing the House Ways and Means proposal to make certain legal immigrants ineligible even if they were disabled as an "extraordinary revocation" of the bipartisan budget blueprint. In addition, by executive action, President Clinton instructed the Labor Department to release guidelines applying a wide variety of federal laws, including the Fair Labor Standards Act, to recipients who were required to work under the new welfare law. This policy set federal minimum wages, overtime pay, child labor, and record keeping requirements as well as requiring protection such as unemployment insurance,

---

11. "$13 Billion in Welfare Cuts Restored," *1997 Congressional Quarterly Almanac*, (Washington, DC: Congressional Quarterly, 1997), pp. 6–31, 6–32.

12. "$13 Billion in Welfare Cuts Restored," pp. 6–32.

the application of antidiscriminatory practices, and the Americans with Disabilities Act. Despite attempts by the Ways and Means Committee and the Education and the Workforce Committee to exempt welfare recipients from these provisions, pressure from the White House and the Senate succeeded in persuading committee members to capitulate.

On June 20, President Clinton sent a letter to Representative John Spratt, Jr., ranking member of the House Budget Committee, stating that he would veto a bill that did not follow the Senate version, restoring SSI and Medicaid benefits for legal immigrants. As a consequence, during final negotiations on the senate floor, Frank Lautenberg of New Jersey offered an amendment to make legal immigrants who were in the United States as of August 22, 1996, eligible for SSI regardless of when they become disabled. In the background of the bipartisan budget agreement, the amendment was passed by a voice vote with little discussion. In the House of Representatives, Republicans modified their minimum wage provisions. Ultimately, the revised bill met the administration's desire to extend SSI and Medicaid to legal immigrants who were in the country on August 22, 1996, it provided funding to help states place long-term welfare recipients into the workforce, it continued Medicaid benefits for disabled children who had lost their SSI benefits, it increased spending on food stamps by $1.5 billion over five years, and it kept the policy that states must pay workfare recipients the federal minimum wage. As a consequence, the administration succeeded in using the budget reconciliation bill to correct what it saw as the greatest weakness of the welfare reform package. It succeeded in changing welfare as we knew it, and it even succeeded in modifying the final product so that it converged with the administration's priorities.

CONCLUSION: MAKING THE PROCESS WORK

The development of a welfare reform policy during the early Clinton administration provides important insights into the nature of the policymaking process. In particular, it demonstrates that when the process breaks down, policymakers tend to diverge from regular channels of communication, and progress in policy formation can be stalled. On the other hand, when participants have confidence that the process is an effective means of voicing concerns, policy initiatives are more likely to come to fruition. In the welfare reform process, competing priorities including health care reform, the crime bill, and balancing the budget meant that, although President Clinton was personally concerned about welfare reform, he did not make welfare reform a clear priority in the first two years of his administration. As a result, the hybrid traditional model of policymaking was used with the economic plan and the crime bill, but was not initially applied to welfare reform. Instead of centralizing the authority and responsibility for guiding the policymaking process with a White House Policy Council, he created a jointly administered task force co-led by an agency and the White House to study the problem. By doing so he doomed the process to continual debate over the details with no accountability for bringing the process to closure. The task force ultimately divided itself into two groups, reflecting the viewpoints of the two directors: orderly deputies meetings did not take place, memoranda to the president focused on policy minutiae and the resolution of disputes among members of the task force rather than more substantive policy matters, and some members of each group doubted that their viewpoints would gain a fair hearing with the president.

Ironically, joint leadership created a process that the participants considered unfair. As faith in the policymaking process broke down, members of the task force moved outside the process and used other means to communicate their viewpoints—such as communicating with the president directly or leaking information to the press. In essence, Senator Moynihan's criticism that the administration espoused an interest in welfare reform but was not getting anything done was correct; however, rather than being a result of a specific initiative to stall welfare reform, the lack of progress was due to a breakdown and misuse of the tools and techniques that characterize an effective policymaking process.

The second phase of welfare reform, in contrast, demonstrated how much more effectively the process can function when the policy initiative is given a mandate and when responsibility and authority are centralized with one entity. Once the DPC was given primary responsibility and authority for welfare reform, regular deputy meetings were instituted, decision-making memoranda were used to evaluate policy alternatives and elucidate strategy, and other tools including polling, and the mobilization of the bully pulpit were used to effectively publicize and promote the administrations objectives. A consensus was much easier to achieve once authority and responsibility had been centralized in the DPC versus when the authority and responsibility had been shared. In the end, all members of the task force and the senior White House staff did not agree with the president's decision to sign the Personal Responsibility and Work Opportunity Act of 1996. Despite this lack of agreement, however, the process enabled the participants to express their views and participate in the decision to sign and reform the Act. With a couple of minor exceptions, there was a consensus among the policymakers that the process, tools, and techniques worked effectively after 1994.

ECONOMIC POLICYMAKING I

The Clinton Economic Plan

THE ECONOMIC PLAN AND THE POLITICAL PROCESS

"It's the economy!" was the mantra of President Clinton and his staff during the 1992 campaign. That slogan helped him win the election by directing public attention toward economic and domestic concerns—including an economic recession, historically high levels of people on welfare rolls, a growing number of Americans with no health insurance—and away from military and international issues where President George H. W. Bush had his greatest successes. Once in office, President Clinton made passage of his economic plan a top priority and fulfilled a campaign promise in creating a National Economic Council (NEC) to parallel the National Security Council (NSC) in importance and in structure. In comparison to the difficulties that characterized the first two years of policymaking in welfare and health care reform, the development of the NEC and the 1993 economic plan are striking policymaking successes. We argue that the structure of the NEC and the policymaking processes it implemented helped to promote the development of the budget and the economic plan in the early Clinton White House. Indeed, as prominent scholars and practitioners have argued, the NEC and the budget process were "island(s) of effective White House process in the 'madhouse' of the early Clinton administration."[1]

---

1. I. M. Destler, "The National Economic Council: A Work in Progress," *Policy Analyses in International Economics* 46 (Washington, DC: Institute for International Economics, November 1996), p. 2; Jeffrey Birnbaum, *Madhouse: The Private Turmoil of Working for the President* (New York, NY: New York Times Books, 1996); Jonathan Orszag, Peter Orszag, and

This chapter analyzes how the tools, techniques, and processes were used by members of the Clinton administration to develop an economic plan and budget that reflected its campaign promises and would ultimately redefine economic strategy at the federal level. The evolution of President Clinton's 1993 economic plan to the 1994 budget can be divided into three periods. During the first phase, the National Economic Council (NEC) was created and its role as the coordinating body responsible for developing the economic plan was legitimated. Throughout this period, there was a general perception among policymakers that the NEC and NEC Director Rubin were honest brokers who could provide access to the president. The second phase began after the president submitted the administration's budget to Congress. While the intensity of executive scrutiny of the budget process generally decreases at this point and does not return until Congress actually begins to vote on budget legislation, several key players, including the Treasury Department, felt excluded from the ongoing budget debates during this period. As a consequence, the legitimacy of the process diminished and criticism of the economic plan from policymakers inside and outside of the executive branch increased. The third phase of policy development began after Congress succeeded in redefining the policy debate in terms of tax increases and government spending. This led to a political struggle in which the administration focused its efforts on securing passage of its budget in the House and Senate. Unlike the inclusive and deliberative process managed by the NEC during the early development of the economic plan, this phase of the process was managed using an economic war room. While the war room was successful, it undercut the legitimacy of the process and raised the political stakes of failure to the administration.

The primary lesson from the economic policymaking process is that centralizing authority in the NEC was effective as long as there was a perception among policymakers that it was an honest broker that could provide an effective and legitimate means for discussing ideas, developing consensuses, and expressing recommendations to the president regarding economic/budget, tax, and trade issues. The success in this regard sets the economic/budget process apart others that were given high priority status, like health care. Yet support of the economic/budget policy process was neither uniform nor constant. When the NEC's role as an honest broker was questioned, or policymakers felt

Laura Tyson, "The Process of Economic Policy-Making During the Clinton Administration." Prepared for the Conference on American Economic Policy in the 1990s, Center for Business and Government, John F. Kennedy School of Government, Harvard University, June 27–30, 2001, pp. 1–86.

excluded or unrepresented by the process, criticism of the process and the policy grew. When these roles were restored, criticism subsided and the policy decision-making process worked more fluidly.

PHASE I: THE ECONOMIC PLAN AND THE NEC

Economic and budgetary problems played a large role in President Bush's defeat in 1992. In addition to rising budget deficits of historic levels and the perceived need to request foreign assistance to pay for cost of Operation Desert Storm and Operation Desert Shield, Congress had demonstrated the capability to reshape federal budget priorities with limited involvement by the executive branch by creating new revenue trends, altering entitlements, slashing defense, and capping domestic discretionary spending in 1990.[2] Seeking to monopolize on President Bush's weakness and avoid his economic pitfalls, Clinton focused on the economy throughout his campaign and began his economic planning well in advance of his inauguration. While large volumes of memoranda were exchanged regarding various components of the budget, two events in particular defined the economic context in which the administration would have to act. The first was a "domestic economic summit" held on December 14–15 of 1992 with Alan Greenspan; the second was the release of projections by the Congressional Budget Office (CBO) showing that the projected budget deficits were much worse than president-elect Clinton's economic team had anticipated.[3] The "domestic economic summit" was crucial because it emphasized the link between deficit reduction, interest rates, and the investment and productivity growth that the Clinton administration wanted to pursue. The Clinton economic team was skeptical of monetary policy and entered office with a plan to stimulate the economy through fiscal policy.

Given this starting point, the domestic economic summit played a critical role in building a collective understanding of the concert between fiscal and monetary policy. Despite the ongoing debate within the administration over a fiscal stimulus package, the December meeting set the foundation for two of President Clinton's major economic legacies: a recognition that there were real economic benefits to be gained from deficit reductions, and a gradual, difficult, and fundamental shift from the use of Keynesian-style fiscal stimuli toward an increasing reliance on monetary policy and the manipulation of interest rates

---

2. Lance LeLoup, "Budget Policy Transformation," in *Presidential Policymaking: An End of Century Assessment,* ed. Steven A. Shull (Armonk, NY: M.E. Sharpe, 1999), p. 215.

3. Congressional Budget Office, *The Economic and Budget Outlook, FY 1994–98* (January 1993), p. 38.

by the Federal Reserve to stimulate or slow the economy. The urgency of the need to lower the deficit was compounded by the release of projections by the Congressional Budget Office (CBO) that showed a major deficit reduction package would be necessary to avoid reaching deficits of half a trillion dollars by the year 2000.

In light of the CBO announcements, Gene Sperling sent a detailed information memorandum to president-elect Clinton on December 23, 1992, summarizing the core of a potential budget proposal and identifying some conflicting priorities that the administration would have to address in order to pursue the economic priorities it specified throughout the presidential campaign (see Box 13-1). Sperling's report summarized the challenges associated with pursuing the president-elect's dual objectives of reducing the federal budget deficit on one hand and reducing the country's "public investment deficit—particularly in life time learning and infrastructure" on the other.[4] Indeed, the memorandum foreshadows many of the difficulties that the administration would have in pursuing the potentially contradictory goals of cutting the budget deficit while increasing investment without pursuing highly controversial options like middle-class tax hikes or social security.

BOX 13-1	**Introduction to Gene Sperling's Information Memorandum to the President**

ECONOMIC OVERVIEW

Gene Sperling

December 23, 1992

INTRODUCTION

You have inherited a two-part challenge of historic proportions. On the one hand, the federal budget deficit threatens to keep capital costs high, drain savings needed to finance private sector investment, and prevent the United States from using fiscal and monetary policy to respond to future recessions. On the other hand, the United States also has a public investment deficit—particularly in lifetime learning and infrastructure. Either challenge by itself could be daunting but manageable. Both challenges together, with their contradictory elements (cutting the deficit, while increasing investment) amount to a formidable task.

---

4. Gene Sperling, "Economic Overview," Memorandum to the president (December 23, 1992), p. 1.

While short-term and long-term decisions are linked together by a vision of investment-led growth and the need for a comprehensive strategy and message, it is still helpful to consider them separately.

The long-term challenge is to increase both public and private investment, so that the United States will enjoy faster productivity growth and a higher standard of living. We can't expect to finish this task or see all the results of a successful productivity-enhancing strategy, even within the next eight years. We can, however, make real progress. You have the capacity to get America back on track, and to create an ethic and understanding of the national imperative to invest in our people and our economic future.

Our short-term challenge is that we are not fully utilizing our current productive capacity. As a result, many Americans are unemployed, underemployed, and underpaid. Developing a short-term strategy involves an assessment of how the U.S. economy will perform over the next six to twelve months, instead of the next six to twelve years. Our capacity to ensure a stronger, investment-led recovery may be the economic challenge we face that will most affect the American people over your first term.

In the short-term, you must decide whether the economy needs a stimulus package, and if so, its size and shape. Furthermore, you have to decide how it should be linked thematically, strategically, and even legislatively with your long-term package.

For the long-term, this memo presents you with a Core Budget. The presentation of a Core Budget is designed to highlight the trade-offs you will have to consider in developing a five year budget. There are a number of unknowns, such as differing views on the feasibility of deep defense cuts or significant savings from improved management. The basic message of the Core Budget is that you can accomplish much of your investment agenda and achieve significant deficit reduction, without resorting to the most controversial options such as middle-class tax hikes or cuts in Social Security. However, if you want to pursue a more aggressive investment agenda, implement universal health care coverage, or reduce the deficit in half in five years, you will have to consider some of the more controversial budget deficit options.

Source: Office of the Presidential Transition, 1992.

Sperling's memorandum concluded by recommending the president-elect make a major speech soon after the inauguration to demonstrate his commitment to tackle these difficult takeoffs and to define the policy agenda by specifying the administration's priorities. In order to define these priorities, Robert Rubin and White House Chief of Staff-designate Thomas McLarty scheduled a meeting of president-elect Clinton's economic team on January 7 in Little Rock.

This meeting defined the economic policy agenda and established budget priorities, including a decision to reduce the federal deficit by $145 billion.[5] In addition, it established the lead role of the nascent[6] NEC in the policymaking process and it set a tone that defined the management style Rubin and the NEC would use to effectively manage the first phase of budget development.

ESTABLISHING THE MANAGEMENT ROLE OF THE NEC

Rubin pursued a preemptive consultative management strategy in preparation for the January 7 meeting. He discussed the meeting's agenda with senior members of the economic team, he negotiated the particular points they intended to argue at the meeting, and then rehearsed their initial statements.[7] The meeting included senior players and many of their deputies, including the president-elect and vice-president-elect, Lloyd Bentsen, Gene Sperling, Leon Panetta, Laura Tyson, Alice Rivlin, Alan Blinder, and Lawrence Summers. During the meeting, Rubin acted as both manager and facilitator. He defined the substance of the meeting broadly but kept it well structured. Rather than presenting his own views, he emphasized his role in assuring the participants they would have an opportunity to express their views and specify their priorities. As a result, despite differences in opinion regarding appropriate budgetary priorities, participants "uniformly found the process fair and productive. They knew how and where presidential policy was made, they knew they would be weighted in personally with their views, and they knew that Rubin would summarize them fairly."[8]

Rubin's strategy at the January 7 meeting was duplicated in the brokering role that he, Sperling, and W. Bowman Cutter created for the NEC. As Cutter argued, "the only way to achieve influence in the White House was to organize and manage a process through which issues get decided. If the process was perceived as fair and effective, agencies would accept it, come to use it, and perhaps even like it."[9] The legitimacy of the process rested on its ability to provide five primary services:[10] First, the NEC offered assurance that they would

---

5. Destler, "The National Economic Council," p. 14.

6. This meeting took place during the transition period before the NEC was formally established by an executive order.

7. Destler, "The National Economic Council," p. 14.

8. Destler, "The National Economic Council," pp. 14–15.

9. Destler, "The National Economic Council," p. 9.

10. Mark Mazur (former NEC member), interview with the author, October 24, 2000.

be able to participate in the process in basic ways—being invited to meetings, having their views heard, and being represented fairly. Second, the NEC provided a conduit for getting messages or concerns to the president quickly. Third, the NEC was able to elicit a presidential decision or reading on an issue when it was needed. Fourth, it served as a source of economic information, including generating informational memoranda to the president on economic issues ranging from the political fallout of deficit reduction, to information about ongoing strikes, or the state of a local economy where the president was about to deliver speech. Finally, because economic policy was a principal focus for President Clinton, participating in economic policy decisions became important to most federal agencies. Many of these agencies sought direct access to the president in order to present their questions and solutions to him in the absence of contrary opinions and, when this was not possible, they often sought to coordinate amongst themselves to keep real choices away from the president so they could maximize their influence over parochial issues.[11]

Establishing a brokering role for the NEC avoided unnecessary conflict with the Council of Economic Advisers (CEA) and enabled Rubin to develop a mutually reinforcing working relationship with Laura Tyson at the CEA, who became his successor as director of the NEC in 1995. In order to avoid competition with other agencies that had process-oriented roles but whose chief responsibilities were the implementation of programs and policies—agencies like the Treasury Department, the NSC, the Office of the U.S. Trade Representative, and the Office of Management and Budget—Rubin made explicit efforts to identify himself as an advocate, representative, and guarantor of access to the president.[12] This latter role was particularly important because while the high degree of presidential involvement in the process meant that no single agency could dominate the process, it also meant that no agency could be left out. Rubin and the NEC became so adept at providing an honest forum for the discussion of ideas that it began to be used for issues that had only a partial connection to economic policy, such as the environment.

THE NEC PROCESS

The National Economic Council includes the president, vice president, ten Cabinet secretaries and administrators of operating agencies, and six heads of staff in the White House and the Executive Office of the President. The core

11. Destler, "The National Economic Council," p. 18.

12. Destler, "The National Economic Council," p. 11.

of the NEC consisted of the Assistant to the President for Economic Policy Robert Rubin and his staff. Between the January 7 meeting and the president's speech before a joint session of Congress on February 17 preparation, principals' meetings were held daily. The principals' meetings were led by Rubin and generally included the secretaries of Treasury, Labor, OMB, CEA, Commerce, and State, and the U.S. Trade Representative, and White House political and legislative people. Deputies committee meetings, led by W. Bowman Cutter, met even more frequently. Cutter organized the NEC staff into "issue clusters" including community development, international, markets and regulation, and science, technology and infrastructure that were intended to change as priorities shifted. The deputies meetings served as the primary fora for interagency discussion and were often characterized by brainstorming and policy debate.

Despite the distinction between principals and deputies, the general organization structure of the NEC was horizontal rather than vertical (see Box 13-2). Rubin and other senior members dealt directly with junior aides and encouraged them to speak out in the regular Monday evening staff meetings. He was seen by members of his staff and those in the broader policy community as an honest broker and a team player. Alan Cohen, who worked extensively on budgetary matters in the executive branch and at the Treasury Department, offered an often-repeated comment from Rubin's staff that he possessed the rare capability of crediting people for their insights and praising people with interesting and insightful ideas.[13] One member of his staff described working in the NEC as follows: first, Rubin selected staffs who were knowledgeable about a wide range of issues and tried to secure a large enough staff to cover all relevant issue for the administration; second, he instilled a team mentality and used a consensus "no sharp elbows" approach to policymaking; third, rather than claiming credit for his staff's ideas, he acknowledged and encouraged the role of individual staff members; and fourth, he articulated a clear set of budgetary priorities, with budget discipline at the top.[14] Thus, while the objective of horizontal management was to create an institution that could react quickly to a changing economic and political circumstances, it had the added benefit of breeding loyalty and respect for NEC.

---

13. Alan Cohen (former Treasury Department official), interview with the author, October 17, 2000.

14. Mark Mazur (former NEC member), interview with the author, October 24, 2000.

| BOX 13-2 | President Clinton's Economic Team |

The Key Players:

Secretary of the Treasury Lloyd Bentsen
Office of Management and Budget Director Leon Panetta
Council of Economic Advisers Chair Laura Tyson
Assistant to the President for Economic Policy and
    National Economic Council Director Robert Rubin

The National Economic Council:

Robert Rubin, Director
W. Bowman "Bo" Cutter, managed the interagency process and international issues
Gene Sperling, led development of Clinton's campaign economic plan
Sylvia Matthews, special assistant to Rubin and de facto chief of staff

The frequency and duration of policy meetings between President Clinton and the NEC intensified in the three weeks prior to the February 17 address. The meetings took place in the Roosevelt Room of the White House, and were often attended by President Clinton. The president was actively involved in the policy formation process and attempted to stimulate debates among the participants.[15] The meetings involved intense discussions and disagreements over a range of issues including investments and the stimulus package (supported by Reich, Sperling, and Brown) versus focusing on deficit reduction (supported by Bentsen, Panetta, and Rivlin), versus others (including Howard Paster and George Stephanopoulos) who argued against cuts that might diminish needed congressional support. In addition, unlike later policy processes, political advisers and consultants (including James Carville, Paul Begala, Stan Greenberg, and Mandy Grunwald, who had run the campaign's media strategy) were brought into the discussion. Both James Carville and Stan Greenberg argued that the president should do something "big" and "bold." Based on the results of survey data from focus groups, Greenberg argued, for example, that the public would support a broad deficit reduction program. Stephanopoulos and Begala opposed this strategy arguing the focus of the campaign had been on helping people rather than deficit cutting. Consistent with

15. Elizabeth Drew, *On the Edge* (New York: Simon & Schuster, 1994), p. 69.

this viewpoint, the president agonized over budget cuts and taxes for the middle class, and fought to promote his investments promised in the campaign.

It is important to note the role of consultants during the early days of the Clinton White House. The majority of political consultants who had worked for Bill Clinton during the 1992 campaign had decided to not join the president's staff in 1993. These consultants saw the monetary advantage of keeping their private consulting operations intact and handling a number of clients besides the president. As a result, they were not involved in the meetings and discussions that led to the development of the economic plan. Instead they participated on an ad hoc basis, often giving their input at the end of the process. This created problems for the policy councils. After weeks of negotiations between the agency members of the NEC, the political consultants would swoop in toward the end of the process and destroy the consensus because they had not been included in prior discussions, either by their choice or the decision of the councils. Since they came into the game late, their objectives were often not fully informed or necessarily relevant to the focus of the policy. Later in the Clinton administration, consultants were included earlier in the process, and some were actually hired onto the White House staff. The most obvious example was Paul Begala, who left the private sector to join the Clinton White House in the second term.

The outcome of the policy debates was an economic plan that focused on deficit reduction and $100 billion in new long-term investment in programs such as job training, rebuilding the nation's infrastructure, education, and promoting high technology, $60 billion in tax incentives and tax breaks for investment in high technology industries.[16] In addition, there were tax increases of $246 billion over five years (with the exception of the BTU [British thermal unit] energy tax, these increases were mostly targeted on couples earning $140,000 and above), and federal spending cuts of $247 billion. While the plan was criticized by Republicans who argued that the deficit reduction was too low and taxes were too high, the budget cuts, taxes, and investments proposed were compromises that reflected the collective judgement of the president and his economic team regarding what type of package would best fulfill the president's objectives and get through the Congress.[17]

---

16. Drew, *On the Edge,* p. 73.

17. Drew, *On the Edge,* p. 74.

COMMUNICATING AND MARKETING THE ECONOMIC PLAN

Recognizing that part of the program would be unpopular and that the president would not be able to carry through on some of his campaign promises, the economic team employed several strategies to market the plan and increase its viability. For example, Panetta, Rivlin, Cutter, and Gore supported a cost-of-living freeze on social security, but Bentsen convinced the president that it would not be supported by Congress. Raising taxes on social security offered an alternative, but would be unpopular. In order to increase the public's acceptance of the tax increases, the economic team decided to leak information that it was considering a cost-of-living adjustment (COLA) freeze for social security recipients, with the intention of backing down from the ensuing uproar and offering a social security tax increase as a more acceptable alternative.[18] In addition, in order to reduce the impact of negative stories in the press regarding tax increases, the economic team encouraged President Clinton to explain and justify his budget proposal—especially the lack of a middle class tax cut—in an Oval Office address on February 15, two days before the presentation of his plan to Congress. Finally, to signal his endorsement of the economic plan, the administration seated Alan Greenspan between Hillary Clinton and Tipper Gore during the February 17 speech.[19]

Despite some modifications, including House and Senate Budget committee decisions to cut the president's proposal by another $63 billion and freeze discretionary spending that potentially threatened some of the president's investment plans, the House and Senate plans did not alter the president's basic emphasis of shifting from consumption spending to investment and deficit reduction.[20] On March 18, the House of Representatives approved the president's budget by a vote of 243–183 with no Republican support.[21] The House also passed the president's stimulus program by a vote of 235–190. And, one week later, the Senate passed its own budget resolution, incorporating the president's program, also with no Republican support.

---

18. Drew, *On the Edge*, pp. 69–70.

19. Bob Woodward, *The Agenda: Inside the Clinton White House* (New York, NY: Simon & Schuster, 1994), p. 139.

20. Drew, *On the Edge*, p. 111.

21. Drew, *On the Edge*, p. 112.

SECURING PASSAGE OF THE BILL

The deficit reduction bill was approved by the House Ways and Means Committee on May 13, but on May 27, the House passed the reconciliation bill by only six points, 219–213.[22] Opposition to the economic plan increased throughout the summer. Congress succeeded in shifting the message away from the promotion of investments and deficit reduction to criticisms of the "tax and spend" strategies reflected in the energy tax and stimulus package. While the NEC was not responsible for congressional politics, it failed to question the need for the stimulus, which proved to be unnecessary by the spring of 1993, and did not anticipate the extent of opposition to the BTU energy tax. Faced with the prospect that the reconciliation bill might not be approbated by the Senate, the Clinton administration altered its policymaking strategy. Rather than using the NEC as a facilitator and manager of meetings designed to air competing viewpoints and work out policy decisions, the administration adopted a war room strategy that it had developed during the 1992 campaign.

"War room" is the name for a rapid response operation that brought together representatives from every department into one room.[23] The war room was effective during the Clinton campaign, and it was used multiple times during the early period of the Clinton administration, notably in the development of health care policy and during the later phases of the 1993 economic plan. While effective for very short and defined periods of time, the war room relies on a very different strategy than that developed by the NEC during the development of the economic plan. It is not an environment that promotes calm, rational decision making or consensus building. The war room must be led by one relatively dictatorial person who can guide the operation to make rapid responses to situations. It is inherently and intentionally reactive not proactive.

Box 13-3 is a memorandum from Paul Weinstein to senior Gore strategist Carter Eskew, sent during the 2000 presidential race, describing how to set up a war room for the Gore campaign. The Gore campaign eventually created a war room in the summer of 2000 called the "kitchen," due to its proximity to the kitchenette in the campaign headquarters.

---

22. Drew, *On the Edge,* p. 171.

23. In this case, Room 160 in the old Executive Office building.

BOX 13-3	The 1992 War Room

March 17, 2000

MEMORANDUM FOR CARTER ESKEW

CC: CHARLES BURSON, BILL KNAPP, LAURA QUINN, DAVID GINSBERG

FROM: PAUL WEINSTEIN

SUBJECT: The 1992 "War Room"

Per David's request, the following summarizes the operations of the "war room" during the 1992 campaign. In 1992, I served as one of Bruce Reed's deputies and as the policy staffer in the war room, where I was responsible for sign-off of all policy paper produced by the campaign. What I describe here is based on my first hand recollections.

Purpose

The purpose of the war room was to provide quick and coordinated rapid response to news events, attacks from the opposing campaign, and other situations that might arise during the course of the general election.

Size

The war room was staffed by roughly thirty individuals. Each office within the campaign—political, policy, opposition research, Arkansas Record, press, communications, scheduling, field, etc.—had a staffer in the room. The staffer was someone with decision-making authority, usually the head of the office or the deputy. Each office had a desk, with a computer, phone, modem in the room. At the center of this operation was James Carville, who served as the campaign's chief strategist. James literally sat in the center of the war room, he had a desk, a conference table and a couch. He and the director of war room operations, Ricki Seidman, coordinated the daily business of the room. Ricki had the final sign-off on any paper produced by the war room staff. There was one staffer who served as the link to the campaign plane, and through her, and only through her, all paper was emailed or faxed to the point person on the plane.

The campaign's senior consultants also had a desk in the war room. Generally, the consultants spent roughly two to three days each week in Little Rock. The consultants who maintained desks in the war room included Stan Greenberg and Celinda Lake (pollster), Mandy Grunwald (media), Paul Begala (strategy), while

(Continued)

(Continued)

others rotated in and out. The rest of the senior officials, including Stephanopoulos, did not actually sit in the war room itself, but rather had offices down the hall. Across the hall from the war room sat the three policy offices—economic (Sperling), domestic (Wright), and foreign policy (Soderberg)—and the opposition research office. The close proximity of these offices to the war room was highly advantageous, since they helped produce the majority of campaign paper. Opposition research had roughly ten staffers and policy had about fifteen.

The war room also had a two full-time writers/editors. These were not speechwriters, but rather individuals with excellent writing and communications skills who took lead in drafting the documents with the considerable input and assistance of the policy and opposition research offices.

The war room had the best equipment available. There were three TV monitors in the center of the room which tracked news programs. VCRs were attached to all three TVs and were ready to record any important information. At the end of the day, a video news summary of the major network news shows was played for the staff. In addition, every staffer had his or her own personal computer (that was unusual at the time). The office had several printers, fax machines for ingoing and outgoing facsimiles, all the online research services (not much of an Internet existed). It also had the only direct email link to the campaign plane.

The plane served as an extension of the war room in some ways. A lead policy person, the press secretary, one of the consultants, and a speechwriter was always on the plane to serve as a link with the candidate. This link, and the interaction of all three with the war room was key to the success of the system, since these three individuals provided much of the "road feedback" on the documents that were being produced and what was needed. They also assisted in getting sign-off, when necessary, from the candidate.

Hours of Operation

The war room was operational 24 hours a day seven days a week from July of 1992 until election day. Sunday was the one exception, when staff were allowed to show up at noon. The day staff arrived at the office each morning at 7:00 am for Carville's morning meeting. It was during this meeting that the day's message and top priorities were set forth. At 7:00 pm, Carville would have a second meeting discussing the day's successes and failures, and previewing the next day's agenda. The day staff were required to stay until midnight. Two individuals served as the overnight staff. They would arrive at 8:00 pm and leave after the morning meeting. These two individuals were responsible for monitoring the overnight news programs and press, and any information about the Bush campaign. At the morning meeting they would report this information which was used to modify that day's message strategy.

Production of Documents

The main function of the war room was to produce rapid response documents. What triggered the production of such a document was usually either a news event or a Bush campaign attack. If we were responding to an attack from the opposition campaign, we tried to respond within one hour (the response process was actually timed by Seidman and Carville). Ricki Seidman would delegate a lead to draft the document usually from either the policy or the opposition research teams. They would work with one of the staff writers in putting together a document with the necessary information. If they needed any information from other offices, the staffer would go directly to the desk for that office in the war room. That person could provide the information, and give clearance for his or her office (at the beginning of the process Ricki would designate who in the war room needed to give clearance, since not every department needed sign-off) After a draft was produced, the consultants were given ten minutes to review. Then the info was sent to the plane, out to the regional press and field offices, to the DNC, and to all the major media outlets.

The war room, however, was responsible for producing more than just rapid response documents. It was also the sign-off point for any public document produced by the campaign, including issue papers, speeches, talking points, op-eds, etc.

The room, and Carville's conference table, served as the ad hoc meeting place for the consultants and other campaign officials.

The key feature that made the war room successful was that there was a representative of each of the main components of the campaign—from policy to opposition research to political—centrally located to produce and sign-off on documents immediately. Collectively, these staffers knew—or had immediate access to knowledge—about details and implications of the policy agenda of the candidate, the opposition's record and agenda, and other information critical to launch or respond to almost any criticism. Equally critical was the close proximity to the campaign's lead strategist to each core component of the campaign. This enabled the campaign to have a disciplined and timely message that was understood and reflected throughout the campaign.

Source: Private memorandum from Paul Weinstein to Carter Eskew, March 2000.

In the 1993 budget process, the war room was managed by Deputy Treasury Secretary Roger Altman, with Ricki Seidman as his deputy. Members of the war room included the primary staff members of the NEC, Treasury, and Communications, as well as consultants including Begala, Greenberg, Grunwald, and Carville. The key objective of the economic team during this period was to secure sufficient votes in the House and the Senate to get the bill passed. To achieve this objective, the war room was charged with responding to any and all charges regarding the economic plan in the same news cycle. In addition, the economic team focused its efforts on those members of Congress whose votes were in question. For example, it worked to reassure the Black Caucus that funds for investments and empowerment zones would be restored, and it reduced the energy tax to 4.3 cents a gallon to secure the vote of Max Baucus of Montana, who said that he would oppose any bill with a gas tax greater than that amount.[24] Once it became clear that Senator David Born would not support the bill, the team focused on securing the vote of at least one of the six Democratic senators who had opposed the bill in its early form—especially Senator DeConcini of Arizona, Richard Bryan of Nevada, Senator Feingold of Wisconsin, and Senator Bob Kerrey. As in the early phase of the process, the White House and the president played an active role. Clinton jogged with uncertain senators, met with caucuses from the House of Representatives, met with senators, rallied the support of the business community, and made numerous phone calls. Ultimately, the Clinton administration narrowly achieved its objective: the House approved the bill by a vote of 218–216, and 51–50 in the Senate, with Al Gore breaking the tie. In the end, in light of the political climate, it was a significant achievement for President Clinton to harness Democratic votes for a deficit reduction package in 1993. The final version of the bill reflected many of the initial aspects of the original economic plan, but certainly not all, the best example being the defeat of the stimulus plan.

In terms of the policymaking process, it is important to understand that the role of the Policy Councils was still developing in 1993. This was the NEC's first test and it is generally considered a success, but the experience also showed that the institution was evolving. The creation of the NEC highlighted the historic trend of centralizing policymaking power in the White House. But, rather than controlling the policy apparatus through an ad hoc basis in which agencies would rebel because they felt they did not have an outlet for their views and opinions, the NEC provided a system for coordinating economic policy in a White House staff one-tenth the size of the smallest cabinet office on the council.

While the NEC was a major step forward in the effort to create a legitimate policymaking process in the White House, it was undermined by the role of political consultants who freelanced around the process and by the use of

---

24. Drew, *On the Edge,* pp. 260–272.

campaign style war rooms which were not effective policymaking operations. For example, rather than reflecting the give and take of competing opinions and ideas under the coordinating leadership of the NEC, in the war room changes were fought for and exchanged as needed to get the votes needed for passage. The ultimate outcome was successful, but the legitimacy of the process was undermined. Congressional support for the final product was also weakened by the shift from the NEC-directed process to the war room-run process. Had there been more coherence to the policy process surrounding consideration of the economic plan in Congress, it is more likely that a more coordinated and consensus bill would have been adopted. However, compared to the health care plan, which was devised totally outside the policymaking apparatus, the 1993 economic plan was a huge victory for the president and for those who believed in the role of the Policy Councils.

CONCLUSION AND LESSONS LEARNED

The purpose of this chapter is not to assess whether the economic plan of 1992 achieved its economic and political goals; rather, it is to analyze how the various tools, techniques, and processes discussed above affected the outcome. It is clear from our discussion that the policymaking process was still evolving throughout 1993. Indeed, it would take another year and a change in the leadership of the White House staff before many of the processes and techniques we have discussed were fully embraced. Some of the delay was the result of a learning curve. A new, young staff trained in the combat environment of a campaign did not readily take to the more time-consuming and deliberate policy process required in government. Those who understood that the running of governments requires a system of consensus eventually won out, but only after the weaknesses of the campaign style of governing became fully clear.

The NEC and the system of decision making it put into place was the exception, not the rule during the early days of the administration. Even with all of Bob Rubin's influence, it took time for everyone in the executive branch to buy into the NEC's policymaking process. As this case study shows, the NEC had early success in putting together a sensible process, but the forays into policymaking by political consultants, pollsters, and media advisers who were not accountable to the system and worked outside of the government occasionally held back the system. As a result, some of the economic policies put forth by the president had neither a sound economic rationale nor political support. This comment is not intended to negate the importance of political consultants. These individuals provide useful services. However, the information consultants provide must be integrated into an accepted process like any other form of information. During the second term of the Clinton-Gore administration, consultants and the information they provided were included in the policymaking processes run by the NEC and DPC. Their information was used early in the process rather than at some last minute. The consultants also avoided—though not completely—end runs around the policy council to the president directly.

Well-run policymaking processes do not guarantee good decisions. But a rational, inclusive policymaking system does help to ferret them out or make them more presentable. One only needs to look at the 1994 Clinton health care plan, which was run outside the NEC and the DPC policymaking processes and which was dominated by political consultants, to understand the dangers of ad hoc policymaking. Despite some difficulties with certain aspects of the policy—especially the fiscal stimulus and the BTU tax—the Clinton-Gore administration created a broad and lasting consensus on three aspects of the national economy: (1) the need for more fiscal responsibility combined with a decline of reliance on Keynesian-style fiscal stimuli and an increase in the reliance on the Federal Reserve and its use of monetary policy to maintain national economic health (understanding the concert between fiscal and monetary policy was one of the great lessons learned by the Clinton administration); (2) the importance of free trade reflected in the pursuit of the North American Free Trade Agreement (NAFTA) and the inclusion of China in the World Trade Organization (WTO); and (3) a recognition that incremental improvements and investments in education, head start, health care, and welfare reform were better than nothing. Although it did not succeed in developing a Marshall Plan–approach to solving social and economic problems, these changes had a profound effect on the nation's economy and the accepted role of the federal government in economic affairs.

ECONOMIC POLICYMAKING II

The Simpson-Bowles Commission Under President Obama

INTRODUCTION

On February 18, 2010, President Obama established the National Commission on Fiscal Responsibility and Reform, a.k.a. "Simpson-Bowles Commission" (SB or "the Commission"), by executive order in response to growing bipartisan concerns over rising national debt and annual federal deficits.[1] At the time, the Congressional Budget Office (CBO) reported a budget deficit of 9.9 percent of GDP or $1.4 trillion, and a national debt of 53 percent of GDP or $7.5 trillion.[2] Although CBO data show that total outlays and revenues returned to historic averages by 2014, government deficits had ballooned during the financial crisis of 2007–2008, and the CBO report in 2010 projected that they would remain unsustainably large without dramatic changes in U.S. budget policy (see Box 14-1). The urgency of this action-forcing event was compounded by expectations of rising future costs of health care and other social services as the baby boomers begin to age.[3]

---

1. A record of activities and documents related to the Simpson-Bowles Commission is available online: http://www.fiscalcommission.gov.

2. Congressional Budget Office, *The Budget and Economic Outlook: Fiscal Years 2010 to 2020* (Washington, DC: CBO, 2010), https://www.cbo.gov/publication/41880.

3. For an overview of fiscal policy issues as seen in 2009, see Center for Effective Government, "Fiscal Policy in 2009: A Review," (December 2009), http://www.foreffectivegov.org/node/10659.

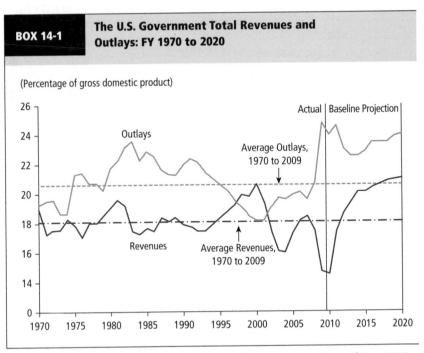

| BOX 14-1 | **The U.S. Government Total Revenues and Outlays: FY 1970 to 2020** |

(Percentage of gross domestic product)

Source: Congressional Budget Office, *The Budget and Economic Outlook: Fiscal Years 2010 to 2020* (Washington, DC: CBO, 2010), https://www.cbo.gov/publication/41880.

These dire economic projections had spurred a congressional attempt to create the "Bipartisan Task Force for Responsible Fiscal Action of 2009."[4] The bill was cosponsored by Kent Conrad (D-ND) and Judd Gregg (R-NH), the top Democrat and the top Republican on the Senate Budget Committee. It called for the creation of an eighteen-member bipartisan commission to study the current and future fiscal condition of the federal government and make recommendations about how to cut the bulging deficit. The bill fell prey to infighting between Republicans committed to a policy of "no new taxes" and Democrats unalterably opposed to a rollback of Obamacare. Consequently, S. 2853 fell seven votes short of the sixty needed to secure passage in the Senate on January 26, 2010. Ironically, it would have succeeded if seven of its original cosponsors—Republican senators Robert Bennett of Utah, Sam Brownback of Kansas, Mike Crapo of Idaho, John Ensign of Nevada, Kay Bailey Hutchison of Texas, James Inhofe of Oklahoma,

4. Library of Congress, https://www.congress.gov/bill/111th-congress/senate-bill/2853.

and John McCain of Arizona—had not withdrawn their support and voted against it on the floor of the Senate.[5]

President Obama responded to the legislative failure by creating the SB through executive order 13513 on February 18, 2010.[6] Because the Commission was created by executive order, there was no guarantee that the Congress would vote on its recommendations. To overcome this limitation, President Obama secured promises from Speaker of the House Nancy Pelosi and Senate Majority Leader Harry Reid to submit the Commission's proposal for an up or down vote if a supermajority of fourteen out of eighteen of the Commission's members supported its recommendations. Thus, the Commission's recommendations would have been voted on in the House and Senate floors under a special procedure similar to fast-track authority given to trade agreements. This admittedly loose commitment was imperative, for although the president had the authority to establish SB, he could not compel Congress to vote on any plan it developed and certainly not in an expedited fashion.[7]

USING THE PROCESS TO OVERCOME A STACKED DECK

SB faced numerous obstacles in its efforts to get legislation enacted into law. Four obstacles were paramount:

- First, the executive order creating the Commission set a very high bar for success. In order for the proposal to be reported to Congress for an expedited vote (a promise made by congressional leadership but not a legal requirement), fourteen of the eighteen members had to vote in favor; this is equivalent to 78 percent of the Commission membership.
- Second, the timetable for devising a plan was very tight. SB was given only seven months to finish its work. This included holding hearings, getting public input, drafting a proposal, reaching a compromise on all

---

5. Louis Jacobson, "McConnell Reversed Position on Conrad-Gregg Budget Commission," *Tampa Bay Times*, PolitiFact.com, (February 1, 2010), http://www.politifact.com/truth-o-meter/statements/2010/feb/01/mitch-mcconnell/mcconnell-reverses-position-conrad-gregg-budget-co.

6. White House, Office of the Press Secretary, "Executive Order 13531—National Commission on Fiscal Responsibility and Reform." (February 18, 2010), https://www.whitehouse.gov/the-press-office/executive-order-national-commission-fiscal-responsibility-and-reform and https://www.whitehouse.gov/the-press-office/president-obama-establishes-bipartisan-national-commission-fiscal-responsibility-an.

7. Paul J. Weinstein, Jr., interview, May 18, 2015.

areas of the budget (including taxes, entitlements, defense spending, domestic discretionary spending, etc.), drafting legislation, and holding a Commission vote.

- Third, as reflected in the defection of co-sponsors from the Conrad-Gregg bill on which the Commission was modeled, issues regarding the deficit and debt, taxing, and spending were highly politicized and polarizing, and support was more tenuous than it appeared.
- Fourth, the Commission conducted its work in the months before a national, mid-term election. When the Commission was established, Democrats held significant majorities in both chambers of Congress. By the summer of 2010, it became increasingly clear that Republicans had a real chance of regaining control of both the Senate and the House. This possibility presented a challenging political dynamic, as Republicans and Democrats became increasingly wary of voting for any plan prior to the election for fear the other side could use it against them in an election. Republicans also felt more empowered and entrenched in their position on taxes (no new revenues) and health care (repeal of Obamacare).[8]

Given these challenges, the SB case presents a provocative challenge: can a president use executive action as a substitute for legislative failure? More specifically, how can the tools, techniques, and processes of policymaking be used to build a consensus among competing stakeholders with regard to politically sensitive and polarizing issues? This case demonstrates that the creation of a representative committee that is willing to consider competing perspectives and hold stakeholders accountable for coming up with viable solutions to a complex problem can succeed in incubating new ideas and "straining towards an agreement." That the Commission was overwhelmed by political forces and received eleven out of eighteen votes, rather than fourteen out of eighteen votes needed, suggests that developing a successful process does not guarantee that the political objectives will be met. On the other hand, the degree of praise and number of references made to the SB demonstrate that the generation of buy-in from a successful process can have positive long-term consequences even if its immediate goals are not met.

---

8. "5 Key Issues in the 2010 Elections," *US News & World Report* (June 11, 2010), http://www .usnews.com/news/slideshows/5-key-issues-in-the-2010-elections/1; and CNN Election Center, *The Issues* (July 15, 2010), http://www.cnn.com/ELECTION/2010/the.issues/.

REPRESENTATIVE MEMBERSHIP

The division of authority over the selection of committee members among the president, the House, and the Senate helped facilitate the sense among Commission members that the views of competing stakeholders would be heard. The Commission members were chosen by President Obama (five appointees), Senate Majority Leader Reid (three appointees), Senate Minority Leader McConnell (three appointees), Speaker Nancy Pelosi (three appointees), and House Minority Leader Boehner (three appointees). The composition of membership—with a balance of Democrats and Republicans, the inclusion of known deficit hawks and social liberals, budget experts, and representatives from the private sector—similarly suggested that a wide range of views would be considered. Furthermore, the combination of Alan Simpson, who is known for his confrontational style, and Erskine Bowles made it likely that the Commission would take on, rather than dodge, important problems. Thus, the incubation of new ideas looked likely.

The members of the commission were as follows:[9]

President's Appointees

Alan Simpson (co-chair; former U.S. Senator—Republican)

Erskine Bowles (co-chair; former White House Chief of Staff—Democrat)

Dave M. Cote (CEO Honeywell International—Republican)

Andy Stern (former president of Service Employees International Union—Democrat)

Alice Rivlin (former Director Congressional Budget Office and Office of Management and Budget—Democrat)

Ann M. Fudge (former CEO Young & Rubicam Brands—Independent)

House Appointees

Representative Paul Ryan (R-Wisconsin)

Representative Jeb Hensarling (R-Texas)

Representative Dave Camp (R-Michigan)

Representative John Spratt (D-South Carolina)

Representative Xavier Becerra (D-California)

Representative Jan Schakowsky (D-Illinois)

---

9. Commission Members, http://www.fiscalcommission.gov/members.

Senate Appointees

Senator Judd Gregg (R-New Hampshire)

Senator Tom Coburn (R-Oklahoma)

Senator Mike Crapo (R-Idaho)

Senator Richard Durbin (D-Illinois)

Senator Max Baucus (D-Montana)

Senator Kent Conrad (D-North Dakota)

President Obama hailed the bipartisan nature of the committee:[10]

> For far too long, Washington has avoided the tough choices necessary to solve our fiscal problems—and they won't be solved overnight. But under the leadership of Erskine and Alan, I'm confident that the Commission I'm establishing today will build a bipartisan consensus to put America on the path toward fiscal reform and responsibility. I know they'll take up their work with the sense of integrity and strength of commitment that America's people deserve and America's future demands.

Former White House Chief of Staff Erskine Bowles and former Senate Whip Alan Simpson responded in kind:[11]

> [Bowles] This is one of the most critically important challenges facing the country today and it has to be addressed in a bipartisan manner. This is not a Republican or Democratic problem–this is a challenge for America.

> [Simpson] We find ourselves in a difficult fiscal situation that is unsustainable. Whatever the results of our work, the American people are going to know about a lot more where we are headed with an honest appraisal of our situation and the courage to do something about it. I am pleased to accept this difficult role and eager to work with Erskine and the members of the Commission.

---

10. White House, Office of the Press Secretary, "President Obama Establishes Bipartisan National Commission on Fiscal Responsibility and Reform" (February 18, 2010), https://www.whitehouse.gov/the-press-office/president-obama-establishes-bipartisan-national-commission-fiscal-responsibility-an.

11. White House, "President Obama Establishes Bipartisan National Commission."

The Commission was given a very small budget that funded the hiring of two staff, an executive director and a junior staffer. Simpson and Bowles met with a number of candidates, and eventually chose former Clinton Domestic Policy Adviser Bruce Reed to be their executive director. Despite minimal funding for staff, Reed was able to put together a team composed of detailees from federal agencies, including the Office of Management and Budget (OMB), Department of the Treasury, the White House Office, as well as a number of assignees from academia and the foundation sector. In addition, several congressional members, in particular Senator Tom Coburn and Representative Paul Ryan, lent the Commission staff resources for short periods of time. These individuals included Joelle Cannon of Senator Coburn's office, Marc Goldwein of the Committee for a Responsible Federal Budget, Meaghan Muldoon from the OMB, Ethan Pollack of the Economic Policy Institute, Ed Lorenzen of the Peterson Institute, Ted McCann of Representative Paul Ryan's office, and Paul J. Weinstein, Jr., of Johns Hopkins University and the Progressive Policy Institute.

OUTREACH

The Commission met on April 27, May 26, June 30, July 28, September 29, and December 1, 2010.[12] The meetings were designed to bring a broad set of issues and stakeholders to the table. Each involved testimonies by experts, stakeholders, or other concerned parties. In April, guest speakers included Federal Reserve Chairman Ben Bernanke, OMB Director Peter Orszag, Rudolph G. Penner, and Robert D. Reischauer. In May, the SB brought in Professor Carmen Reinhart, an expert on financial crises, and Carlo Cottarelli, the director of fiscal affairs from the International Monetary Fund, to talk about the aftermath of the financial crises and the fiscal outlook in advanced industrialized countries, respectively. In June, CBO Director Doug Elmendorf presented information on the mid- and long-term fiscal challenges facing the United States. In July, Maya MacGuineas, president, Committee for a Responsible Federal Budget; and Barry Anderson, former head, Budget and Public Expenditures Division, OECD, testified. In September, Paul Posner, the director of the public administration program at George Mason; Janet St. Laurent, managing director, Defense Capabilities and Management, GAO; and Patricia Dalton, managing director, Natural Resources and Environment, each presented. In addition, on June 30, the NCFR held a public forum and heard testimony from more than ninety groups and

---

12. Commission meetings, http://www.fiscalcommission.gov/meetings.

individuals from among experts, advocacy groups, think tanks, and concerned citizens. In short, they conducted a wide range of outreach to share ideas and gain a broad base of expertise.

ASSIGNING ACCOUNTABILITY AND PUTTING ISSUES ON THE TABLE

In addition to public outreach, the Commission created several working groups headed up by members of the committee to encourage "buy-in" on a final plan. These included the Discretionary Working Group, the Mandatory Working Group, and the Tax Reform Working Group. The Discretionary Working Group, headed by Representative Spratt and Senator Coburn, made the most progress on a number of issues. A general consensus formed around the idea of cutting both categories of spending, and using budget caps, points of order, and seques-tration as ways to enforce the spending reduction targets if Congress was unable to meet those targets through itemized spending cuts. The subcommittees focusing on Social Security and non–health care entitlements also experienced progress. The subcommittees on health and taxes found little or no common ground due to the position of both parties on those issues.

Toward the end of August, it became clear to Commission Chairmen Simpson and Bowles that relying on the subcommittees to come up with com-promise proposals for each topic area was not possible in the limited time frame available. To accelerate the process, the Chairmen directed the Commission staff to draft a plan based on what they thought would garner a majority of members. The plan was intended to be bold enough so that members who voted for it could justify their support by arguing that the plan would actually fix myriad problems. They set the following goals:[13]

1. Stabilize the debt and cut it as a percentage of GDP over time;
2. Return spending to pre-2008 levels (before the financial crisis and the advent of the stimulus);
3. Cut the corporate and individual tax rates to levels not seen since the Reagan era;

---

13. National Commission on Fiscal Responsibility and Reform, *Co-Chairs' Proposal* (November 2010), http://www.fiscalcommission.gov/sites/fiscalcommission.gov/files/documents/CoChair_Draft.pdf; Marc Goldwein and Paul J. Weinstein, Jr., "Less Is More: The Modified Zero Plan for Tax Reform," *Progressive Policy Institute* (April 2011), http://www.progressivepolicy.org/publications/policy-memo/less-is-more-the-modified-zero-plan-for-tax-reform/.

4. Raise revenue, not through marginal rate increases but rather by closing the myriad tax loopholes that cost the government over $1 trillion each year. Cap revenue at 21 percent of GDP;
5. Make the tax code more progressive;
6. Reform Social Security to make it sustainable and also more progressive (greater benefits to lower-income individuals);
7. Reduce health care spending to cover some of the burden of the newly enacted ACA (Obamacare).

On November 10, the *Co-Chairs' Proposal* was released to the Commission members.[14] It specified ten guiding principles and values, and it offered five recommendations to meet them:[15]

1. Enact tough discretionary spending caps and provide $200 billion in illustrative domestic and defense savings in 2015;
2. Pass tax reform that dramatically reduces rates, simplifies the code, broadens the base, and reduces the deficit;
3. Address the "Doc Fix" not through deficit spending but through savings from payment reforms, cost-sharing, and malpractice reform, and long-term measures to control health care cost growth;
4. Achieve mandatory savings from farm subsidies, military and civil service retirement;
5. Ensure Social Security solvency for the next 75 years while reducing poverty among seniors.

The plan included discretionary spending cuts, three alternatives for comprehensive tax reform, and recommendations for mandatory spending including reforming social security.

Reaction was mixed initially, but over the next month the plan began to gain traction, particularly as members offered changes. Republicans coalesced increasingly around the low tax rates and corporate tax reform. They also appreciated that spending cuts were greater than revenue increases. Democrats liked the initial stimulus spending, the higher revenues, and funding for infrastructure from a hike in the gas tax. At the same time, neither side was totally

---

14. National Commission on Fiscal Responsibility and Reform, *Co-Chairs' Proposal.*

15. National Commission on Fiscal Responsibility and Reform, *Co-Chairs' Proposal.*

pleased. Some Republicans were appalled by the cuts in defense spending while some Democrats flinched at the idea of raising the retirement age for Social Security. Importantly, most members agreed not to criticize the plan in public unless they offered alternate proposals. Members also trusted the two chairmen, who avoided criticizing the Commission members even when some tried to undermine their proposal.[16]

THE OUTCOME

The final plan, *The Moment of Truth: Report of the National Commission on Fiscal Responsibility and Reform,* was released on December 1, 2010.[17] The proposal reflected the input of all of its stakeholders. While the final plan represented a compromise that required everybody to give up some of their desired goals, it succeeded in reducing the federal deficit by nearly $4 trillion, stabilizing the growth of debt held by the public by 2014, reducing debt 60 percent by 2023 and 40 percent by 2035. Outlays were projected to equal 21.6 percent of GDP in 2015, compared to 23.8 percent in 2010 and would fall to 21.0 percent by 2035. Revenues would rise from 14.9 percent in 2010 to 19.3 percent in 2015 and would equal 21.0 percent in 2035.

Based on a "Plausible Baseline," which closely resembled the Congressional Budget Office's Alternative Fiscal Scenario, the plan achieved roughly $2 in spending cuts to $1 in revenue increases. It assumed that the 2001/2003 tax cuts were extended except for those above $250,000, the estate tax and Alternative Minimum Tax would continue at 2009 levels, the Medicare physicians pay freeze would continue and war spending would decrease based on current administration policy.

The final plan was broken down into six major components (savings are 2012–2020): [18]

1. Discretionary Spending Cuts: $1,661 billion of discretionary spending cuts by putting in place discretionary spending caps into law lower than what is projected to be spent;

---

16. Paul J. Weinstein, Jr., interview with the author, May 18, 2015.

17. The White House, "The National Commission on Fiscal Responsibility and Reform: The Moment of Truth," (December 2010), http://www.fiscalcommission.gov/sites/fiscalcommission .gov/files/documents/TheMomentofTruth12_1_2010.pdf.

18. The White House, "The National Commission on Fiscal Responsibility and Reform."

2. Tax Reform: $995 billion in additional revenue with $785 billion in new revenues from tax reform by lowering income and corporate tax rates to their lowest levels in decades (since the Reagan era) and broadening the tax base by eliminating the vast majority of tax expenditures (and combining the rest into several super tax incentives, for college, retirement, homeownership, and family). An additional $210 billion in revenue is also raised in other revenue by switching to the Chained CPI and an increase in the federal gasoline tax;

3. Health Policies: $341 billion in federal health care savings by reforming the Sustainable Growth Rate for Medicare, repeal the CLASS Act (which has already happened), increase Medicare cost sharing, reform health-care tort, change provider payments, increase drug rebates, and establish a long-term budget for total federal health care spending after 2020 to GDP + 1 percent;

4. Other Mandatory Policies: $215 billion in other mandatory savings by moving to the Chained CPI for all inflation-indexed programs, reform the military and civil service retirement system, reduce farm subsidies, and reduce student loans and various other reforms;

5. Social Security: $238 billion in Social Security reform, to be used to ensure the program is sustainably solvent in the infinite horizon by slowing benefit growth for high and medium-income workers, increase the early and normal retirement age to 68 by 2050 and 69 by 2075 by indexing it to longevity, index cost of living adjustments to the Chained CPI, include newly hired state and local workers after 2020, increase the payroll tax cap to cover 90 percent of wages by 2050 and creates a new minimum and old-age benefit;

6. Process Reform: Budget Process Reforms by creating discretionary spending caps and caps total federal revenue at 20 percent of GDP.

An additional $673 billion is saved due to lower projected spending interest payments as a result of lower deficits.

CONCLUSIONS AND LESSONS FOR THE POLICYMAKING PROCESS

Simpson and Bowles acted as honest brokers. They understood that getting a super majority vote would require bringing all of the commission members into the process. At the same time, letting the individual members drive the process (which is what occurred initially) did not produce any significant progress or compromises. The subcommittee on taxes, for example, did not produce any type of plan despite meeting regularly. So Simpson and Bowles had to take the lead and design a first draft themselves.

Shaping the process by drafting the Chairman's Proposal was politically sensitive. The plan had to feel like one the members would have put together. Simpson and Bowles needed to incorporate what the players at the table wanted without alienating a majority of members. The focus on increasing revenue through the elimination of tax expenditures instead of through higher marginal rates was the key in getting both Democrats and Republicans on board. It allowed Democrats to claim they were increasing revenues and Republicans to argue they were reforming the tax code and cutting rates.

They key to success was their plan incorporated ideas from most members and both parties. So even though Simpson and Bowles were the authors of the plan, their proposal also included principles, ideas, and specific proposals from members and therefore the plan was viewed as being fair. In addition:

a. The staff remained neutral and worked to provide information to Commission members no matter their political views;

b. The Commission held one hearing where the public could comment and others where the public could attend. But there were also a number of private, internal meetings where the members, particularly elected officials, would feel comfortable bargaining and having honest discussions. This built a certain camaraderie among those from both sides;

c. The Commission also included some non-elected officials from the business community, think tank world, and labor unions. These individuals helped to provide some outside views that challenged the "inside Washington" mindset and reduced the amount of groupthink. It also put people from different sides in the same room. One example was the relationship between Dave Cote of Honeywell and Andrew Stern of SEIU, who worked together on tax reform. Another example was former Clinton Budget Director Alice Rivlin and Republican Congressman Paul Ryan who developed a reform plan for Medicare;

d. The final plan was broad and sweeping. It cut tax rates and lowered marginal rates (Republican preference), raised revenues (Democrat preference), cut domestic discretionary spending (Republican preference), and cut defense spending while increasing spending on investments (Democrat preference). While none of the members would have voted for all of these proposals if they were presented individually, combining them in a single package made the solution palatable.

Most agreed it would address the deficit issue in a real way. If you are going to ask elected officials to vote for something that is going to upset the constituents, including some of those in their base, you better give them a proposal that is big, sweeping, and will fix the problem. Asking those same officials to vote for something that will make people unhappy and doesn't get the job done is bad politics and bad policy.

Even a good process cannot always overcome politics. Though all members praised the process, the SB did not achieve the supermajority approval it needed to get expedited consideration in the House and Senate. On the other hand, a majority of Commission members did support the final plan. This success demonstrates that bipartisanship is possible on difficult issues when the process was considered legitimate and the final plan included good ideas from both sides.

SECURITY POLICYMAKING I

Desert Shield and Desert Storm Under George H. W. Bush

SECURITY CRISES AND THE POLITICAL PROCESS

In the previous chapters, we showed that centralizing authority, responsibility, and accountability for a particular policy in a policy council can enhance policy process legitimacy. It proved to be a turning point for welfare reform and a primary reason for the success of the NEC. At the same time, however, it is important to recognize that centralizing the process does not guarantee that it will be considered legitimate unless all stakeholders believe that the policymaking process provides an effective means of voicing their views to the president or those responsible for its development. During the development of welfare reform and the economic plan, the level of support for the policy was highest when stakeholders felt that they were part of the process and it declined when they questioned their ability to voice their opinions and concerns through the established channels.

Policymaking processes developed during crises often differ from those used in noncrisis situations. Especially when there is a potential for military action, policymaking tends to be more centralized and the involvement of participants within and outside of the executive branch tends to be more limited than would otherwise be the case. Consequently, one might expect the policymaking processes regarding a response to Iraq's invasion of Kuwait in 1990 to be different from those developed to address the economic and welfare issues presented in previous chapters. Furthermore, one might expect stakeholders within and outside of the executive branch to be more tolerant of a reduction in access to key decision makers than would otherwise be the case. We argue, however, that even in crisis conditions where the process is expected to be highly centralized, a consensus within the executive branch is more likely to form and support for the policy is likely to be broader when policymakers believe that the process provides an effective conduit for expressing their views to the president or the designated decision-making body. Policymaking during Desert Shield and Desert Storm demonstrates that procedural legitimacy is important under crisis and noncrisis conditions. When a formal policymaking process is not developed or the process in place is not perceived to provide a viable conduit to the key decision makers, policymakers are likely to circumvent established channels and undermine the process and the resulting policy— either intentionally or unintentionally.

The policymaking process used for formulating a response to Iraq's invasion and occupation of Kuwait on August 2, 1990, reflected this phenomenon. The policymaking process was highly centralized within a core group of decision makers known as the "group of eight" or the "war council." The core group included President George H. W. Bush, Vice-President Dan Quayle, Chief of Staff John Sununu, National Security Adviser Brent Scowcroft, Secretary of Defense Dick Cheney, Chairman of the Joint Chiefs of Staff Colin Powell, Secretary of State James Baker, and Deputy Adviser on National Security Affairs Robert Gates. The heavy reliance on a small group of senior advisors like this is a common characteristic of decision making in crisis situations.[1] Indeed, Bush's reliance on his so-called war council during the Gulf War was similar to John Kennedy's use of his "executive committee" during the Cuban Missile Crisis, and Lyndon Johnson's use of the "Tuesday lunch group" during the Vietnam conflict.[2]

---

1. Robert Art, "Bureaucratic Politics and American Foreign Policy," *Policy Sciences* 4, 4 (1973), pp. 467–490; John R. Oneal, "The Rationality of Decision-Making During International Crises," *Polity* 20, 4 (1988), pp. 598–622; Jonathon Bendor and Thomas Hammond, "Rethinking Allison's Models," *American Political Science Review* (1992), pp. 301–322; Andrew Bennett, "Models of Crisis Decision-Making and the Experience in the 1990–1991 Gulf War," Paper presented at the American Political Science Association Conference, Chicago, September 1992, pp. 3–4.

2. James P. Pfiffner, "Presidential Policy-Making and the Gulf War," in *The Presidency and the Persian Gulf War,* ed. Marcia Lynn Whicker, James P. Pfiffner, and Raymond A. Moore (Westport, CT: Praeger, 1993), p. 7.

Prominent scholars have argued that there is little evidence that President George H. W. Bush sought to promote debate among competing viewpoints when formulating his policy decisions during the Gulf War.[3] While the NSC served as the primary coordinating body for policymaking and deliberation, members of the war council had privileged access to the president and input into policy decisions. As a result, some of the administration's key policymakers were excluded from the decision-making process at critical points throughout the crisis—including the decision to make the liberation of Kuwait a priority of U.S. policy, the decision to double U.S. troops in October of 1990, and the decisions to end the containment strategy using sanctions and rely primarily on a military strategy from November 1990 to January 1991. As a consequence, some outside of the inner circle engaged in behavior that complicated the signal or actions the Administration was seeking to accomplish. Furthermore, because the president did not take full advantage of the NSC process, even those in Bush's war council were occasionally surprised by important policy developments.

The objective of this chapter is not to evaluate the policy decisions that President George H. W. Bush made during Desert Shield and Desert Storm. Rather, it is to examine how the tools, techniques, and processes discussed in the earlier sections of this textbook change when a multiple advocacy strategy is not used. To do so, the process through which several key decisions leading up to Desert Storm were made will be examined.

RESPONDING TO THE CRISIS

This chapter addresses two turning points in the policymaking process during the Gulf Crisis: the initial crisis response to the invasion of Kuwait in August of 1990, and the noncrisis decision to double U.S. forces and pursue a military response in lieu of economic sanctions in October and November. We argue that a reliance on a highly centralized and relatively closed decision-making process in each situation reduced support for the chosen policies.

President George H. W. Bush centralized decision making during the Gulf Crisis in the National Security Council (NSC) and a small core group of top decision makers known as his war council. As in the previous cases, the principal decision makers relied heavily on the work of the policy

---

3. Pfiffner, "Presidential Policy-Making and the Gulf War," p. 7.

council's deputies committee, which was responsible for framing key memoranda and issues.[4] The NSC deputies committee was chaired by Brent Scowcroft's deputy at the NSC Robert Gates, and included staff from the Department of State, the Department of Defense (DOD), the Joint Chiefs of Staff (JCS), the Central Intelligence Agency (CIA), Treasury, the Attorney General's Office, and occasionally Commerce and other agencies.[5] While a general consensus existed among these policymakers regarding the need to respond to Iraq's invasion of Kuwait, there were substantial disagreements over how best to define the problem, what objectives took priority, and how to achieve them. There were major disputes over the objectives of U.S. involvement, the buildup of military forces, the likelihood and timing of military action versus the viability of the policy of containment using economic sanctions, and the need to secure congressional approval.

Critics have argued that the Bush administration should have consulted more widely within the executive branch and with Congress before making its August decision to commit U.S. troops to the defense of Saudi Arabia and the liberation of Kuwait, and again before making its decision to double U.S. forces and promote a military solution to the problem.[6] The first set of decisions took place during a period of intense crisis and uncertainty from August 2 through August 5. Time was limited and the Administration was responding to a clear act of aggression against a U.S. ally that possessed a large quantity of strategic resources upon which other allies relied. Under crisis circumstances like these, the ability to consult with others is generally limited and the tendency for decision making to become centralized is strong. In contrast, the decisions to double U.S. forces and pursue a military option in lieu of relying on economic sanctions were not made under crisis conditions. These decisions were made in October and November under conditions that did not impose the same time or informational constraints that characterized the initial decisions made during the first week of August. They represented major changes in U.S. policy. Yet, despite the lack of crisis conditions, they were also made using a highly centralized

---

4. Lauren Holland, "The U.S. Decision to Launch Operation Desert Storm: A Bureaucratic Politics Analysis," *Armed Forces and Society* 25, 2 (1999), p. 222.

5. Holland, "The U.S. Decision to Launch Operation Desert Storm," p. 222.

6. Robert Spitzer, "The Conflict Between Congress and the President Over War," in *The Presidency and the Persian Gulf War,* ed. Marcia Whicker, James Pfiffner, and Raymond Moore (Westport, CT: Greenwood, 1993), pp. 34–35.

decision-making process without reaching a consensus between executive branch players and without congressional consultation or permission—indeed, the announcement of the troop increase was strategically delayed until after the November 6 elections. Failure to use a more inclusive policy-making process in both cases resulted in criticism and conflicting actions taken by key participants that complicated decision making and potentially undermined the policy decisions.

THE INITIAL RESPONSE

On August 1, immediately following confirmation that an Iraqi invasion of Kuwait was underway, Brent Scowcroft convened an interagency deputies committee directed by the NSC to assess the situation and develop an initial response.[7] The deputies committee agreed to recommend a series of measures that could be quickly taken, including freezing Iraqi and Kuwaiti assets in the United States, moving a squadron of F-15s to Saudi Arabia (pending Saudi approval), and securing a condemnation of the invasion by the UN Security Council. In response to these recommendations, White House Counsel Bowden Gray wrote a set of executive orders freezing the assets that the president signed the next morning (see Box 15-1). In addition, U.S. UN Ambassador Thomas Pickering negotiated with members of the United Nations Security Council (UNSC) which voted 14–0 in favor of UNSC Resolution 660, condemning Iraq's aggression, demanding that it withdraw its troops from Kuwait, and demanding that the dispute is resolved through negotiations.[8]

BOX 15-1	Summary of Executive Orders
12722	2 August 1990. Froze Iraqi assets and prohibited transactions with Iraq.
12723	2 August 1990. Froze Kuwaiti assets and prohibited transactions with Kuwait.
12724	9 August 1990. Strengthened the previous orders freezing assets and prohibiting trade with Iraq.
12725	9 August 1990. Strengthened the previous orders freezing assets and prohibiting trade with Kuwait.

---

7. George Bush and Brent Scowcroft, *A World Transformed* (New York, NY: Alfred Knopf, 1998), p. 304.

8. Bush and Scowcroft, *A World Transformed*, p. 414.

12727	22 August 1990. Ordered to active duty selected elements of the reserves.
12728	22 August 1990. Allowed the president to suspend promotions, retirement, or separation of members from the Armed Services.
12734	14 November 1990. Allowed the president to redirect military construction funds to priority projects in the Gulf.
12742	8 January 1990. Gave the president the power to direct industry to produce necessary war-related goods over domestic products.
12743	18 January 1991. Allowed the president to call up the reserves for up to twenty-four months if needed.
12744	21 January 1991. Designated the Persian Gulf region as a war zone for the purposes of the troops taxes extensions and exemptions.
12750	14 February 1991. Designated the Persian Gulf region as the Persian Gulf Desert Shield area for tax purposes.
12751	15 February 1991. Authorized the secretary of veterans affairs to provide health care for wounded personnel from the Gulf Crisis.

Source: Andrew Leyden, *Gulf War Debriefing Book: An After Action Report* (Grants Pass, OR: Hellgate Press, 1997), p. 107.

After its immediate actions on August 1 and 2, the Administration's initial policy response to Iraq's invasion was ostensibly developed in a series of NSC meetings between August 2 and August 5. The decision-making process throughout this time was centered in the National Security Council; however, actions by the president and individual members of the war council at key turning points in the evolution of U.S. policy suggest that the NSC did not play a role comparable to that of the NEC during the development of Clinton's economic plan. Procedural legitimacy demands authority and accountability beyond that associated with holding meetings. In Chapter 1, we argued that it will be lacking unless all the players believe that their views can be exchanged and dissenting views can be expressed to the president.

Two examples of this occurred early in the crisis in August and September, a third involved the U.S. decisions to double U.S. forces and promote a military option. The first example involves actions taken by Secretary of Defense Cheney when he became dissatisfied with the NSC process because, despite ostensibly being in charge of defense policy, he did not feel that his views and preferred options were given sufficient attention in the NSC meetings.

On August 2, during the first NSC principals meeting following the invasion, CIA Director William Webster provided an intelligence briefing summarizing Iraqi actions, Robert Kimmitt summarized diplomatic actions in the United Nations Security Council, and Treasury Secretary Nicholas Brady presented an analysis of the potential oil profits that Iraq would receive from Kuwait production and the implications of a potential Iraqi incursion into Saudi Arabia.[9] The participants defined the problem in terms of access to oil. They also identified preventing Iraq from selling oil and blocking any effort to invade Saudi Arabia as important U.S. policy objectives. CENTCOM Commander General Schwarzkopf presented two military options for achieving these objectives. One involved retaliatory strikes by carrier-based aircraft, the other involved the execution of Operations Plan 90–1002 designed for the general defense of the Saudi Peninsula.[10] The plan called for a massive ground and sea assault involving 100,000–200,000 troops and was expected to take several months to implement. No decision was made regarding these two options.[11]

According to Bob Woodward's account of the meeting, Secretary of Defense Cheney was dissatisfied because he did not believe that briefing had provided the president with a full range of military options—especially the use of air and sea power to conduct immediate or surgical strikes against Iraq.[12] Given what he saw as a failure of the NSC process to provide a forum for presenting a fuller range of views, Secretary Cheney ordered Admiral Bill Owens and Air Force Colonel Garry Trexler to generate additional options involving the immediate use of sea and air power, including the potential use of surgical air strikes, which JCS Chairman Powell opposed.[13] By "pulsing the system"—using informal ties to sample various services for options—Secretary Cheney thus bypassed the NSC process and sidestepped the Joint Chiefs of Staff, which held a competing viewpoint.[14]

We argued above that going outside the policymaking process undermines the procedural legitimacy of the process and increases the likelihood that those excluded will challenge the outcome regardless of the policy chosen.

9. Holland, "The U.S. Decision to Launch Operation Desert Storm," p. 222.

10. Bob Woodward, *The Commanders* (New York, NY: Simon & Schuster, 1991), p. 228.

11. House Armed Services Committee, *Defense for a New Era: Lessons of the Persian Gulf War* (U.S. GPO, 1992), p. 84, cited in Bennett, "Models of Crisis Decision-Making."

12. Woodward, *The Commanders*, pp. 234–36.

13. Woodward, *The Commanders*, pp. 234–36, 239.

14. Woodward, *The Commanders*, p. 235.

Consistent with this viewpoint, when he learned of their activities, Powell chastised Owens for "freelancing out of this office." He demanded that "all information and options for the services to the Secretary come through him and the Joint Chiefs" and he argued that all chiefs and services in the JCS were to act together by reaching a consensus rather than promoting individual service-based solutions.[15] The fact that Powell and Cheney disagreed on the appropriate strategy for responding to Iraq is not the most important issue. Instead, the primary lesson from this exchange is that when the process fails to provide a means for participants to express their viewpoints and engage in debates about options they identify as important, even very senior policymakers are likely to go outside existing channels. This is critical because the highly centralized nature of the decision making during this crisis did not mean that the central policymakers were able to reach a consensus on all matters related Iraq, nor did it mean that the president was able to act independently of others in the executive branch. We argued in Chapter 1 that procedural legitimacy becomes increasingly important in securing political support for a policy when there is disagreement over proposed strategies or outcomes. Maintaining political support is important because even though the policymaking process is highly centralized, the president remains highly dependent on others in the executive branch to promote and implement his policy decisions.

An inclusive process is essential even when the issue at hand involves military conflict. For example, as much as President Bush and Secretary of Defense Dick Cheney tried to circumvent Powell's authority during the early deliberations over military options, they were inevitably compelled to rely on him to prepare the military force that would determine the success of the war against Iraq, just as Powell had to depend on General Norman Schwarzkopf to implement the plan.[16] The president tried to overcome the legitimacy deficiencies of his policies throughout the conflict by securing the backing of the United Nations and the Desert Shield and Desert Storm coalition members. He also sought to rebuild his credibility with Congress by seeking congressional endorsement of UN Resolution 678 authorizing the use of force before taking offensive action. To achieve these objectives, Bush relied heavily on the efforts of all members of his administration to promote his policy and secure support from each of these groups (see Box 15-2).

---

15. Woodward, *The Commanders*, pp. 238–9.

16. Holland, "The U.S. Decision to Launch Operation Desert Storm," p. 221.

BOX 15-2   **Impromptu Remarks by the Chief Executive**

Impromptu remarks by the president or other high ranking individuals can complicate the policymaking process. While it is often difficult to tell whether such remarks are mistakes or intentional indications of U.S. policy decisions, they can give the impression of disorder in the policymaking process, they may suggest that certain individuals had privileged access to the president, and they can send mixed signals about U.S. intentions or policies.

For example, during the NSC meeting on August 4 at Camp David, the debates centered around prioritizing U.S. objectives and what military response options were appropriate. A consensus was reached that the first objective was keeping Saddam out of Saudi Arabia.[17] There were discussions about oil, ground troops, air power, Operations Plan 90–1002, and Saudi Arabia, but no specific decision or options paper was or had been written that specified the administration's goals and their implications.[18] However, August 5, when returning from Camp David, reporters asked about the U.S. response and President Bush answered,[19]

> I am not going to discuss what we're doing in terms of moving forces, anything of that nature. But I view it very seriously, not just that by any threat to any other countries, as well as I view very seriously our determination to reverse this awful aggression. And please believe me, there are an awful lot of countries that are in total accord with what I've just said, and I salute them. They are staunch friends and allies, and we will be working with them all for collective action. This will not stand, this aggression against Kuwait.

The statement implies that U.S. objectives included reversing the Iraqi invasion of Kuwait in addition to deterring an attack against Saudi Arabia and defending Saudi Arabia if it was attacked. Such an interpretation implies objectives that go well beyond those discussed or debated during the NSC meetings that had taken place.[20] On August 8, President Bush attempted to qualify his statement arguing that while the U.S. would seek the immediate, unconditional and complete withdrawal of Iraqi forces from Kuwait, the U.S. military would be used only for the "military objective" of defending Saudi Arabia and other friends in the Gulf, but the decision had effectively been made and announced.[21] After several additional impromptu comments of this type, Bob Gates and Brent Scowcroft began the practice of joining Bush on his campaign stops in case questions arose related to the Gulf.[22]

---

17. Bush and Scowcroft, *A World Transformed*, p. 328.

18. Woodward, *The Commanders*, pp. 259–260.

19. Bush and Scowcroft, *A World Transformed*, pp. 332–333.

20. Bush and Scowcroft, *A World Transformed*, p. 333; Woodward, *The Commanders*, pp. 260.

21. Woodward, *The Commanders*, pp. 277.

22. Bush and Scowcroft, *A World Transformed*, p. 389.

Lack of a clear process often results in leaks to the press that can undermine both the process and its objectives. On September 16, stories appeared in the *Washington Post* and the *Los Angeles Times* in which Air Force Chief General Michael Dugan leaked information about U.S. objectives and strategies in the Gulf.[23] The articles stated that the Joint Chiefs of Staff had decided that air power would be critical and that a single military service (the Air Force) would be the driving force in the U.S. response to Iraqi actions. In addition to promoting policymaking and operational strategies that the Chairman of the JCS disagreed with and neither he, nor Cheney or Scowcroft was prepared to support, the article provided details about the deployment of U.S. forces in the region and assessed their readiness to enter battle. None of the central decision makers had been notified in advance that the stories were forthcoming. In response, with President Bush's clearance, Cheney relieved General Dugan of his command.

In this example, a stakeholder in the policy process decided that the NSC process had not given his agency's preferences (for air power over ground forces) adequate consideration. As a consequence, he used the press as a way to deliver his policy preference to the president. This backfired in three ways. First, Air Force Chief General Michael Dugan was removed from the process, thus reducing input from an Airforce perspective. Second, it made the policymaking process look less legitimate and thoughtful. Third, it provided potentially damaging information about U.S. forces on the ground.

This example highlights how secondary policy officials can capitalize on disagreements at the highest levels to sabotage policy. It further demonstrates that centralizing the process without providing a conduit for other stake holders to express their views and concerns can be counterproductive. Far from generating an expedient, cohesive policy at the top level, the president was given a more limited set of options.

CONTAINMENT AND THE DECISION TO DOUBLE U.S. GROUND FORCES

Despite their drawbacks, closed decision-making processes are more common and more likely to be tolerated under crisis conditions like those in August and September of 1990. The second major turning point in Gulf War policy took place in non-crisis conditions. Yet despite the change in context, the policy choice to promote a military option rather than relying

---

23. Woodward, *The Commanders*, pp. 290–296. Rick Atkinson, "U.S. to Rely on Air Strikes if War Erupts," *The Washington Post* (September 16, 1990), p. A1. "Top AF General Bounced: Dugan Told Press of Gulf Bomb Plans" *Los Angeles Times* (September 17, 1990), p. P1, column 6.

on economic containment and the related decision to double U.S. ground forces were made by a small number of individuals using a very restricted policymaking process. As a result, these policy processes faced many of the same problems experienced in September and October.

Despite a general consensus on the use of economic sanctions as an important immediate response to the Iraqi invasion, disagreements persisted within and outside the executive branch regarding the ability to rely on economic containment and the need for and shape of military action. Brent Scowcroft and Dick Cheney were consistent proponents of military action. In contrast, there was a long list of supporters for continuing economic containment: Powell, Baker, Undersecretary of Defense for Policy Paul Wolfowitz, Schwarzkopf, Lieutenant General George Lee Butler, as well as Admiral William Crowe, Jr., and General David Jones, both former Joint Chiefs of Staff, and most members of the UN coalition.[24] Their viewpoints were expressed in a series of congressional testimonies, public statements, and newspaper reports throughout the fall.

Despite these differences, the policy decisions were made by a small group of policymakers with what has been described as little or no formal discussion of the benefits or limitations of economic containment.[25] According to Bob Woodward's account, during September and October of 1991, Chairman Powell expressed concern that the NSC meetings had been casual about discussing the various alternatives and clear decisions about options rarely emerged.[26] Given the perceived limitation of the NSC process, Chairman Powell articulated his desire to debate the options and express his preferences for pursuing economic containment versus military action in individual meetings with Cheney, Scowcroft, and Baker. Powell eventually succeeded in raising his concerns to the president in a small meeting in the Oval Office with the president, Cheney, and Scowcroft. Powell specified the economic alternatives to military action, but he declined to express a personal preference for containment to a military option.[27]

---

24. Holland, "The U.S. Decision to Launch Operation Desert Storm," p. 223.

25. Holland, "The U.S. Decision to Launch Operation Desert Storm," p. 224.

26. Woodward, *The Commanders*, pp. 301–302.

27. Woodward, *The Commanders*, pp. 41–42, 302–303.

The decisions to pursue offensive military action evolved in a series of stages. The decision to increase the number of ground troops was reached in October. With that decision, war became even more likely.[28] On October 10, a small group of decision makers including Powell, Cheney, Wolfowitz, and other members of the JCS met to review offensive war plans presented by Marine Major General Robert Johnston, General Schwarzkopf's chief of staff.[29] On General Schwarzkopf's instruction, Johnston argued that he needed roughly double the force level he currently had (in terms of the Air Force, Navy, Marines, and Army troops) to guarantee success, and that there was a window of opportunity between January 1 and February 15 that would be conducive for offensive action.[30] On October 11, Johnston repeated the briefing for President Bush in the **situation room**.

This was followed by a series of meetings among military leaders.[31] On October 17, Lieutenant General George Lee Butler, director of J-5, the JCS Planning and Policy Staff, sent Powell an options memorandum that identified four possibilities: (1) maintain the status quo to deter and defend; (2) prepare for long-term containment, increasing the pressure of sanctions that would have to be in place for six months to one year to be effective; (3) go to war; (4) up the ante by adding sufficient forces for a credible offensive threat.[32] Butler recommended the second option and advised against going to war. On October 21, Powell traveled to Saudi Arabia to meet with Schwarzkopf and assess U.S. ground forces. Schwarzkopf reported that he was not persuaded that an offensive military operation was viable and that such an operation would require roughly double the current forces on the ground. Powell told Schwarzkopf that he would support the doubling of force levels, but that no decision about offensive action had been made.

On October 24, President Bush met with Cheney and indicated that he was leaning toward adding the forces necessary to carry out offensive

---

28. Holland, "The U.S. Decision to Launch Operation Desert Storm," p. 224.

29. For a discussion of the negotiations over military strategy that took place at that meeting, see Woodward, *The Commanders*, pp. 304–307.

30. Woodward, *The Commanders*, pp. 306.

31. For a discussion of these meetings and a bureaucratic politics perspective on the decision making process, see Bennett, "Models of Crisis Decision-Making."

32. Woodward, *The Commanders*, pp. 308.

operations, but that nothing could be announced until after the November 6 elections.[33] On October 25, during interviews on morning news programs on ABC, CBS, and NBC, Cheney suggested that troop increases were likely by arguing that, "We are not at the point yet where we want to stop adding forces," and that it was conceivable that the U.S. would increase its forces by as many as 10,000 troops.[34] According to Woodward's account, the announcement reflected a decision to increase troops and forgo economic containment that had been decided by Scowcroft, Sununu, and President Bush without a "full airing of views."[35] Indeed, Powell and Schwarzkopf both learned of the policy decision from the new reports, and General Schwarzkopf reportedly had to explain it to his Saudi Arabian contacts without any guidance from Washington.

On October 30, President Bush met with Baker, Cheney, Scowcroft, and Powell in the situation room to decide whether to switch to an offensive military option (see Box 15-3). According to Woodward's account, Powell was struck again by the informality of the discussions, the lack of organization to the proceedings as options were discussed, and the casual nature with which ideas were exchanged.[36] Powell succeeded in presenting Schwarzkopf's recommendation to double the U.S. military force and he received the president's approval for that action. At the same time, however, Powell felt that he had not been given permission to raise the issue of containment with the president and that his advice in that regard would not be welcomed. President Bush approved the increase in forces verbally during the meeting, and did so formally the next day, but he insisted that the decision not be released until the congressional elections had passed.

Echoing Powell's concern about the policymaking process, Brent Scowcroft noted that President Bush had come to the conclusion in early or mid-October that it was necessary to liberate Kuwait and that doing so would require using force.[37] He also noted that this was, ironically, only a general impression and did not result from a specific meeting or debate about going to war, setting out

---

33. Woodward, *The Commanders*, pp. 311.

34. Woodward, *The Commanders*, pp. 312.

35. Woodward, *The Commanders*, pp. 312.

36. Woodward, *The Commanders*, pp. 318–320.

37. Bush and Scowcroft, *A World Transformed*, p. 382.

BOX 15-3   Memorandum to the President

In advance of the meeting on October 30, Brent Scowcroft wrote a memorandum to the president outlining his opinion and recommendation. In the memorandum, he argued as follows:

> Our basic objective at this point ought to be to regain momentum and take the initiative away from Saddam. This requires a two-track strategy: on the diplomatic side, a renewed push for full and unconditional Iraqi withdrawal as called for by Security Council Resolution 660; on the military side, accelerated preparations that provide a real alternative should diplomacy fail. One way of implementing this strategy would be giving an ultimatum to Saddam demanding that he withdraw fully from Kuwait (and release all hostages while permitting the legitimate government to return) by a certain date. I would argue that the date certain should be around the end of the year, some five months since the attack and the imposition of sanctions. . . .
>
> I believe this general approach is preferable to sticking to sanctions. It does not appear that sanctions alone will accomplish what we seek in the foreseeable future. Meanwhile, the hostages remain hostage and Kuwait is being destroyed and resettled by others. The coalition shows signs of fraying at the edges because of disagreements over such issues as the use of force, the need for full Iraqi withdrawal, the restoration of the Sabahs, and the Palestinian issue.

Source: George Bush and Brent Scowcroft, *A World Transformed* (New York: Alfred Knopf, 1998), p. 392.

---

war aims, or setting out the strategic military objectives for the coalition and U.S. forces.

Similarly, upon reviewing the war plans, Paul Wolfowitz, Undersecretary of Defense for Policy, echoed Powell's concern about the lack of access and apparent lack of debate in the decision-making process. His assessment was that decisions were largely made in closed and frequent meetings between Bush, Baker, Cheney, Scowcroft, and Powell without the presence of staff or the participation of others outside of the group. As a result, he was "worried that the administration had transitioned to the decision on the offensive option without a lot of clear thought. There was little or no process where alternatives and implications were written down so they could be systematically weighted and argued."[38]

On November 8, at a news briefing, President Bush announced, "I have today directed the Secretary of Defense to increase the size of U.S. forces committed to Desert Storm to ensure that the coalition has an adequate offensive military option should that be necessary to achieve our common goals."[39] The November 8 announcement of the escalation provoked congressional critics to demand a more meaningful congressional role.[40] As a result, securing congressional support became particularly important. Once the announcement had been made, the Administration set about building congressional support, gaining UN authorization for military action, and securing agreement from the coalition that "all necessary means" would be used to eject Saddam Hussein's forces from Kuwait if he did not pull out by the deadline of January 15, 1991. The UN resolution passed on November 29. Congress gave its approval on January 12.[41]

On January 15, 1991, President Bush met with members of his war council—including Quayle, Baker, Cheney, Scowcroft, Powell, Sununu, and Gates—to sign a top-secret National Security Directive authorizing the execution of Operation Desert Storm, provided that there was no last minute diplomatic breakthrough and that Congress had been property notified.[42] At the same time, the president authorized Cheney to sign a formal executive order authorizing Schwarzkopf to execute Desert Storm pursuant to the warning order on December 29. Powell wrote the executive order; both he and Cheney signed it and faxed it to Schwarzkopf. The Gulf War that ensued lasted 42 days. Kuwait was liberated.

CONCLUSION

While the NSC served as the primary coordinating body for policymaking and deliberation throughout Desert Shield and Desert Storm, George H. W. Bush also established a de facto war council of individuals with privileged access to the president and input into policy decisions. Thus, his strategy did not

---

38. Woodward, *The Commanders*, pp. 320–321.

39. Woodward, *The Commanders*, pp. 324.

40. Spitzer, "The Conflict Between Congress and the President Over War," p. 35.

41. Public Law 102–1 (H.J. Res. 77), January 23, 1991.

42. Woodward, *The Commanders*, pp. 366–367.

represent the "multiple advocacy" approach to policymaking which we argued in Chapter 1 is likely to increase the perception of the legitimacy and efficacy of the policymaking process. Because the president did not take full advantage of NSC procedures, and because some members of Bush's team had less privileged access, even those in Bush's war council were occasionally surprised by policy developments. Furthermore, some of those outside of the inner circle leaked information or engaged in behavior that complicated the Administration efforts. President Bush succeeded in gaining support from the United Nations, Desert Shield and Desert Storm coalition partners, and the U.S. Congress. He also succeeded in deterring an attack against Saudi Arabia and in liberating Kuwait. The success of these policy outcomes should not, however, minimize the lessons this case provides about the potential hazards of relying on a centralized policymaking process that does not provide a means for stakeholders to voice their views.

SECURITY POLICYMAKING II

The Surge and Iraq War Under George W. Bush

CHANGING POLICY

On January 10, 2007, President George W. Bush addressed the nation from the Oval Office and made a striking announcement: the United States would soon deploy more than 20,000 additional troops to the ongoing war in Iraq. This policy, called "The New Way Forward," later became known as "The Surge."[1] As noted in the previous chapters, President George W. Bush prided himself on taking action that challenged public opinion. In making this decision, he did precisely that. The public was war weary and unhappy with the way that the president was handling his job. Recent Gallup polls indicated that 82 percent of respondents had a mostly or very unfavorable view of the war, and 63 percent of respondents disapproved of the way President Bush was handling his job.[2] On November 7, 2006, Republicans lost their majorities in the House and Senate in a midterm election that was widely considered to be a referendum on the war in Iraq. Furthermore, several key stakeholders in the military, the Department of State, and Congress had recommended that the president draw down the number of American troops. Worse yet, by the fall of 2006, it had become clear that conditions on the ground were deteriorating and many within and outside of the executive branch recognized that the United States

---

1. George W. Bush, "The New Strategy in Iraq: Primetime Address to the Nation," Washington, DC (January 10, 2007), http://www.presidentialrhetoric.com/speeches/01.10.07.html.

2. Gallup, Foreign Affairs: Iraq, http://www.gallup.com/poll/1633/iraq.aspx.

was at risk of losing the war. Despite pressures to draw down U.S. forces, The New Way Forward called for a significant increase in the numbers of troops on the ground as well as expanded involvement by the State Department and a variety of military and civilian actors focused on small-scale activities, humanitarian relief, and reconstruction projects and services.[3]

The ability of the Bush administration to change U.S. strategy in Iraq under these conditions raises important questions for the art of policymaking. How does an administration that is committed to an unpopular war that all of its political forces are driving it to abandon agree partway with its critics while still salvaging the mission? More specifically, how did the tools, techniques, and processes of policymaking enable the president to get key stakeholders in the military, Department of State, and Congress to reevaluate standing policy in the war in Iraq and then double down on the bet by dramatically increasing U.S. military and civilian personnel on the ground rather than continuing or accelerating the transition to Iraqi-led operations?

The policymaking process served multiple roles throughout this period. In 2005, it was principally focused on implementing and executing U.S. policy. This policy focused on training and equipping Iraqi Security Forces so that they could defeat the insurgents in their country. President Bush articulated the "National Strategy for Victory in Iraq" at the U.S. Naval Academy on November 30:[4]

> As the Iraqi security forces stand up, their confidence is growing and they are taking on tougher and more important missions on their own. As the Iraqi security forces stand up, the confidence of the Iraqi people is growing—and Iraqis are providing the vital intelligence needed to track down the terrorists. And as the Iraqi security forces stand up, coalition forces can stand down—and when our mission of defeating the terrorists in Iraq is complete, our troops will return home to a proud nation.

---

3. National Security Council, "Highlights of the Iraq Strategy Review," Briefing Slides (January 10, 2007). http://2001-2009.state.gov/p/nea/rls/78589.htm.

4. White House, Office of the Press Secretary, "Our National Security Strategy for Victory in Iraq: Helping the Iraqi People Defeat the Terrorists and Build an Inclusive Democratic State," (November 30, 2005) http://georgewbush-whitehouse.archives.gov/news/releases/2005/11/20051130-2.html.

President Bush set broad policy parameters and regularly communicated with military commanders and others about Iraq. At the same time, he generally delegated oversight of the "stand up, stand down" policy to his principals, especially Secretary of Defense Donald Rumsfeld. He also publically expressed high praise and deference to the operational recommendations of General George Casey, the Commanding General of the Multinational Force-Iraq, and General John Abizaid, the Commander of United States Central Command.

The policymaking process shifted in 2006 due to three factors.[5] The first was an objective assessment of the deteriorating circumstances on the ground. Despite initial optimism about the Iraqi elections in December of 2005, the Iraqi government proved to be incapable of resolving sectarian divisions and governing effectively. With the bombing of the Al-Askari Mosque in Samarra on February 22, 2006, violence escalated and continued to worsen throughout much of the year. The second factor was a divergence between what current strategy suggested should be happening and what was actually taking place. The third factor involved the president's questioning of the basic premises on which the strategy was based.

As sectarian violence increased in 2006, the policymaking process shifted to policy evaluation and policy development. During this period, the NSC acted as an honest broker and incubator of ideas by encouraging stakeholders to evaluate U.S. policy in Iraq and by conducting parallel reviews within the NSC. The NSC promoted debate by holding stakeholders accountable for divergences in policy expectations and outcomes, by asking tough questions about the assumptions behind U.S. policy, and by putting policy options on the table.

As President Bush's views on the surge solidified, the role of the NSC shifted increasingly to promoting the president's policy preferences and bringing competing stakeholders on board with the surge. Though fluid, these efforts likely began as early as June of 2006. They intensified in November following the mid-term elections, the authorization of a formal interagency review of Iraq policy by the president, and personnel changes in the military and the Office of the Secretary of Defense. In November and December, the NSC focused on building support with the Department of State and the military. Once the surge was formally announced on January 10, 2006, the process shifted back to policy implementation and execution.

---

5. Stephen Hadley (former national security adviser), interview with the author, January 12, 2015.

The objective of this chapter is to demonstrate how the tools, techniques, and processes of policymaking bolstered presidential leadership and facilitated presidential management of key political stakeholders who disagreed about the appropriate course of action in an unpopular and failing war. Many detailed accounts of the surge have been written.[6] We supplement these accounts with specific insights from National Security Adviser Stephen Hadley and others involved in the process to examine how they viewed the process and the lessons they gleaned from this experience. We do not evaluate whether the surge or other policy decisions taken throughout the War in Iraq were the best of all available options.

THE UNPREDICTABILITY OF BEING AN HONEST BROKER

Two core principles shaped National Security Adviser Stephen Hadley's management style:[7] (1) Keep the president at the center of the decision-making process. As President Bush declared, he was "the decider."[8] (2) Give the president access to options from a broad range of sources so that he could make the best possible policy decisions. Giving the president access to options from a broad range of sources meant acting as an honest broker and incubator of ideas. Keeping the president at the center meant keeping options open until he made a decision and then bringing stakeholders to his chosen position.

With regard to Iraq, Hadley was emphatic that the policymaking process was not designed to choreograph strategy and get the president to say "yes" to the surge. Rather, it was designed to give him the breadth of information needed to make that very important decision. To reinforce this point, he recounted a request from President Bush when he was first appointed as National Security Adviser in which the president said, "I want you to be an honest broker in the

---

6. Steven Metz, "Decision-Making in Operation Iraqi Freedom: The Strategic Shift of 2007," in *Operation IRAQ FREEDOM Key Decisions Monograph Series*, ed. John R. Martin (2010), http://www.StrategicStudiesInstitute.army.mil/.

7. Stephen Hadley (former national security adviser), interview with the author, January 12, 2015.

8. In a Rose Garden ceremony on April 18, 2006, President Bush famously responded to questions regarding Secretary of State Rumsfeld by arguing, "I have strong confidence in Don Rumsfeld. I hear the voices, and I read the front page, and I know the speculation. But I'm the decider, and I decide what is best. And what's best is for Don Rumsfeld to remain as the Secretary of Defense." White House, Office of the Press Secretary, "President Bush Nominates Rob Portman as OMB Director and Susan Schwab for USTR," (April 18, 2006), http://georgewbush-whitehouse.archives.gov/news/releases/2006/04/20060418-1.html.

process. I want people to feel that this is an open process, that they have access to me, and that nobody's putting their finger or their thumb on the scales."[9]

Acting as an honest broker among competing stakeholders does not guarantee that the process will generate new and better ideas or produce a consensus. For example, in the face of growing concerns about sectarian violence in Iraq, the National Security Staff organized a meeting with the president and senior advisers at Camp David to debate current strategy in Iraq. According to Peter Feaver, Special Adviser for Strategic Planning and Institutional Reform on the National Security Council Staff, he and other NSC staff members had wanted to model the June 12 meeting on a planning exercise used by President Eisenhower to develop U.S. policy toward the Soviet Union called Project Solarium.[10] To encourage long-term strategic thinking, President Eisenhower divided top foreign policy advisers into groups responsible for analyzing and defending competing policy propositions with potentially irreconcilable differences.[11] The groups debated, often challenging one another rather than pushing for a consensus. The president participated in the debates and challenged the presenters. He then made a decision, everybody saluted, and the chosen policy was implemented. In contrast to this model, Bob Woodward describes the meeting at Camp David as dominated by a series of presentations focused on General Casey's argument for continuing the "stand up, stand down" policy of building up Iraq forces.[12] The next day, President Bush and National Security Adviser Hadley visited Iraq to assess Iraqi Prime Minister Nouri al-Maliki and evaluate the situation on the ground. On their return, President Bush held a press conference in the Rose Garden where he called for patience and asked people to give U.S. strategy more time to succeed:[13]

---

9. Stephen Hadley (former national security adviser), interview with the author, January 12, 2015.

10. Peter Feaver, (former national security adviser), interview with the author, February 22, 2015. See also Peter Feaver, "The Right to Be Right: Civil-Military Relations and the Iraq Surge Decision," *International Security* 35, 4 (2011), pp. 87–125.

11. Michèle A. Flournoy and Shawn W. Brimley, "Strategic Planning for U.S. National Security: A Project Solarium for the 21st Century," Princeton University: The Princeton Project on National Security, September 27, 2006.

12. Bob Woodward, *The War Within* (New York, NY: Simon & Schuster, 2008), pp. 9–12.

13. The White House, Office of the Press Secretary, Press Conference of the president (June 14, 2006), http://georgewbush-whitehouse.archives.gov/news/releases/2006/06/20060614.html.

The challenges that remain are serious, and they will require more sacrifice and patience. And our efforts are well worth it. By helping this new government succeed, we'll be closer to completing our mission, and the mission is to develop a country that can govern itself, sustain itself, and defend itself, and a country that is an ally in the war on terror.

Consequently, rather than copy the Project Solarium process of hashing out differences in potential strategies and developing a long-term strategic plan, the Camp David meeting resulted in a reaffirmation of existing policy in Iraq.

The Iraq Study Group (ISG) provides another example of an effort to encourage stakeholders to express their viewpoints that ultimately produced the desired outcome but had unintended consequences. The ISG, also known as the Baker-Hamilton Commission, was appointed by Congress on March 15, 2006, to evaluate the current and future situation in Iraq and offer policy recommendations for U.S. policy. Peter Feaver argues that the creation of the ISG was encouraged by the White House as a means of bolstering the Bush administration's current strategy of transferring the responsibility for Iraqi security to the Iraqis and drawing down the number of U.S. troops.[14] To play this role, opposition from some within the White House had to be overcome and the commission needed to be perceived as unbiased. Hadley played a key role in getting the White House to agree to the ISG (a) standing up and having full access to information (a crucial condition), and (b) accepting the ISG as an independent, truly bipartisan entity.[15] The solution to the second condition, first raised and discussed in conversations between Congressman Frank Wolf and Former Ambassador to NATO David Abshire (president of Center for the Study of the Presidency), was to appoint individuals in equal numbers from both parties, selected for both their prominence and seniority. It was also agreed that members of the ISG would not be actively involved in the coming presidential campaign and that they would not be in highly visible positions in the policy debate that was already brewing. The ISG members would also follow a strict rule of not leaking information throughout the process.

The composition of the commission was designed to enhance its credibility by including wise and widely trusted individuals from across the political spectrum. James A. Baker, III (R) and Lee H. Hamilton (D) served as co-chairs. Other members included republicans Lawrence S. Eagleburger, Robert Gates,

---

14. Peter Feaver (former national security adviser), interview with the author, February 22, 2015.

15. Jay M. Parker (member of the Iraq Study Group), interview with the author, May 22, 2015.

Edwin Meese III, Alan Simpson, and Supreme Court Justice Sandra Day O'Conner, and Democrats Vernon E. Jordan, Jr., Leon E. Panetta, William J. Perry, and Charles S. Robb.[16] Also crucial to the process was Richard Solomon, then-president of the U.S. Institute of Peace (USIP). He provided much of the infrastructure through USIP, which served as the funnel for the congressional funds. Hamilton also provided several key staff including Ben Rhodes, his then-assistant at the Wilson Center, and Chris Kojm from the 9/11 commission. Others included Dan Serwer, who helped coordinate advisers and the "Group of Experts" from USIP, the Center for Security Policy, the Baker Center, Center for Strategic and International Studies, and a group of independent scholars, experts, and experienced government officials who became known as the "Group of Experts."[17]

The Commission ultimately made an extensive list of recommendations. Some—including the phased withdrawal combat forces—overlapped strongly with the "stand up, stand down" policies currently being promoted by the administration.[18] Its support for a limited surge—that the president would highlight—was actually intended to secure conditions on the ground necessary to make the "stand up, stand down" policy possible. Unfortunately, by the time the ISG delivered its report on December 6, 2006, the NSC was focused on promoting the president's view that the existing policy was no longer viable and a surge was needed. Peter Feaver summarized the outcome as follows:[19]

> In other words, it ended up doing the thing that it had been launched to do, but the facts on the ground had changed in the interim and we no longer wanted to see that advice. And because of the Kabuki theater nature of this, it wraps the description of its advice as if it's a *bold* departure from our current strategy, when in fact, people in the know recognize that's Casey's next slide on what to do next. And now here's the real irony. The final product of what

---

16. Despite some strong objections to his initial appointment, Rudy Giuliani was in the ISG for about two months or less. After missing all the initial meetings but attending and holding forth on the ISG and Iraq policy at a number of unauthorized press conferences, he "agreed to step down," after a conversation with Baker and Hamilton. He was quickly replaced by Ed Meese.

17. Jay M. Parker (member of the Iraq Study Group), interview with the author, May 22, 2015.

18. James A. Baker, III, and Lee H. Hamilton, Co-Chairs, Lawrence S. Eagleburger, Vernon E. Jordan, Jr., Edwin Meese III, Sandra Day O'Connor, Leon E. Panetta, William J. Perry, Charles S. Robb, Alan K. Simpson, "The Iraq Study Group Report" (December 6, 2006), http://www.usip.org/isg/iraq_study_group_report/report/1206/index.html.

19. Peter Feaver (former national security adviser), interview with the author, February 22, 2015.

they produced was essentially recommending back to us a continuation of the existing strategy.

Jay Parker, a member of the ISG, interprets the impact of their report more broadly:[20]

The original intent of the ISG was never to validate or attack any particular strategy. The goal was to independently assess the facts as they were known at the time, to provide recommendations on multiple points based on the teams assessment and analysis, and to put those forth for consideration by those in Congress and the White House a number of options grounded in the independent assessment. It was then up to others to forge those into strategy. The independent credibility of the group was meant to provide a degree of top cover for discussion.

In fact, at the initial congressional meeting this need—to have a place out of the light and heat where genuine discussion and dialogue could occur—was identified and strongly supported. On the one hand, it was depressing that "the world's greatest deliberative, democratic body" felt itself unable to actually deliberate on the most important choices a nation must make. On the other hand, at least they were willing and able to support a venue where the discussion could take place.

With the ISG's report released many things were put on the table for discussion, the surge among them. Several key folks from the expert working groups later were drawn into the arena and did take part in the debates and policy formulations. Some of these individuals had initially felt shut out of the discussions before the ISG gave them an entry point. I personally think those who dismiss the report had either overstated its potential or understated the inevitable sub level steps and second order effects, or both. It was never going to end the war, nor was it going to legitimize and mobilize support for the war's aggressive continuation, despite those who viewed its presence with great hope or great fear. It is a lesson in the role of those small, seemingly off-line, little-more-than-footnote, but truly essential actions in a complex policy process.

---

20. Jay M. Parker (member of the Iraq Study Group), interview with the author, May 22, 2015.

The president expressed appreciation for the report and highlighted its assessment that the situation in Iraq had deteriorated badly. However, rather than using the report to bolster the "stand up, stand down" policy as the NSC staff had initially hoped, the president focused on one caveat contained in the report that helped bolster his decision to change U.S. strategy from transferring responsibility to providing population security through a surge of military and civilian forces in Iraq. The caveat in the report notes:[21]

> Because of the importance of Iraq to our regional security goals and to our ongoing fight against al Qaeda, we considered proposals to make a substantial increase (100,000 to 200,000) in the number of U.S. troops in Iraq. We rejected this course because we do not believe that the needed levels are available for a sustained deployment. Further, adding more American troops could conceivably worsen those aspects of the security problem that are fed by the view that the U.S. presence is intended to be a long-term "occupation." We could, however, support a short-term redeployment or surge of American combat forces to stabilize Baghdad, or to speed up the training and equipping mission, if the U.S. commander in Iraq determines that such steps would be effective.

> We also rejected the immediate withdrawal of our troops, because we believe that so much is at stake.

The so-called Council of Colonels provides another example in which an interagency process may not produce a particular outcome even if you think you know what is coming. In late September of 2006, Chairman of the Joint Chiefs of Staff General Peter Pace convened a group of sixteen men from the four military services to conduct a systematic review of the U.S. global war on terrorism including the role of the war in Iraq. On November 20, 2006, a summary of the Council of Colonel's recommendations was reported in the *Washington Post*.[22] The article highlighted three policy recommendations including "Go Big," "Go Long," and "Go Home." The "Go Big" option reflected the idea of a surge involving a large increase in U.S. troops to bring the

---

21. Baker et al., "The Iraq Study Group Report."

22. Thomas Ricks, "Pentagon May Suggest Short-Term Buildup Leading to Iraq Exit," *Washington Post* (November 20, 2006), http://www.washingtonpost.com/wp-dyn/content/article/2006/11/19/AR2006111901249.html.

sectarian violence under control. However, when the Joint Chiefs of Staff presented their proposal to the NSC-directed interagency committee, it recommended accelerating rather than changing the current strategy. The recommendation was given despite accounts that suggest that the Council of Colonels and General Casey had been asked by the Secretary of Defense and White House to express their views of the surge and its viability with the use of five brigades. Despite expressing some frustration given knowledge of the Colonels' recommendations, Feaver noted that the institution of the Joint Chiefs of Staff is not intended to play the role of honest broker; rather, it is intended to evaluate the options given to it and present those it deems most appropriate to others.[23] Indeed, the assessment of the JCS reflected ongoing concerns by Generals Casey, Abizaid, Schoomaker, and others that a surge in troops would not bring down sectarian violence in Baghdad and that attempts to expand U.S. forces as suggested could be detrimental to the military.[24]

SPARKING DEBATE AND INCUBATING IDEAS

Acting as an honest broker is not a passive activity. In may involve managing formidable stakeholders who feel strongly about the policies they are pursuing and the positions they are defending. Hadley recounted an exchange with a reporter that focused on this point:

> The reporter asked, "Well, if Condoleezza Rice, a formidable figure close to the president, couldn't knock heads among Powell, Cheney and Rumsfeld and create order, how are you going to do it?" I said, "I have no intention of trying. Yes, they are 600-pound gorillas. But I have a 1200-pound gorilla right down the hall that loves to make decisions called the president of the United States. So if we have a disagreement among the principals, we're going to take that disagreement down the hall, we're going to put it to the president, the president is going to hear our arguments, he's going to make a decision, and they are all professionals, they are going to salute, and carry out his decision. That's how we are going to run the process.[25]

---

23. Peter Feaver (former national security adviser), interview with the author, February 22, 2015.

24. Woodward, *The War Within*, pp. 241–244.

25. Stephen Hadley (former national security adviser), interview with the author, January 12, 2015.

Whether they are 600-pound gorillas or not, getting people to conduct a critical review of a policy that they have been focused implementing and defending against critics inside and outside of the administration can be difficult. Hadley argued that doing so may require "breaking a little china"—by which he meant asking tough questions, holding stakeholders accountable for variations between expectations and consequences of policy, and by placing desired policy options on the table. He argued further that one of the goals of the NSC between May and September was "unsticking the system" by getting each of the relevant agencies to start questioning the current strategy and looking for alternatives. Hence the use of outside groups with independent credibility.

BREAKING SOME CHINA

During the summer, the president reportedly expressed increasing frustration over the number of U.S. forces killed in action. Hadley recounted one such instance as follows:[26]

> At one point, President Bush looked up from reading the morning intelligence report and said, "Hadley, this strategy isn't working." And I agreed with him. And he said, "We need to develop a new strategy." That started the process that eventually resulted in the surge decision he announced in January of 2007.

Hadley requested and was given permission to encourage senior military leaders to conduct full strategy review. As recounted by Bob Woodward, he and Deputy National Security Adviser Meghan O'Sullivan did so by compiling a list of tough questions for Secretary Rumsfeld, General Pace, General Casey, General Abizaid, and Ambassador Khalilzad about conditions on the ground and U.S. strategy in Iraq.[27] The questions were probing and provocative. They asked about the underlying premise and objectives of U.S. strategy, the level of sectarian violence, the capacity of Iraqi forces, the role and political capacity of Prime Minister Maliki, and whether additional resources would be needed to bring security to Baghdad over a reasonable time frame. Following the meeting, Meghan O'Sullivan, who Peter Feaver credits for being one of the

---

26. Stephen Hadley (former national security adviser), interview with the author, January 12, 2015.

27. Woodward, *The War Within*, pp. 71–79.

first to identify the failure of existing strategies on the ground, reportedly distributed a summary of the July 22 meeting to the participants that began with an overarching question: What has changed about the strategic situation in Iraq, and do these changes warrant alteration in military and political strategies?[28]

A meeting on August 17 involved additional "breaking of china" and the assertion of a policy position by the president. President Bush met with Hadley and Generals Casey, Abizaid, and Pace as well as Phillip Zelikow from the State Department to evaluate the deteriorating situation on the ground. Based on Woodward's account of the meeting, after dismissing the notion that the United States could leave prematurely, the president challenged the generals:[29]

> We must succeed. We will commit the resources to succeed. If they can't do it, we will . . . [to Rumsfeld] If the bicycle teeters, we're going to put the hand back on. We have to make damn sure we cannot fail. If we stumble, we have to have enough manpower to cope.

Bush told Bob Woodward that his intent was to send a message to Rumsfeld and Casey: "If it's not working, let's do something different . . . I presume they took it as a message." [30]

Pressure to consider alternative solutions can also come from outside of the administration. One particularly prominent example of this involves actions taken by Retired U.S. Army Vice Chief of Staff General Jack Keane and Frederick Kagan from the American Enterprise Institute.[31] General Keane had extensive experience in Iraq, was serving on Secretary Rumsfeld's Defense Policy Board, was an early contributor to the ISG, and had extensive contact with General Petraeus, General Peter Pace, and Lieutenant General Ray Odierno (who was General Casey's Deputy in Iraq in charge of tactical ground operations). He met with President Bush, Secretary Rumsfeld, General Peter Pace, General Petraeus, and NSA Hadley in the fall of 2006 to personally express his concern about the problems with U.S. strategy in

---

28. Woodward, *The War Within*, pp. 72–78.

29. Woodward, *The War Within*, p. 94.

30. Woodward, *The War Within*, p. 99.

31. Metz, "Decision-Making in Operation Iraqi Freedom," pp. 24–25.

Iraq.[32] Together with Frederick Kagan, Keane led a study group at the American Enterprise Institute that promoted a shift in strategy from training Iraqi Security Forces (ISF) to providing population security and controlling sectarian violence. Most significantly, they argued that their recommendations were consistent with U.S. counterinsurgency policy, but that strategy could not be implemented effectively by the ISF.[33]

In addition to interacting directly with key stakeholders, Kagan wrote a report that specified their criticisms, outlined their policy recommendations, and provided guidelines for implementation.[34] On December 27, 2006, Keane and Kagan also published their argument in the *Washington Post* and reportedly had disseminated briefings to key stakeholders.[35] Keane and Kagan clearly broke some china by dismissing the findings of the ISG and challenging those in the military who wanted to keep the focus on training the ISF rather than providing population security. They argued that the administration's push to democracy had failed to stem the violence and that the key to success lay in beating the insurgency and providing the forces necessary to do so. While the specific impact of their actions cannot be known, Steven Metz's assessment is highly probable: "While the AEI report did not lead President Bush in new directions, it made him aware of the feasibility of a surge, despite less enthusiasm from the Pentagon or CENTCOM [United States Central Command]."[36]

PRESENTING NEW IDEAS

The NSC also shaped the process by developing its own internal reviews, by encouraging others to consider options that aligned with those the president preferred, and by capitalizing on an external review that bolstered its position. The Department of State and the National Security Council developed their own internal reviews of Iraqi policy in October and November. David

---

32. Woodward, *The War Within*, pp. 129–138.

33. Frederick W. Kagan, "Choosing Victory: A Plan for Success in Iraq," Phase I report of the Iraq Planning Group at the American Enterprise Institute, January 25, 2007, http://www.aei .org/wp-content/uploads/2011/11/20070111_ChoosingVictoryupdated.pdf.

34. Kagan, "Choosing Victory."

35. Jack Keane and Frederick W. Kagan, "The Right Type of 'Surge.' Any Troop Increase Must Be Large and Lasting," *Washington Post* (December 27, 2006), http://www.washingtonpost .com/wp-dyn/content/article/2006/12/26/AR2006122600773.html.

36. Metz, "Decision-Making in Operation Iraqi Freedom," p. 25.

Satterfield, Senior Adviser to the Department of State/Coordinator for Iraq, sent a memo to Secretary of State Rice on October 31 in which he concluded that the current strategy of seeking a national unity government "offered only a small and diminishing chance of success over the next two years" and that a change in strategy was necessary to protect Shia and Sunnis from a full-blow, civil conflict.[37] He recommended shifting to a mixed strategy in which the United States would reduce its forces, but not leave. Given this assessment, Satterfield and Rice tried to get President Bush to tone down his rhetoric regarding the goals in Iraq, but the president disagreed. Satterfield's arguments never got traction.

Two weeks later, Meghan O'Sullivan offered a memo titled, "The New Way Forward: Four Organizing Constructs." In it, she developed four options for Iraq: [38]

- Adjust at the margins and stay with the current strategy;
- Target our efforts and limit American exposure to sectarian violence;
- Double down by significantly increasing political and military efforts in Iraq;
- Bet on Maliki by enhancing political and security forces to the Iraqi leadership.

Rather than choosing a particular strategy, she left all four options on the table.

In response to O'Sullivan's memo, Hadley commented,[39]

> There was Meghan's memo, she writes . . . an interesting memo about the ratio of troops you need to put down an insurgency and shows that we don't have them in Iraq. This raises the question of where can we get the additional troops. I said well, the premise of our strategy is that we will train Iraqis to do that goal. Meghan comes back and says that the Iraqi Army is not viewed as an honest broker by the Iraqis . . . [and thus] cannot play the role that you need them to play. It's going to have to be Americans and other outside allies. Very important insight.

---

37. Woodward, *The War Within*, p. 188.

38. Woodward, *The War Within*, pp. 191–192.

39. Stephen Hadley (former national security adviser), interview with the author, January 12, 2015.

For Hadley, this memo raised two management challenges: How could he enhance the credibility of O'Sullivan's assessment and then get the military to consider her recommendation? Hadley chose to seek external validation and then share her evaluation informally. He did so by asking his deputy, J. D. Crouch, to solicit a feasibility assessment by Navy Captain William Lutie: [40]

> Without telling Meghan, I asked Bill Lutie, a former DoD planner, "So if you were going to do a surge, how would you do it and what kind of troops you would need?" Because I wanted to check on what I was hearing from Meghan and Brett by somebody else to see whether the surge was plausible, somebody who was a planner (Meghan wasn't a planner), whether it was plausible, and whether we had the troops to do it. So Bill comes in with a memo in October and basically says, "We can do this." Well that's reassuring.

Lutie delivered his assessment, "Changing the Dynamic in Iraq," on October 11.[41] In it, he recommended a "surge" in U.S. forces and the doubling of the Iraqi army to "secure and hold" Baghdad and other hotspots.[42] In the spirit of incubating new ideas by putting the surge proposal on the table, Hadley presented Lutie's memo to General Pace, Chairman of the Joint Chiefs of Staff.

> All of this was done transparently, with the principals and with the president. . . . When I got it [Bill Lutie's memo] back, the first person I gave it to wasn't the president of the United States. I don't think the president of the United States ever saw it. First person I gave it to was Pete Pace. I brought Pete over and said, "Pete there's a discussion about the surge. I had this work done by Bill Lutie because I wanted to know whether it was realistic. Here it is for your own internal use, 'cause you're the military, you're the ones who do military planning. . . . Make such use of it as you will but I wanted you to have it. [43]

---

40. Stephen Hadley (former national security adviser), interview with the author, January 12, 2015.

41. Woodward, *The War Within*, p. 161.

42. Woodward, *The War Within*, p. 170.

43. Stephen Hadley (former national security adviser), interview with the author, January 12, 2015.

In late October, Hadley and Rice agreed they needed to pool their teams, bringing together Meghan O'Sullivan and Peter Feaver from the NSC and David Satterfeld from State. On November 10, President Bush formally authorized an interagency review headed by Hadley's deputy, J. D. Crouch. The team included Crouch, O'Sullivan, and Feaver from the NSC, and Zelikow and Satterfeld from the Department of State, as well as representatives from the Department of Defense, the Director of National Intelligence, the CIA, and the Department of the Treasury.

PROMOTING THE PRESIDENT'S AGENDA

The authorization of a formal interagency review with representation from the NSC, Department of State, and other organizations provided the means for moving the assessment of Iraqi policy forward. Escalating violence (October was one of the most violent months on record) and Republican losses in the mid-term election on November 7 added a sense of urgency by suggesting that the window for implementing change was closing. President Bush's announcement on November 8 that Donald Rumsfeld had resigned also added momentum. While Secretary Rumsfeld had been a strong backer of the "stand up, stand down" policy, he assisted moving the process forward by writing a memo arguing that U.S. policy in Iraq "is not working well enough" and is calling for "a major adjustment."[44] While provocative given Rumsfeld's longstanding opposition to the change, the appearance of his memo in the press gave President Bush an opportunity to discuss the possibility of changes in U.S. policy and let the public know that he would be announcing a new strategy.[45] As the administration moved toward this goal, the NSC shifted its focus to bringing others to the president's position.

The honest broker process had succeeded in getting many different stakeholders to acknowledge the challenges in Iraq. Unfortunately, it had not led to a consensus on the best strategy for addressing them. Michael Gordon recently published a transcript of a meeting that took place in November of 2006 that demonstrates the extent to which key stakeholders in the Department of State and National Security Council continued to disagree about the best strategy to

---

44. See the memo from the *New York Times,* http://www.nytimes.com/2006/12/03/world/middleeast/03mtext.html; See also the story from the *Public Broadcasting Service,* http://www.pbs.org/newshour/bb/middle_east-jan-june08-surge_03-11/.

45. James Klatell, "Adviser: Bush Not Swayed by Iraq Panel," CBS/AP (December 3, 2006), http://www.cbsnews.com/news/adviser-bush-not-swayed-by-iraq-panel/.

pursue in Iraq.[46] The transcript reveals Secretary of State Rice's ongoing concern that the existing strategy was failing and her belief the United States should refocus its efforts on "core interests" such as fighting al Qaeda, limiting Iranian aggression, averting mass killings, and recovering the initiative in the Middle East. She is broadly supported by Philip Zelikow, Counselor of the Department of State, who emphasizes the rise of sectarian violence and the risk to the United States of expending its forces in an effort to defeat sectarian violence militarily rather than fighting terrorism. Meanwhile, David Satterfeld, Senior Adviser to the Department of State/Coordinator for Iraq, argued that U.S. security efforts had become focused on the Green Zone and that the central government was too weak to provide security beyond that point. To correct this, he recommended supporting specific Iraqi Security Force units who would be willing to advance American interests.

In contrast, Meghan O'Sullivan highlighted the dangers of failing to manage the sectarian violence and increase security. Hadley questioned whether or not we could provide sufficient levels of security to achieve the objectives that Rice specified. Rice did not think so. Hadley argued that expanding the U.S. military presence could help bolster security. Brett McGurk, on the National Security Council staff, supported the buildup by arguing that a large U.S. troop presence had succeeded in providing security when facing counter-insurgencies. He expressed concern, however, that the United States had never had sufficient troops in Baghdad to do so. Zelikow argued that this could take six to eight U.S. brigades; this would take time and the risks were huge. Hadley warned that drawing down U.S. forces could create conditions for a regional Sunni and Shia clash. Feaver argued that they had a small window of time in which to operate.

The exchanges reflected in this transcript reflect the same type of back-and-forth debate that Bob Woodward describes occuring among President Bush and the principals on Sunday, November 26.[47] Specifics aside, the exchange demonstrates that even as late as November of 2006, there was no consensus among key players in the Department of State and National Security Council about

---

46. Michael R. Gordon, "The Secret Surge Debate," *Foreign Policy* (March 17, 2013), http://foreignpolicy.com/2013/03/18/the-secret-surge-debate/. The transcript corresponds closely to a summary of meeting that Bob Woodward describes taking place on Sunday, November 26, in Woodward, *The War Within*, pp. 244–248.

47. Woodward, *The War Within*, pp. 244–248.

how to fix the problems in Iraq. Hadley's assessment of the situation suggests that there was a lot of work to do:[48]

> The Chiefs and the Chairman of the Joint Chiefs Pete Pace are not on board, and Condi isn't on board. . . . . So the first week in December, what is happening is that the president has four, maybe five NSC meetings in various venues and with various degrees of formalities. And he's asking questions, and his questions are both to satisfy himself that he is moving in the right direction towards the surge, but also to bring his principal national security advisers to that place as well.

President Bush placed a high value on aligning various stakeholders with his policies. Hadley attributes this to several factors. First, the president wants to verify that he is making the best policy choice. He holds his team in high regard and respects their opinions. If he cannot convince trusted advisers like Condoleezza Rice, then there is something wrong. Second, the president does not want a split among his cabinet. With a hostile external environment outside of the White House, internal splits could incapacitate the administration. Third, the president wants the people who are going to implement the policy to believe in it. This would motivate them to do well, and it would empower them when defending the policy against its many potential critics.

The NSC focused many of its actions in December on bringing Condoleezza Rice, Peter Pace, and the Joint Chiefs of Staff on board. Bringing these stakeholders on board involved a combination of persuasion, compromise, and direct intervention by the president. Three issues were paramount. These included a shift in the U.S. mission from training Iraqi forces to providing population security and defeating the insurgency, the number of troops needed to achieve those objectives and the consequences that would have on the ability of the military to achieve other "core" missions, and the willingness of Prime Minister al-Maliki to accept an increase in U.S. forces without opposition or interference.

Throughout the month, ongoing negotiations took place among Hadley, Rice, Petraeus, Gates and the other principals. Megan O'Sullivan and General

---

48. Stephen Hadley (former national security adviser), interview with the author, January 12, 2015.

Keane actively took advantage of their connections to the various stakehold-ers to promote the president's agenda.[49] O'Sullivan worked with Petraeus, who tried to persuade General Ray Odierno (Casey's deputy and tactical ground commander) that since the mission had shifted to providing popula-tion security, counterinsurgency tactics required providing as many troops as possible.[50]

The president himself played a central role in bringing U.S. military leaders and Prime Minister al-Maliki on board. On December 13, President Bush and Vice President Cheney met the Joint Chiefs of Staff to address their concerns about a change in U.S. strategy and a potential surge in U.S. forces in Iraq. Rather than summoning them to the White House, the president signaled his respect by joining the group in a secure conference room in the Pentagon known as the "Tank."[51] At the meeting, the president asked for their input. He also sought to mollify concerns by General Schoomaker and others about an increase in land forces.[52] Despite challenging his commanders, President Bush signaled his respect by always supporting them in public and by nominat-ing General Casey for the position of Chief of Staff of the Army in January. He also helped to bring the Joint Chiefs of Staff and the Department of State on board by broadening both the mission and participation in the mission itself. Winning the peace meant expanding civilian participation on the ground, and developing provisional reconstruction teams that included civilian as well as military personnel involved in providing basic services and reestablishing a functional society.

On November 30 and again on January 4, President Bush spoke directly to Prime Minister al-Maliki to secure his unequivocal support for at least two additional brigades.[53] Al-Maliki responded in a nation-wide speech on January 6, 2007, arguing that "Iraqi troops would lead a new assault against insurgents and militias, with U.S. help as needed."[54] The president and Hadley agreed that the U.S. mission could proceed.

---

49. These exchanges are detailed in Woodward, *The War Within*, pp. 270–321.

50. Woodward, *The War Within*, p. 300.

51. Fred Barnes, "How Bush Decided on the Surge," *The Weekly Standard*, 13, 20 (2008).

52. Metz, "Decision-Making in Operation Iraqi Freedom,".

53. Woodward, *The War Within*, pp. 257, 311.

54. Mark Kukis, "Maliki's Last Stand?" *Time* (January 5, 2007) http://content.time.com/time/world/article/0,8599,1574410,00.html.

Hadley provided the following synopsis of the month: [55]

> During the month of December, the president is bringing his national security principals on board. He finally gets Condi to say okay I'm okay with more troops, as long as they're not doing the same thing they're doing, and the president says no we have a different strategy. So Condi is on board. Gradually, Pete Pace has come around, the military is almost there. Bob Gates, now back from Iraq, is involved in this process, and is coming on board with the surge. The final piece of course is the meeting the president has in the Tank with the Chairmen. At this point it's pretty clear that he's got the commanders in the field more or less on board. But the Joint Chiefs, (who don't fight wars, they only raise the forces for the wars), are not on board because they think the strain will break the force. So, the president is also bringing the Chiefs along by meeting their objections to a surge because at the end of the day, he also understands that a split between the president and his military over a military strategy in wartime is a prescription for failure.
>
> Ultimately, mostly everybody's on board. So when he announces the surge—knowing that the country is going to be stunned, and that all the Democrats in Congress and a good chunk of Republicans are going to think it's the craziest idea they ever heard of since the Baker-Hamilton report got everybody thinking we were about to step down—the president is confident he's got his administration behind him.

CONCLUSION

Changing policy is difficult, especially when doing so means escalating military and civilian involvement in a war that lacks public support. Such a change is particularly challenging if it is driven by the White House and is not supported by top military commanders in the field, the Joint Chiefs of Staff, or the Secretary of State. The National Security Council played a critical role in getting these stakeholders to reevaluate standing U.S. policy and consider

---

55. Stephen Hadley (former national security adviser), interview with the author, January 12, 2015.

alternatives. Its experiences provide several insights into the dynamics of the policymaking process:

- The National Security Council used the policymaking process to provide the president with a wide range of information and ideas from multiple sources;
- Serving as an incubator of ideas often required the NSC to "break some china" by asking tough questions and holding stakeholders accountable for divergences between policy predictions and outcomes;
- Acting as an honest broker helped generate concern that the situation in Iraq was deteriorating, but it did not generate a consensus on an appropriate solution;
- Once the president had made a decision, it was important to build support and bring other stakeholders on board rather than asking them to simply salute and carry out the order. Doing this required acknowledging their concerns. It also meant engaging a wide variety of public and private figures, including the president of the United States.

PRACTICE SCENARIOS

PRACTICE SCENARIOS

The art of policymaking is the art of leading people and managing problems by using a process that enables the president and other key government officials to make and implement the best possible decisions for the nation. When used effectively, the tools, techniques, and processes of policymaking enhance the president's ability—and the ability of those he charges with the responsibility to act—to lead the policymaking process. The tools, techniques, and processes also help the president manage policymaking by providing staffing functions, by coordinating the agencies and departments within the Executive Office of the President, by designating accountability, and by monitoring policy implementation and execution. We argue, in particular, that the policymaking process operates best when the authority, responsibility, and accountability for a particular policy are clearly specified and all policymakers with a stake in the policy believe that the process provides a legitimate and effective means of voicing their concerns to the president or those responsible for policy development.

As we argued above, the perceived legitimacy and effectiveness of the process of policymaking can be as important as achieving a specific policy outcome to members of the policymaking community. When the process is considered to be illegitimate or ineffective, policymakers will circumvent the process and use other means—such as leaking information to the media, ignoring the established chains of command, and/or using alternative means to contact the president or other key decision makers directly—to promote their objectives. Such activities undermine the policymaking process because they tend to present the president, the decision makers responsible for the policy at hand, and the public at large with a biased view of the issue. Furthermore, they often spark retaliatory actions by others who do not share the critic's views. The end result may be an ill-considered policy or, even more likely, political deadlock on both the issue at hand and other policy proposals considered important to political opponents. The tools, techniques, and processes help establish systems of decision making that enable the effective participation of all relevant policymakers. When these tools, techniques, and processes are applied appropriately they can facilitate policymaking; when they are ignored the process tends to unravel.

In this chapter, we present several scenarios that require action by the executive branch. The objective is for students to practice using the tools, techniques, and processes analyzed in this book. The scenarios involve different sets of issues—including a domestic problem over a texting ban, security and political problems associated with Russian intervention in Ukraine, and environmental and trade concerns in the context of the U.S.-European Transatlantic Agenda for the twenty-first century. Although the reader may lack some of the issue-specific information needed to reach a final policy decision, the reader can design a policymaking process to acquire that information and develop potential policy responses to each of these issues.

The key to successful policymaking is to develop an effective and legitimate process for creating and implementing policy in response to an action-forcing event. Box 17-1 provides a ten-step checklist for developing an effective and legitimate process. Each step is summarized with references to the earlier sections of this book to make it easier for students to reference information.

BOX 17-1 **A Ten-Step Policy Process**

Step 1: Assess the context, issues, and implications of the action-forcing event. Given these factors, identify all necessary and appropriate participants to be included in developing a policy response. Identify a coordinating entity (e.g., the appropriate policy council) that will set up and manage the process.

Step 2: Develop a specific timetable for the policy response. The timetable should include the date for a final decision by the president. It should also specify how much time each agency, department, or other policymaking entity has to develop policy options. In addition, the coordinating entity should establish a specific meeting schedule, agenda items, and deadlines for completion of all intermediary steps.

Step 3: The coordinating entity will direct a series of interagency meetings. The first meeting should entail an overview of the problem and potential solutions from each participating agency's perspective.

Step 4: If there is an immediate consensus, the coordinating entity should identify one lead agency to work with the others in developing a single proposal for the agency principals. If there is no immediate consensus, the coordinating entity should identify the agencies that will be given primary responsibility for developing competing policy proposals.

Step 5: If there are competing proposals, the coordinating entity should try to build a consensus around one or two of the competing options (or as few of the options as possible). Some proposals may be modified to make them compatible, while some agencies are likely to drop competing proposals in light of debates within the working group.

Step 6: Once a consensus around one or two proposals has been developed, a draft decision memorandum should be prepared for the agency principals. Public support for the various options can be tested by polling before the decision memorandum is formally presented to the president or the chief decision makers.

Step 7: If all of the department heads and agency principals agree on the decision memorandum, it can go forward to the president. If not, further principals' meeting(s) may be needed to find consensus. To preserve legitimacy and buy-in, no agency should be prevented from putting forth a dissenting proposal in the final decision memorandum.

Step 8: The president makes a decision or asks for more options and/or information.

Step 9: Assuming the president chooses one of the options proposed in the decision memorandum, the coordinating entity should direct the appropriate agencies or departments to implement the president's decision. If legislation is needed, a Legislative Referral Memorandum (LRM) will be written by the OMB and an accompanying Statement of Administration Position (SAP) will be drafted by the relevant agency and circulated to Congress along with the legislation.

(Continued)

(Continued)

> If the president chooses to take regulatory or executive action to implement the policy, no SAP will be produced and the process will proceed through the existing regulatory and legal channels.

Step 10:   Decide whether the president or a specific agency or department will take the lead in announcing the policy decision. The White House or designated agency or department will then prepare press paper/fact sheets and question and answer sheets that will communicate and market the proposal to Congress and the public at large.

Scenario One: Texting While Driving

All around the country there have been bans to make driving while talking on a handheld phone illegal. Many states and cities have also made it illegal to text and drive. The primary rationale for these bans is that some studies found driving while talking on the phone or texting causes accidents.

Prior to their implementation, some experts wondered about how effective the bans would be, particularly among some of the more at-risk groups like teen drivers. In December 2009, a teen interviewed by Reuters said that most drivers, especially teen drivers, would simply ignore the bans and continue to text and drive and talk and drive. In states where the bans are in effect, police are ticketing people for talking on handheld phones while driving. However, law enforcement officers note that catching a driver texting is very difficult.

Some lawmakers are calling for nationwide bans on texting while driving. There are already national laws against texting and driving for federal employees, and in 2010 the U.S. Department of Transportation issued a new rule that would ban bus drivers and drivers of large trucks from texting while driving. The ban would impose a hefty $2,750 fine on drivers caught violating the ban.

Assess whether this constitutes an action-forcing event. If it does, design a policy process to develop a response following the ten-step policy process in Box 17-1. Consider the roles and views of some of the following stakeholders:

Agencies

Attorney General/Department of Justice

Director of the Office of Management and Budget

Secretary of Treasury

Chair of the Federal Communications Commission

Director of the Office of Science and Technology Policy

White House Offices

White House Chief of Staff

Domestic Policy Council Director/Adviser

National Economic Council Director/Adviser

Chief of Staff to the Vice President

White House Counsel

White House Director of Congressional Affairs

White House Communications Director

White House Director of Political Affairs

White House Director of Public Liaison

Staff Secretary

Outside Advisors

Pollster

Scenario Two: Ukraine Crisis

More than 3,000 people have been killed in the continuing crisis in Ukraine. Pro-Russian separatists are fighting government forces in eastern Ukraine. President Viktor Yanukovych fled the country in February of 2014 after months of violent protests in the capital against his refusal to sign a deal that would have created closer ties between Ukraine and the European Union (EU). Since then, more than one million people have been displaced by the conflict, which has raised underlying tensions between ethnic Ukrainians, Russians, and other minorities in the former Soviet republic. Fear of Russian incursions is growing in the Baltic. Lithuania, Latvia, and Estonia have asked for U.S. and NATO assistance. Russian actions in Syria and a surge of refugees are increasing tensions across Europe.

NATO has said it will form a 4,000-strong force able to go into action in 48 hours in response to an attack against any of its alliance members, under Article 5 of the Washington Treaty. It remains divided, however, on how best to respond to incidents in Ukraine and other non-NATO countries.

Assess whether this constitutes an action-forcing event. If it does, design a policy process to develop a response following the ten-step policy process in Box 17-1. Consider the roles and views of some of the following stakeholders:

Agencies

Secretary of State

Secretary of Defense

Secretary of Treasury

Chairman of the Joint Chiefs of Staff

Director National Intelligence

White House Offices

White House Chief of Staff

National Security Council Director/Adviser

Chief of Staff to the Vice President

White House Director of Congressional Affairs

Scenario Three: U.S.–European Environmental Negotiations

Environmentalists and the fishing industry in the United States have become increasingly concerned by the depletion of fish stocks throughout the northern Atlantic. They have joined forces in a coalition calling for the United States to press Europe to address this problem in a way that can promote the growth of fishing stocks for future consumption and conservation.

In two days, the president will be addressing an ongoing meeting between the United States and members of the EU in Madrid to set a Transatlantic Agenda for the twenty-first century. During several months of preparatory negotiations, two difficult issues were settled: burden-sharing regarding the reconstruction of Afghanistan and the establishment of a cooperative agreement aimed at eliminating trade barriers between the United States and the EU. The remaining issue is, however, the most contentious. It involves the establishment of a multilateral agreement to manage the use of living resources in the Atlantic Ocean. The issue has become a matter of increasing international concern as fish stocks have declined and international competition over remaining commercial species has become more vicious.

The dispute has divided Europe, pitting Spain, Portugal, Italy, and France against the UK and Germany. The former group argues against additional multilateral management and supports increased privatization of the oceans, with no restrictions other than possibly extending the exclusive economic zones (EEZs). Canada has joined the latter countries in seeking a multilateral management regime to control fishing throughout the Atlantic. Canadian representatives argue that privatizing the oceans will lead to maritime conflicts similar to the 1995 incident when Canadian patrol boats fired on a Spanish fishing vessel near the 200-mile Exclusive Economic Zone limit off of Newfoundland to stop it from overfishing.

Assess whether this constitutes an action-forcing event. If it does, design a policy process to develop a response following the ten-step policy process in Box 17-1. Consider the roles and views of some of the following stakeholders:

Agencies

United States Trade Representative

Secretary of the Interior

Secretary of Commerce

Secretary of Agriculture

Secretary of State

Secretary of Treasury

Chair of the Council on Environmental Quality

Chair of the Council of Economic Advisers

White House Offices

White House Chief of Staff

National Economic Council Director/Adviser

National Security Council Director/Adviser

Chief of Staff to the Vice President

White House Director of Congressional Affairs

GLOSSARY

Action-Forcing Event: A potential or existing situation that necessitates presidential action or review. Examples of action-forcing events include the onset of a military conflict that threatens the United States, an upcoming vote on important legislation, and the issuing of an executive order by the president.

Adhocracy Model: Policymaking management model that is highly decentralized and encourages creativity at the expense of accountability. It does rely on regularized and systematic patterns of providing advice to the president.

Administration Policy: Policy becomes "administration policy" when the Office of Management and Budget prepares a Statement of Administrative Policy (SAP). See also **Statement of Administrative Policy (SAP).**

Agency/Department: An "agency" or "department" is a federal entity that is chartered by Congress or the president to develop policies, run programs, and issue and enforce regulations.

Agency-Owned Issues: As part of the Legislative Referral Memorandum (LRM) process, executive agencies may oversee and coordinate issues without direct presidential involvement. The strategy of identifying "agency-owned" issues allows the president to stay out of potentially contentious debates on issues or legislative proposals that are not of major importance to the country as a whole. See also **Legislative Referral Memorandum (LRM).**

Buy-in: Support for a proposal. Gaining buy-in from all interested parties is equivalent to achieving a consensus the proposal should move forward.

Cabinet-Level Status: Status granted to agencies or individuals that Congress has determined should serve as preeminent advisors to the president and whose programs and responsibilities are of vital national interest. The president can include the heads of particular agencies in his cabinet, but only Congress can grant the whole agency cabinet status. Cabinet agency heads are included in the presidential line of succession.

Carrots: Policy tools that use incentives, rather than penalties, to achieve a policy goal. Examples include grants, prizes, tax incentives, and loans.

Centralized Management Model: Policymaking model that centralizes the decision-making process among a key set of senior officials who serve to filter information to the president. The process emphasizes that accountability and information flow vertically toward the top.

Central Limit Theorem: A theorem that provides the mathematical justification for making inferences about a population based on a sample.

Cognitive Bias: An unmotivated decision-making bias that results from an inability of individuals to process excessive or insufficient amounts of information. Individuals exhibiting a cognitive bias will tend to interpret information and events in ways that conform to what they expect to see, given their beliefs about how the world works and their understanding of the specific context at hand.

Concurrence/Nonconcurrence Sheet: A document circulated to agency senior staff before a memorandum from an interagency working group is submitted to a cabinet secretary. Each member of the senior staff must express his or her viewpoint on the memorandum before it is submitted.

Confidence Interval: When calculating poll results, the range of the unknown variable within a population estimated from a sample and the confidence level that the range covers its true value.

Congressional Review Act: The federal legislation that requires agencies to submit new regulations to the Congress and the General Accounting Office (GAO) before they can take effect.

Decision-Making Memorandum: One of the primary means of communicating and exchanging ideas in the policymaking process. It plays a critical role in agenda setting, policy formation, and policy implementation. The most important of these roles is setting agenda by identifying which events have sufficient importance to the executive and to the United States of America to necessitate the policymaker's attention.

Deputy: An individual who is directly subordinate to the head of an agency, department or office.

Deputy Level: Events or meetings that generally involve only deputies.

Dial Group: See **Focus Group**.

Efficiency Criterion: One of the primary means used to evaluate policy options. This approach measures policy efficiency by determining the relationship between the value of the ends and the value of the means.

Executive Orders: Presidential directives that carry the force of law. These orders derive their legal authority from the Constitution, treaties, and statutes. They do not require the approval of Congress to take effect, but they can be overturned by Congress (with the passage of a law) or by a future president.

Fact Checking: Checking a public statement or release for factual errors. Sometimes factual discrepancies are incredibly subtle. What appears to be factually accurate to a speechwriter may, in fact, be a major error to a policymaker.

Focus Group: A group of individuals with specific similar characteristics who are asked to view or listen to a speech, commercial, or policy statement and state their degree of approval or disapproval of certain phrases, words, or proposals.

Groupthink: A situation in which decision makers in a group begin to evaluate and rationalize problems collectively, develop illusions of invulnerability and unanimity, view other groups and opponents as less capable, tolerate only self-censorship, and pressure internal dissenters to conform.

Independent Agencies, Departments, and Bureaus: Entities that exist within the executive branch, and whose leadership are typically nominated by the president, but are not directly overseen by the White House. These agencies tend to have certain characteristics that enable them to avoid political pressure (to some extent) from the White House and Congress. These include full or partial self-funding, terms of office that do not coincide with those of elected officials, or membership allotments that are unaffiliated or cross political parties.

Information Memorandum: A memo providing information on an issue/potential action item requiring a decision at a later date. Unlike the decision-making memorandum, the information memorandum should not make policy recommendations. See also **Decision-Making Memorandum**.

Interagency Working Group: A working group that involves several agencies and is directed to develop a policy proposal or position on a policy area.

Leaks: "Approved leaks" refer to information that is intentionally provided to the media in an informal manner in order to mobilize public support. "Unapproved leaks" refer to information that is provided to people outside of the formal decision-making apparatus without the knowledge or consent of the executive. Unapproved leaks can weaken the president by making the internal control mechanisms seem irrelevant and thus promoting chaos within an administration.

Legislative Referral Memorandum (LRM): The formal oversight process run by OMB to resolve policy conflicts and guarantee that resulting legislation or actions are consistent with the policies and objectives of the president. The guidelines for the LRM process are set out in OMB Circular A-19.

Mall Intercept Method: A method of polling in which passers-by are asked for their opinions regarding a variety of issues.

Motivated Bias: Bias that results from a subconscious tendency to interpret information in ways that match some underlying motivation. In other words, people tend to see what they want to to see. In such circumstances, the policy decision is usually made first and is followed by extensive justifications and rationalizations.

Multiple Advocacy Model: Policymaking model designed to expose the president to competing arguments and viewpoints in a systematic manner.

Non-Program Offices: These include an agency's budget office, the office of the general counsel, the office of the chief of staff, and an agency's policy and research office.

Office of Management and Budget (OMB): One of the most powerful agencies in the federal government, OMB is located in the Executive Office of the President (and physically across the street from the White House). The agency is charged by Congress to prepare the president's budget submission each year and to maintain the federal government's books. The agency is also responsible for overseeing the management of programs and the review of federal regulations.

Passback: Typically in November, OMB "passes back" drafts of agencies' budgets for the next fiscal year, kicking off last-ditch negotiations before OMB prepares a final budget proposal in January. Passbacks require agency budgeteers to revise the drafts and address any concerns with OMB officials.

Policy Authorization Tool: A tool that provides the legal basis to implement policy. Examples of policy authorizing tools include legislation, executive authority, treaties, and legal precedents.

Policy Implementation Tool: The means by which a policy is designed to achieve a goal or a set of goals. Examples include targeted tax incentives, grants, regulations, and media campaigns.

Principal: The head of an agency, department, or office.

Principal Level: Events or meetings that generally involve only principals.

Procedural Legitimacy: Legitimacy derived from the process by which decisions are made.

Proclamations: Ceremonial statements made by the executive that are of general interest (such as declaring National Flag Day). Occasionally, however, they are used for substantive statements of general policy (such as Lincoln's Emancipation Proclamation) or for announcements of certain presidential decisions.

Program Offices: Offices that run the specific programs that Congress has established by statute. Examples include Head Start, Pell Grants, and food stamps.

Public Policy: The sum of government activities, whether pursued directly or through agents, that have an influence on the lives of citizens.

Random Sample: A sample group from a population in which all elements of the population have an equal chance of being chosen or a known probability that they will be missed.

Reliable Question: A polling question that will be interpreted the same way by different respondents or by the same respondent at different times.

Sequential Approach: An approach to policymaking that divides the policymaking process into a series of sequential stages—including problem identification, formulation, adoption, implementation, and evaluation—and categorizes policy actions as they vary from stage to stage.

Situation Room: The situation room is located in the basement of the West Wing of the White House. It serves as a base of operations and provides support for the NSC and the President when managing sensitive issues and crises.

Spin: Marketing efforts used to promote support for a particular policy. Policy spin is factual evidence presented in a way to support a proposal or position. It is not meant to mislead but rather to inform the public in a way that puts a proposal in the best light.

Statement of Administration Policy (SAP): Statements that provide a direct and authoritative way for the administration to let the Congress and, via the press, the American people know the views of the president on a particular bill or legislative issue.

Strain Toward Agreement: The motivation of policymakers with common as well as competing interests to reach a collective solution to the problems at hand.

Stakeholders: Individuals, agencies, departments, and interest groups in the policymaking community with vested interests in the issues or policies at hand.

State of the Union (SOTU): An annual address presented by the president of the United States to the United States Congress. The address can be given by correspondence, but since the Wilson presidency, it has typically been delivered by the president before a joint session of Congress. The address reports on the condition of the nation and allows the president to outline his legislative agenda and national priorities to Congress.

Statistical Inference: A process of analyzing data to infer information about a population. It enables pollsters to use a small sample of individuals to provide a reasonably accurate picture of a much larger population.

Tax Credit: One type of targeted tax incentive that reduces one's tax liability (what a taxpayer owes).

Valid Question: One that clearly reflects the underlying issue that the analyst is interested in.

Views Letters: To assist the president in deciding his course of action on a bill, OMB may request that each interested agency submit a "views letter" that specifies its analysis and recommendation of a particular policy proposal within 48 hours. OMB then prepares a memorandum to the president on the enrolled bill, comprising these views letters along with its summary of the bill. OMB identifies significant issues raised by various agencies and provides its recommendations.

War Room: A rapid response operation that brings together representatives from every department into one room.

Weekly Report: A mechanism that provides decision makers with important information on a regularly scheduled basis.

West Wing: Since it was first constructed under President Theodore Roosevelt, the West Wing of the White House has served as the office building of the senior members of the White House staff. The building contains the Oval Office, the vice president's office, and the National Security Council's situation room, where the president's staff monitors the world 24/7.

INDEX